THE PHILOSOPHY OF
Edmund Husserl

THE PHILOSOPHY OF
Edmund Husserl

The Origin and Development
of His Phenomenology

By E. PARL WELCH

1 9 6 5

OCTAGON BOOKS, INC.

NEW YORK

376332
A

Reprinted 1965
by special arrangement with Columbia University Press

OCTAGON BOOKS, INC.
175 FIFTH AVENUE
NEW YORK, N. Y. 10010

LIBRARY OF CONGRESS CATALOG CARD NUMBER: 65-16781

Printed in U.S.A. by
NOBLE OFFSET PRINTERS, INC.
NEW YORK 3, N. Y.

To Cassil

ACKNOWLEDGMENTS

A LTHOUGH due acknowledgment has been given when occassion has arisen to the works of those men to which I have turned for guidance, I would like to record my particular indebtedness to the following: E. Levinas, *La Théorie de l'intuition dans la phénoménologie de Husserl;* Georges Gurvitch, *Les Tendances actuelles de la philosophie allemande;* Joachim Bannes, *Versuch einer Darstellung und Beurteilung der Grundlagen der Philosophie Edmund Husserls;* Werner Illemann, *Husserls Vorphänomenologische Philosophie;* Friedrich Weidauer, *Kritik der Transzendental-Phänomenologie Husserls;* Maria Brück, *Ueber das Verhältnis Edmund Husserls zu Franz Brentano vornehmlich mit Rücksicht auf Brentanos Psychologie;* Theodor Celms, *Der phänomenologische Idealismus Husserls;* Andrew D. Osborn, *The Philosophy of Edmund Husserl;* Eugen Fink, *Die phänomenologische Philosophie Edmund Husserls in der gegenwärtigen Kritik,* and *Was will die Phänomenologie Edmunds Husserls?;* Marvin Farber, *Phenomenology as a Method and a Philosophical Discipline.* To Gerhart Husserl, who is now residing in the United States, I owe my thanks for assistance in the sketch of his father's *Lebenslauf.* In addition, I would like to acknowledge my gratitude to Professor Edgar S. Brightman of Boston University and Dr. Hendrikus Sjaardema of Los Angeles, California, for the invaluable service which they rendered me by reading the manuscript and offering many helpful suggestions. Finally, thanks are due to the University of Southern California Press for permission to reprint in this volume the two chapters which were published in 1939 under the title, *Edmund Husserl's Phenomenology*. Although changes have been made to meet certain needs, the chapters remain substantially the same.

E. PARL WELCH

Madison, New Jersey
December 2, 1941

CONTENTS

PART TWO

TRANSITION TO PURE PHENOMENOLOGY

PART THREE: CONCLUSION

FIVE QUESTIONS CONCERNING PHENOMENOLOGY

ABBREVIATIONS

Ideen. *Ideen zu einer reinen Phänomenologie und phä-nomenologischen Philosophie.*

LU II. *Logische Untersuchungen,* Vol. II, Part 1.

LU III. *Logische Untersuchungen,* Vol. II, Part 2.

Nachwort. *Nachwort zu meinen Ideen zu einer reinen Phänomenologie.*

PA. *Philosophie der Arithmetik.*

PES, I, II. Brentano, Psychologie vom empirischen Standpunkt. 2 vols.

Prolegomena. Logische Untersuchungen, Vol. I.

INTRODUCTION

EDMUND GUSTAV ALBRECHT HUSSERL was born in the small Moravian town of Prossnitz, April 8, 1859. Since Moravia was then a part of the Austrian Empire, he was an Austrian by birth. At the age of ten, having finished his elementary education, he was sent to Vienna to enter secondary school. After studying at the Leopoldstädter Realgymnasium in Vienna and the Deutsches Staatsgymnasium in Olmütz, he qualified for entrance into a university.

The young student did not enter the University of Leipzig in 1876 with an especially impressive record. The only subjects in which he had excelled were mathematics and the natural sciences. Somewhat of the reflective type, he was apparently of the persuasion that there was no good reason to concentrate upon any subject which did not attract his attention. It has been written that his fellow students even considered him a "sleepyhead," and that they were astonished when he once announced his desire to study astronomy.

From 1876 to 1878 Husserl spent most of his time at the University of Leipzig attending courses in physics, philosophy, mathematics, and astronomy. Although he attended lectures in philosophy under Wilhelm Wundt, even that great thinker failed to excite his interest in the study of philosophy or psychology. In 1878, owing to his proclivities toward mathematics, he transferred to the Friedrich Wilhelm University of Berlin.

In Berlin he had the rare opportunity of studying under three of the foremost mathematicians of the times: Kronecker, Kummer, and Weierstrass. The greatest of these was Weierstrass, and it was under his and Kronecker's influence that Husserl became vitally interested in the philosophy and the arithmetization of mathematics. As opposed to those who regarded the concept of space as the sole foundation of mathematics, these men were arguing for the concept of number and, more particularly, that of the integral number. But more important than all this, under them he received an enviable training in the disciplines of rigorous thinking. While Weierstrass and Kronecker were stimulating the imagination of Husserl the mathematician, Friedrich Paulsen was instilling in him a desire to study philosophy. He seized upon Husserl's reflective capacities and directed his thinking into channels that were destined to prove productive of profound insights.

Although he was focusing his attention more and more upon philosophy, in 1881 Husserl transferred to the University of Vienna to finish his mathematical studies. In 1883, having studied under Leo Königsberger, he received his degree of Doctor of Philosophy. His dissertation, *Beiträge zur Theorie der Variationsrechnung,* dealt with the calculus of variations, interest in which had first been aroused by Weierstrass in the summer of 1879.

In the winter semester of 1882–83, Weierstrass had called Husserl to Berlin to act as his assistant. However, in the winter of 1883–84, the great mathematician, owing to illness, did not lecture, and Husserl hastened back to Vienna to study philosophy.

When Husserl arrived in Vienna, he found the city still buzzing with scandal about Franz Brentano. In 1873 Brentano had retired officially from the Catholic University of Würzburg. In 1869 the Catholic liberal party of

Germany had adopted his formulation of arguments op-
posing the dogma of infallibility, and as a result he not
only had to withdraw from the priesthood but was forced
to sacrifice his professorship at the university. The year
following his official retirement, his *Psychologie vom
empirischen Standpunkt* was published (1874), and he
was invited to Vienna as professor of philosophy. Here he
was destined to meet the most tragic part of his career, for
in 1880 he wanted to marry but the Austrian law forbade
this of an ex-priest; in order to escape so drastic a regulation he went to Leipzig, resumed his German citizenship,
married, and returned to the University of Vienna—as a
Privatdozent.

In 1881, while working on his dissertation, Husserl had
gone out of "mere curiosity" to hear the man about whom
everyone was gossiping. While attending these lectures, he
had been so favorably impressed by Brentano that now,
two years later, he welcomed the opportunity to return
to Vienna to study under him. During the years 1884 to
1886 he not only pursued ardently the study of philosophy
under Brentano's tutelage but enjoyed a close personal relationship with the famous psychologist. Husserl was particularly impressed not only by the manner in which he
was introduced to the philosophies of Hume and Mill but
by Brentano's treatment of ethics and logic. It was during
this time that he also became persuaded of the value of
Bernard Bolzano's *Wissenschaftslehre.* Bolzano's theory of
science contained not only a conception of the nature of
science that later influenced Husserl deeply, but it likewise introduced to Husserl "the doctrine of proposition-
in-itself, of an idea-in-itself, and of truth-in-itself that
Husserl was later to use in developing a theory of universals for himself."[1]

The manner in which Brentano linked philosophy and

[1] Osborn, *The Philosophy of Edmund Husserl,* p. 18.

science was an inspiration to Husserl. Philosophy must, above all, be "scientific." Husserl understood this to mean that the philosopher must constantly bear in mind the need for rigorous discipline and rigid investigation. Although he had been interested in the way that Paulsen and Wundt viewed the relationship between science and philosophy, their emphasis lay more on the biological sciences. Brentano, on the other hand, was the philosopher writing about psychology and lecturing on logic and it was he who drew Husserl's attention to the importance of investigating the field and scope of logic as a "strict" science.

In 1886 Husserl, on the advice of Brentano, went to the University of Halle as an assistant under Stumpf, where he obtained a thorough grounding in psychology. A year later, on the sixth of July, 1887, he became a *Privatdozent* under Stumpf on the philosophical faculty at Halle. Husserl's philosophic career had begun. His first publication, *Philosophie der Arithmetik,* was published four years later.

In 1900 Husserl went to Göttingen, where he remained until 1916, when he was called to Freiburg as Heinrich Rickert's successor. For fourteen years he held this professorship until, in 1930, he was made emeritus professor.

For almost forty years, until his death in April, 1938, Husserl was busy laying the foundations for a philosophic *Weltanschauung* which would contain a reasonable justification for the richness and magnitude of all human experiences. A careful study of his phenomenology shows a deep insight into realms of experience of which the realist, the idealist, the personalist, and the pragmatist have hardly dreamed.

The purpose of this book is not only to trace the course of Edmund Husserl's philosophic development from his

Philosophie der Arithmetik (1891) to *Méditations cartésiennes* (1931), but also to give as explicit a statement as possible of what I believe to be the principal tenets of his fully developed "phenomenology."[2] Since the movement has long since succeeded in establishing itself as a potent factor in German and European philosophy, as attested by the bibliography given at the end of this book, it is neither necessary nor desirable to write an apologia for phenomenology. This is not to insist, of course, that Husserl has carved himself a permanent niche in the halls of philosophy. Only time itself can prove that. It is simply to suggest that this movement, judged by its vigor and influence, is already too well entrenched in European philosophy to require any "defense." In any case, understanding must precede defense or attack, and for this reason, the remarks to follow, with the exception of the final section, are deliberately expository. In this respect I have tried to follow the advice of Bernard Bosanquet, who, I belive, said somewhere in his *Contemporary Philosophy* that it was bad taste to mix exposition and criticism, the truth of which is certainly confirmed by such inadequate treatments of phenomenology as are to be found in Charles W. Morris' *Six Theories of Mind* and Hans Driesch's attacks in his *Die Logik als Aufgabe* and his "Die Phänomenologie und ihre Vieldeutigkeit." When one reads these works, as well as others, one is reminded of what Schopenhauer said at the beginning of his *Kritik der kantischen Philosophie:*

Es ist viel leichter, in dem Werke eines grossen Geistes die Fehler und Irrtümer nachzuweisen, als von dem Werte desselben eine deutliche und vollständige Entwickelung zu geben.

[2] While this volume was in preparation there appeared (1939) Husserl's *Erfahrung und Urteil: Untersuchungen zur Genealogie der Logik,* ed. by Ludwig Landgrebe. Neither this work nor materials in the new journal *Philosophy and Phenomenological Research* (a quarterly which began publication in September, 1940) are touched upon in this volume.

Yet this book embodies a hope as well as a purpose, since it aspires to contribute to a clarification of Husserl's philosophy. Although phenomenology has made a deep, if not indelible impression in Europe, there are still comparatively few American philosophers who are intimately conversant with it. It will be noted, for instance, how relatively few American names appear in the bibliography. Why? Naturally it is impossible to speak with absolute authority on this matter. Undoubtedly it is due in part to the difficulty of translating the works of the scholars within the movement, a difficulty aggravated by Husserl's insistence almost from the very beginning upon creating a vocabulary exclusively his own. This in itself might conceivably be justified, were it not that the vocabulary which he created was so abstruse. Although it is questionable whether this was necessary, the damage has been done, and it behooves those who are interested in the movement to dispel as many ambiguities as possible by explaining Husserl's peculiar use of traditional terms and the meaning of his new ones.

It is hardly necessary that I acknowledge that mine is only one of many possible interpretations of Husserl's philosophy. It may or may not be the correct one, although of course this would depend upon who was the judge. Be that as it may, I certainly do not find myself in agreement with several of those who are avowed phenomenologists, let alone with those who have chosen to become antagonists of phenomenology. It is difficult to concur, for instance, with the view of some that Husserl's principal contribution is to be found in a new philosophical method.[3] Rather do I align myself with the *Gegenstands-*

<hr />

[3] Salmon, "The Starting Point of Husserl's Philosophy," *Proceedings of the Aristotelian Society,* Vol. XXX, 1930; Chandler, "Professor Husserl's Program of Philosophic Reform," *Philosophical Review,* XXVI (1917), 634 ff.; and Linke, "The Present Status of Logic and Epistemology in Germany," *The Monist,* Vol. XXXVI, 1926.

theorie group, particularly Max Scheler, Moritz Geiger, and Joseph Geyser, whose interpretations stress the "noematic" or objective character of Husserl's phenomenology rather than that which is found in its subjective side. In short, the more I examine Husserl's works, the more the conviction grows that his real contribution is to be found in the development of a novel epistemology which dissolves the impasse between idealism and realism by going beyond them both. With the idealists he objects to realism's dementalization of the world; this is seen in his insistence upon the substantiality of the pure Ego. On the other hand, he endorses the realists' contention that idealism has long been unjustified in its implicit or explicit attempt to emasculate the world of all but those aspects which can be called mental or *geistig;* this is evident from his doctrine of categorical intuition and the intentionality of consciousness. For this reason Husserl's philosophy is not to be classified either as idealism *or* realism. There is no reason whatever to call it anything but phenomenology —although it must not be confused with Hegel's system.

Nor can I agree with those who hold that the *Logische Untersuchungen* was Husserl's greatest work, an attitude exemplified, for instance, by Andrew D. Osborn's statement in *The Journal of Philosophy*[4] that it was "undoubtedly his greatest work," and that "the *Ideen* (1913), with its more systematic presentation of phenomenology, never rose to the same heights as *Logische Untersuchungen,* of which it is largely a highly refined and difficult restatement." But unhappily Osborn does not try to substantiate either of these statements. It follows from this, moreover, that I cannot understand how he holds that the *Vorlesungen zur Phänomenologie des inneren Zeitbewusstseins* (1928) and *Méditations cartésiennes* "more closely approximate the *Logische Untersuchungen*" than *Ideen zu*

[4] Vol. XXXVI, No. 9, April 27, 1939.

*einer reinen Phänomenologie und phänomenologischen
Philosophie.* This might be true if he meant the second
volume only; certainly it is not true of the first, which, if
seen in the proper light, is obviously a struggle on the part
of the author to divorce himself from his earlier psychologism. The same criticism holds for Traugott Konstantin
Oesterreich,[5] who, in spite of his excellent and sympathe-
tic interpretation of Husserl's works up to and including
the *Ideen,* and the compliment which he intended to pay
him, was hardly correct when he affirmed that *Logische Untersuchungen* "can certainly be designated as the most influential and consequential work appearing in the new century." To be sure, it might be the "most influential" insofar
as it contributed to the collapse of psychologism. It would
not follow from this, however, that it was the "most consequential," since it barely introduces Husserl's phenomenology, which, as every careful student knows, reached its
fruition in *Ideen.* It is this latter work, therefore, which
I myself would designate as the most consequential. However true this may be, without doubt such statements contribute greatly to the general misunderstanding of Husserl's phenomenology, since they emphasize his developmental period at the expense of his crowning achievement
as exemplified in *Ideen;* they fail, in short, to recognize
Logische Untersuchungen simply for what it is, namely,
the reflection of a growing, faltering mind rather than the
fruition of a mature philosopher. But a man must be
judged not so much by the process he undergoes as by
the fruits of his development, and in this case the acme
of Husserl's thinking is found in his strictly phenomenological philosophy, i. e., in *Ideen.* For this reason, as contrasted with those mentioned above, the conclusion forces

[5] Oesterreich, "Die reine Logik und die Phänomenologie," in Friedrich
Ueberweg, *Grundriss der Geschichte der Philosophie* (12th ed., 1923), IV, 504 ff.

itself that his writings since 1913, the principal of which were *Formale und transzendentale Logik* (1929) and the *Méditations cartésiennes*, comprise more an elaboration than a transformation of the philosophy set forth in *Ideen*. Nevertheless, in what follows considerable attention is devoted to the earlier phases of Husserl's philosophic growth, because of the conviction that a knowledge of the developmental stages of a philosopher's outlook will throw a great deal of light on the final phase of his thinking, and, indeed, that the latter can hardly be understood without the former.

There are a few, of course, who have tried to dismiss Husserl by making him look ridiculous, but they are hardly worthy of consideration, since, for the most part, they show scarcely one iota of understanding of his phenomenology. As a case in point, mention might be made of Hans Driesch's remarks in the article adverted to above, where he holds that Husserl's philosophy is to be described as wishful thinking, or, to use his own words, that "Alles ist auf Wunsch gegründet," and hence that "Die Phänomenologie . . . ist eine Gefahr für die strenge Philosophie." Oddly enough, he was forced to these quaint conclusions after making what to Husserl is itself an absurd demand, namely, that it be explained how essences could be empirically known and "scientifically" demonstrated. Driesch, indeed, reflects a stodgy scientism from which Husserl fought so violently to liberate philosophy, and he who does not understand this cannot claim to comprehend the founder of phenomenology.

In February, 1929, upon the invitation of *l'Institut d'Etudes germaniques* and *la Société de Philosophie,* Husserl delivered a series of lectures at the Sorbonne, entitled *l'Introduction à la phénoménologie transcendentale,* which was later published under the title *Méditations cartésiennes*. In these lectures Husserl for the first time described in detail his indebtedness to Descartes when he said, in part, that

The new impulses which phenomenology has received have been from R. Descartes, the greatest thinker of France. It is by the study of his *Méditations* that nascent phenomenology transformed itself into a new type of transcendental philosophy. It could almost be called a neo-Cartesianism, although it would be obliged to reject almost all the doctrinal content known as Cartesian, since it has given to certain Cartesian theses a radical development.[6]

Continuing in this vein, Husserl affirmed, however, that a really significant philosophical renaissance could not consist in merely reviving a system of Cartesian meditations, let alone in adopting them as a whole; nevertheless, in the spirit of Descartes its real direction must be upon the deep significance of a radical return to the "pure *cogito* Ego" and in reviving the eternal values which spring from it. It was such interest and emphasis which led to the origin and development of his transcendental phenomenology. This is the reason that a great similarity is found between Descartes' *cogito* Ego and Husserl's theory of transcendental subjectivity, since, as Husserl himself argued, they both represent "the ultimate and apodictically certain domain upon which should be founded every radical philosophy."[7]

Furthermore, Husserl sympathized with Descartes' desire for a "universal science" which would be "authentic" in the sense of possessing "absolutely certain foundations." While comparing his and Descartes' methods, he argued

that the *Epoche* is the universal and radical method by which I seize myself as pure self, with the life of pure consciousness

6 *Méditations cartésiennes*, p. 1.
7 *Ibid.*, p. 16.

which is proper to me, life in and by which the objective world in its entirety exists for me, precisely as it exists for me. All that is the "world," all spatial and temporal being, exists for me; it is, so to say, made for me, a fact just as I experience it, perceive it, remember it, thinking in the manner of judgments, of existence or value, of desire, of anything. All these Descartes designated, as is known, by the term "cogito." Truly the world is for me nothing else than that which exists and is valid for my consciousness in a similar *cogito*.[8]

Using the Cartesian term, Husserl thus defined consciousness in terms of *cogitationes;* all of its universal and particular meaning, all its existential validity, can be called exclusively "cogitations" of the pure Ego. Consequently, the existence of the natural world presupposes, as an existence *en soi anterieure,* the pure Ego and its experiences. The realm of so-called natural existence thus has only "an authority of second degree, and always presupposes the transcendental domain." [9] It is for this reason, Husserl declared, that there is required a transcendental phenomenology with a transcendental *Epoche* as its method for examining the essentiality of the existential world, and to this end he developed his philosophy. Accordingly, as Husserl's philosophic thinking progressed, there was a gradual yet inescapable shifting of emphasis from the data of consciousness to the act of seizing the datum. Out of this grew his epistemological doctrine of intuition. Yet Husserl firmly believed he had escaped Descartes' dualism by refusing to have anything to do with his precursor's distinction between *"res cogitans"* and *"res extensa."* The perennial problem of how the knower can "get out of himself" to know that which is known yet independent of him, did not dog Husserl for the very reason that "objective" and "subjective" became for him simply two complementary parts of the same stream of experience. More-

8 *Ibid.,* p. 18.
9 *Ibid.*

over, there is a richer realm of experience which Descartes was unwilling to admit. The intentionality of consciousness discloses a relation with a realm of essential Being (*Eidos*) which is beyond the cognizance of mere psychological consciousness and its "natural standpoint." The full import of all this has, of course, received considerable elaboration in its proper place in the following pages.

PART ONE

FROM MATHEMATICS TO QUASI-PHENOMENOLOGY

CHAPTER ONE

Husserl's

PRE-PHENOMENOLOGY

T HE PRINCIPAL TASK of psychology, Brentano had
avowed, was to study "perceiving," and he employed
the scholastic term "intention" to describe the relation between subject and object in the act of perceiving. An object perceived is an object intended. Since there can be no
perception without intention, and since only "phenomena" (or appearances) are perceived, psychology, according to Brentano, would obviously be "the science of psychical phenomena." [1] The subject contains "within itself"
an object intentionally, and the object is thus present in
perception in "immanent objectivity," the scholastic term
employed by Brentano signifying "in the form of psychical phenomenon." The *act* of intending, not the intended object, is that which is to be investigated by
psychology.

The important thing about the doctrine of intentionality, Brentano believed, is that it demonstrated that consciousness is consciousness *of* something. Consciousness
is "prepositional":

Every psychical phenomenon is characterized by what the
scholastics of the middle ages called the intentional (also

---

[1] *Psychologie vom empirischen Standpunkt*, I, 13. Hereafter referred
as as *PES*, I, II. The relation between Brentano and Husserl is further
discussed in chap. ii, § 7(a), pp. 75–81 f., and chap. vi, § 2, pp. 224–
29 f.

mental) inexistence of an object, and which we (although acknowledging its possible ambiguity) would call the relation to a content, the direction to an object (under which is not to be understood a reality), or immanent objectivity. Everything, although not in the same way, contains something as object in itself. In the idea something is ideated, in judgment something is acknowledged or denied, in love loved, in hate hated, in desire, desired, etc.[2]

Continuing this line of argument, Brentano held that physical phenomena could not be so characterized. Hence it is possible to define psychical phenomena as those "which contain in themselves, intentionally, an object." [3] Brentano was careful to emphasize that he was not arguing for the "reality" of the object in the physical world outside the perceiving object, but that the object is merely a "mentally immanent" object. Nothing is required but the ideating subject itself. For instance, the centaur, as an ideated object, exists only in the imagination. Hence the intentional characteristic of consciousness is a guarantee not of any real or unreal object, but solely of the subject.

All psychology is "empirical." Yet merely to distinguish it as the science of psychical phenomena in contrast with natural science, which is interested in physical phenomena, is not sufficient. Within psychology itself there is a distinction between "psychognosis" and genetic psychology. [4] Psychognosis is "descriptive," or phenomenal psychology; it is the theory of psychical phenomena. Its method is strictly empirical, since it rests on inner experi-

[2] *PES*, I, 124–25: By "mental inexistence" of an object Brentano did not mean a *Seinsweise* of the thing in consciousness, but that the experient "has something" as an object with which he is spiritually (*geistig*) concerned or to which he relates himself. Brentano was accustomed to saying, *"Ich mache (habe) etwas zum Object."* For a concise yet excellent analysis of Brentano's emphasis upon primary or psychical phenomena, compare Brightman's "The Finite Self," in *Contemporary Idealism in America.*

[3] *PES*, I, 125. Note Brentano's relation to Aristotle.

[4] *Ibid.*, I, xvii.

ence or "secondary consciousness," which "accompanies" every primary consciousness. Genetic psychology, on the other hand, investigates the *causal* relationships of consciousness; it concerns itself with the laws according to which psychical phenomena come and go.

Although Husserl did not accept *in toto* all of Brentano's psychology, the doctrine of intentionality of consciousness proved to be of permanent value and influence.[5] He undoubtedly had Brentano's definition of genetic psychology in mind whenever he classified psychology as a "natural science." Later, however, he believed he had considerably improved upon this concept by rejecting the theory that intentionality cannot demonstrate, or is no guarantee for, the objectivity of an object. If consciousness is prepositional, it must be in relation with real or ideal objects. This enlargement of Brentano's doctrine of the intentional character of consciousness marked a real cleavage between teacher and disciple.

§ 1. *Student of Mathematics*

In 1886 Husserl, upon the advice of Brentano, went to the University of Halle to study under Carl Stumpf,[6] who in turn had studied under Hermann Lotze, E. H. Weber, and Gustav Fechner. Stumpf took a deep interest in him and provided him with a systematic foundation in psychology. He was invited to remain as a Privatdozent, and his *Habilitationsschrift* was entitled *Ueber den Begriff der Zahl* (1887). In this work he applied Stumpf's psychological theories to the philosophy of mathematics, and the ideas contained therein constituted the core of

5 Husserl later averred (1930) that it was Brentano's "conversion of the scholastic concept of intentionality into a descriptive root-concept of psychology that alone made phenomenology possible." "Nachwort zu meinen Ideen zu einer reinen Phänomenologie," p. 564. Hereafter referred to as "Nachwort."

6 *Logische Untersuchungen* (1900–1) was dedicated *"in Verehrung und Freundschaft"* to Carl Stumpf.

PRE-PHENOMENOLOGY

later.

The task which Husserl assumed in the *Philosophy
of Arithmetic* was an "epistemological study of arithmetic."[7] Brentano had convinced him that any genuine
philosophy of mathematics must begin with a philosophic
examination of the first principles of mathematics; this
viewpoint was earlier articulated by Husserl as follows:

A final removal of the real and inherent difficulties of all the
problems which constitute the dividing line between mathematics and philosophy can first be expected when, in their
natural order, those concepts and relations which in themselves are simpler and logically prior—and here in a wider
sense more complicated and dependent in accordance with
the measure of their dependence—are subjected to analysis.
The first member of this order is the concept of number;
therefore, every philosophy of mathematics must begin, perforce, with the concept of number.[8]

Husserl, with this in view, began his first book with a
philosophic examination of mathematics. Although he did
not confine himself solely to arithmetic, it was not long
until he found himself involved in the difficult questions
of theory and methods, and more especially the logical
examination of formal arithmetic and the doctrine of
multiplicity. Because of his preoccupation with such
speculations, he inadvertently entered upon a philosophic
career, and consequently the second volume of his *Philosophy of Arithmetic,* originally intended as a continuation of his philosophy of mathematics, was never published.

In this work Husserl had betrayed his allegiance to the

[7] *Philosophie der Arithmetik,* I, p. vi. Hereafter referred to as *PA.*
Since a copy of this book was unavailable, all quotations are from Osborn, *The Philosophy of Edmund Husserl,* and Illemann, *Husserls vorphänomenologische Philosophie.*

[8] *Ueber den Begriff der Zahl,* Preface.

prevailing psychology. This is clear in the outline of the subject matter in the preface to the first volume, in which it is asserted that the first part is to deal with

the psychological questions which are connected with the analysis of the concepts of multiplicity, unity, and number as far as they are given to us really and not through indirect symbolism. The second part then considers the symbolic ideas of multiplicity and number and attempts to show how the fact that we are almost entirely confined to symbolic concepts of number determines the meaning and object of arithmetical numbers.

The logical investigations of the arithmetical algorithm—still comprehended as the arithmetic of number—and the justification of the calculatory realization of the quasi-numbers arising from the inverse operations, the negative, imaginary, fractional and irrational numbers, will be contained in the first part of the second volume.[9]

The foundation of the concept of number is the psychological grounding of the concept of multiplicity. Husserl accepted Weierstrass's theory that the concept of multiplicity must both logically and psychologically precede the concept of number, and even that of cardinal numbers, which possess logical priority to ordinal numbers. So much of a psychologist was Husserl at this period that he concluded that the concept of multiplicity was neither a categorical nor a class concept, but is first won in an act of abstraction or "reflection." By this he meant the "active apperception" of certain elements of representations out of those psychical factors which, after Wundt, he chose to call the concept of totality (*Inbegriffsvorstellung*) .

Every object of ideation (*Vorstellung*), whether psychical or physical, abstract or concrete, whether given through sensation or phantasy, can arbitrarily be united with any one or several to a totality and, accordingly, likewise be counted.

---

[9] *PA*, pp. vii–viii; Osborn, *The Philosophy of Edmund Husserl*, p. 36.

For instance: certain trees; sun, moon, earth, and Mars; a feeling, the moon, and Italians, etc. We can in all these instances speak of a totality, of a multiplicity, and of a definite number.[10]

Husserl summed up this uniting of individual elements by means of a psychical act in the term "collective connecting" (*kollektive Verbindung*). This signifies the significant characteristics of the concept of totality. Accordingly, totality and multiplicity originate in the mind's activity, in the act of knowing; as such, it is clear that totality and connection do not constitute a relationship existing between objects themselves.[11] The grammatic expression of this psychical uniting of objects is found in the simple word "and."[12]

The importance of this commitment is clear. Husserl was avowedly a member of the "psychologistic" school.[13] Individual elements of experience are not united "in themselves," but find their totality or wholeness in certain acts of conscious activity. Perceived contents, since they possess no inherent interrelationship, remain constituents of the thinking and relating mind. "In this sense the contents are simultaneously present, they are one, and with reflection upon this union of separated (*gesonderten*) contents through complex psychical acts arise the universal concepts of multiplicity and definite number."[14]

Thus Husserl, the Kantian psychologist: our "world"

10 *PA*, p. 11; Illemann, *Husserls vorphänomenologische Philosophie*, p. 12.

11 *PA*, p. 15; Illemann, *op. cit.*.

12 This concept had been held by Bolzano, but with this difference: for Bolzano, the concept of totality was logical, whereas with Husserl it was psychological. It might well be argued, since Brentano had acquainted Husserl with Bolzano's works, that Husserl borrowed his theory from Bolzano.

13 Cf. chap. ii, pp. 30–48, for an analysis of Husserl's later attitude toward psychologism.

14 *PA*. p. 45; Illemann, *op. cit.*, p. 14.

is a world constructed by reflection and abstraction upon and from psychical contents; ours is not a world of "experienced" objects, but a "mental" world of contents "constructed" by complex "psychical acts." Of a world of objects in which connections and relations obtain in and for themselves nothing can be said, since all (genuine) knowledge is limited to psychical phenomena.

After 1891, instead of completing the second volume of the *Philosophy of Arithmetic,* Husserl engaged in a long period of profound thinking upon the whole subject matter, the fruits of which were two important writings, in which his changing concepts are clearly perceptible; they were "Psychologische Studien zur elementaren Logik" (1894) [15] and "Bericht über deutsche Schriften zur Logik aus dem Jahre 1894" (1897).[16]

In these publications Husserl disclosed that he was gradually estranging himself from his original psychologistic outlook. His attention was first directed to "formal arithmetic." Considering the problem of the psychological basis of pure mathematics, he had begun to criticize his own psychologistic standpoint, with the result that he shifted his interest from mathematics to logic. The need of a logical discipline as exact as that of mathematics gradually forced itself upon him. Yet in spite of the fact that he was slowly becoming aware of the inadequacy of his previous theories, actually he did not make much progress, since he was still struggling to explain the sphere of logic and epistemology on the basis of both genetic and descriptive psychology. For instance, he once argued that "no theory of judgment can be final which does not sup-

15 *Monatshefte,* XXX (1894), 159–61.

16 *Archiv für systematische Philosophie,* III (1897), 216–44. Cf. his later treatment of German logic dusing the period 1895–99 in "Bericht über deutsche Schriften zur Logik," *Archiv für systematische Philosophie,* IX (1903), 113–32, 237–59, 393–408, 523–43; X (1904), 101–25.

port itself on a deep study of descriptive and genetic relations of perception and representation." [17] In a few years, however, he completely abandoned this standpoint as futile.

§ 2. *Husserl Renounces Psychologismus*

During the ten years preceding the turn of the century, Husserl, the psychologistic mathematician, changed into Husserl, the "quasi-phenomenological" logician. The articulation of this transition is found in the first volume of his *Logische Untersuchungen,* which he called *Prolegomena zur reinen Logik.*[18] In the preface of *Prolegomena* he aptly described the renunciation of his psychologistic position, the manner in which it gradually came about, and the results he hoped would accrue from the step he had taken. Because of its extreme importance, it is best to allow Husserl to speak for himself of his repudiation of psychologism; he said, in part:

The logical investigations, whose publication I began with this *Prolegomena,* have grown out of peremptory problems which have repeatedly retarded and finally stopped the progress of my attempts, throughout many years, to accomplish a philosophic clarification of pure mathematics. Besides the questions relative to the origin of the fundamental mathematical concepts and insights, those efforts were concerned more particularly with the difficult questions of mathematical theory and method. That which, according to the contentions of traditional or otherwise reformed logic had appeared easily understandable and clear, namely, the rational nature of deductive science with its formal unity and symbolic method, presented itself to me as obscure and problematic in the study

---

[17] "Psychologische Studien zur elementaren Logik," p. 187; Illemann, *op. cit.,* p. 32. This article proved to be the last published by Husserl as a member of the psychologistic school.

[18] *Logische Untersuchungen,* Vol. I, v f., 4th ed., 3 vols., 1928. Halle, a. d. S. The first volume of the *Logische Untersuchungen* will hereafter be referred to as *Prolegomena.* Vol. II, in two parts, will be referred to as *LU II* and *LU III* respectively.

of actually given deductive sciences. The deeper I penetrated analytically, the more did it become clear that contemporaneous logic in no way approximates the actual science which it is nevertheless called upon to clarify.

The logical examination of formal arithmetic and the theory of multiplicities afforded me special difficulties. . . . It forced me to considerations of a very general kind which arose in the narrow mathematical sphere, and to endeavor to attain a general theory of the formal deductive systems. Of these problems which assailed me, only one needs to be indicated here.

The obvious possibility of generalizations, e.g. inflections, of formal arithmetic, whereby it can be applied to the quantitative field without essentially changing its theoretical character and calculatory method, must awaken the insight that the quantitative by no means belongs to the most general nature of mathematics . . . and the calculatory methods based upon it. When I then became conversant, in "mathematical logic," with a mathematics which in fact was free of quantity—even as an indispensable discipline of mathematical form and method—and which treated of both the old syllogisms and new forms of inference, there became formulated for me the important problems surrounding the general nature of mathematics, the natural relationships or contingent boundaries obtaining between the systems of quantitative and non-quantitative mathematics, and more particularly, for example, the relation between the formalism of arithmetic and the formalism of logic. It was to be expected that I must then advance to the even more fundamental problems of the nature of the form of knowledge as distinct from the matter of knowledge, as well as the questions surrounding the meaning of the difference between formal (pure) and material determinations, truths, and laws.

But further, and in a quite different direction, I found myself involved in problems of general logic and epistemology. I had started from the prevailing view that it is psychology from which the logic of the deductive sciences must expect its philosophic clarification. Of necessity psychological studies occupy a predominant place in the first (and only published) volume of my *Philosophie der Arithmetik*. This psychological foundation could never entirely satisfy me in certain respects. Where it treated of the question of the origin of mathematical concepts or of the developing of practical methods—which indeed are psychologically determined—the psychological analyses appeared clear and instructive. Yet as soon as a transition from the psychological connections of thinking to the logical unity of the content of thought (the unity of theory) was completed, no genuine continuity and clarity manifested themselves. Even more so was I harassed by the fundamental dubiety concerning the manner in which the objectivity of mathematics and of science in general was compatible with a psychological grounding of the logical. Since in this manner my whole method, which was supported by the convictions of the prevailing logic—to clarify science logically by psychological analyses—came to uncertainty, I saw myself increasingly forced to general critical reflections upon the nature of logic, and at the same time, upon the relation between the subjectivity of knowing and the objectivity of the content of knowledge. Left without succor from logic everywhere when I sought clarification of definite questions, I was finally compelled to suspend completely my philosophico-mathematical studies until I had succeeded in advancing to sure clarity in the fundamental problems of epistemology and the critical understanding of logic as a science.

The course of development has necessitated estranging myself, in matters of fundamental logical convictions, from the men and works most responsible for my scientific unbringing; on the other hand, I have very nearly approached a number of scholars whose work I was unable earlier to evaluate according to their worth and which, therefore, I had ignored all too much. . . . As regards the candid criticism I have made against psychologistic logic and epistemology, I might recall the words of Goethe: *"Man ist gegen nichts strenger als gegen erst abgelegte Irrtümer."*[19]

This confession discloses one of the most remarkable reversals of position to be found in modern philosophy. Indeed, it represents Husserl, the mathematician, coming

[19] *Prolegomena*, Preface, pp. v–vii.

of philosophic age, and with it is to be found, from practically every standpoint, an entirely new thinker, e.g., an indifference toward matters once considered important, an awareness of the significance of epistemology and logic as contrasted with mathematics, and a repudiation of psychologistic tenets hitherto considered to be basic. It must be borne in mind, however, that although all these, and much more, are to be found in the *Prolegomena*, Husserl was by no means the phenomenologist he became in later years. The whole volume, with the exception of the last chapter, treating of "Die Ideen der reinen Logik," represents a struggle within and against himself to divest his mind of those ideas and theories which he had once so firmly held to be essential. The net positive results of this long yet fruitful travail of Husserl's can be summarized as fourfold: the preliminary establishment of logic as *Wissenschaftslehre;* the critical analysis of psychologism; the rejection of the antipsychologizers; and, finally, the formulation of the threefold task of logic as the Science of science. In the chapter to follow these will be treated in the order named.

CHAPTER TWO

Husserl's

QUASI-PHENOMENOLOGY

HUSSERL began his *Logische Untersuchungen* by pointing out that since John Stuart Mill, and owing principally to his influence, logic had developed in three ways: metaphysical, formal, and psychologistic; the last, unfortunately, had become most prevalent. As a logician, he would investigate this trend of *Psychologismus* with the purpose of disclosing wherein it is insufficient to meet the demands of logic as a science. Its incompetency becomes clear once it is seen how it

shows us unity of conviction only as regards the limits of discipline in its essential aims and methods; but it can be said without fear of exaggeration that there has hardly been any consideration in these teachings, particularly in regard to the objective meanings of traditional forms and doctrines, of the word from *bellum omnium contra omnes*.[1]

§ 1. *Logic as Wissenschaftslehre*

But Husserl was interested in much more than a polemic against psychologistic logic. In common with Kant, he would examine, among other things, the foundations of science. He observed, for instance, that science is con-

---

[1] *Prolegomena*, p. 4. Husserl took pains to emphasize that his use of the term "psychologism" had no "contemptible" connotation (*ibid.*, p. 52). His definition and critical analysis of psychologism are treated at length in the present chapter, § 2, pp. 30 f.

vinced of, and uses, what it calls "universal truths." Science blandly assumes the "validity" of these truths and employs them without question. Husserl inquired, Does not this assumption require an examination of *Principienfragen?* It does, and the task belongs to logic. Yet, if logic is to investigate these principles, it must first win respect as a science in and for itself. But is logic justified in claiming this status? A consideration of this question would disclose its proper domain, methods, and aims.

It must first be asked, however, What is science? Husserl held that one way to define a given science is on the basis of its aims; these, in turn, are contained in the proper sphere of each science itself:

> The definitions of science reflect the steps of its development; as science progresses there follows theoretical knowledge of its objects, limitations, and sphere. . . . The sphere of a science is an objective, closed unity; it cannot be arbitrarily declared where and how we might delimit spheres of truth. The realm of truth is ordered objectively in spheres; according to these objective unities the investigations must direct and constitute themselves as sciences. There is a science of numbers, a science of the formations of space, of animal beings, etc.; not, however, sciences of prime numbers, of trapezes, of lions, or even of all of them taken together.[2]

A science, then, can be defined according to the realm which it investigates.

There are, however, two dangers constantly besetting science: that of defining too narrowly the sphere of any given science; and, even worse than this, the *Gebietsvermengung,* the mixing of the heterogeneous so that it allegedly constitutes "a unity." The net result of such mixing is a complete misunderstanding of objects to be examined, the fixation of invalid aims, and the incommensurable methods employed to examine these. As a case in point Husserl would first show

[2] *Ibid.,* p. 5.

that the prevailing, i. e., psychologistically founded, logic is shamelessly guilty of these things and that, through the misunderstanding of theoretical foundations and the mixing of spheres growing out of this, the progress of logical knowledge has been essentially retarded.[3]

Since Husserl would combat the claim that logic is a discipline of psychology by articulating what logic as a science is, he enumerated four problems:

1. Is logic a theoretical or practical discipline (*Kunstlehre*)?

2. Is it independent of other sciences, particularly psychology and metaphysics?

3. Is it a formal discipline or, as it is commonly said, does it have to do with "the mere form of knowledge"; or does it give regard to its "matter"?

4. Does it have the character of an a priori and demonstrative discipline, or is it empirical and inductive?[4]

All these questions are really interrelated, and answers to them can be subsumed under two groups: one school says that logic is a theoretical discipline, independent of psychology, yet at the same time formal and demonstrative; the other argues that it is dependent upon psychology. In the latter case logic is deprived of the character of a formal and demonstrative discipline in the sense, for instance, of arithmetic, and its members hold that it is an "art." However, Husserl refused to align himself with either group, and from the outset stated his position as follows:

We assume as starting-point the almost commonly accepted definition of logic as an art, and establish its meaning and justification. There naturally arises the question of the theo-

---

[3] *Ibid.*, p. 7.

[4] For a careful and more critical analysis of Husserl's earlier viewpoint of logic, cf. Gotesky, "Husserl's Conception of Logic as *Kunstlehre* in the *Logische Untersuchungen*," *The Philosophical Review*, July, 1938, pp. 375 f.

retical foundations of this discipline, and particularly its relation to psychology. Essentially (if not entirely) this is a problem of the cardinal question of epistemology, the objectivity of knowledge. The result of our investigation is the elaboration of a new and purely theoretical science, which constructs the most important basis for every doctrine of art, of scientific knowledge, and possesses the character of an a priori and purely demonstrative science. It is as Kant and other representatives of a "formal" or "pure" logic intended, but it was not correctly conceived or established according to its content and latitude. As final consequence of these meditations there results a clearly comprehensive idea of the essential content of the disputed discipline whereby is given, of itself, a clear position regarding the controversial problems at hand.[5]

Husserl thus introduced his standpoint, his problem, and the manner in which he intended to deal with it.

These introductory statements reflect his intention of entering immediately the realm of epistemology, i. e., that he will deal with problems of logic from the standpoint of epistemology. To examine the field and process of logic meant, according to him, to investigate the problem of the "objectivity" of knowledge. In order to clarify this position he inquired whether logic ought to be considered "normative." That he held it to be an "art" has already been mentioned. The first question to be treated, then, is how Husserl would characterize art in and for itself, and what he meant by saying he will disclose the "theoretical imperfection" of the particular sciences.

The artist (his argument ran) proceeds in his work on the basis of a theoretical knowledge of laws, which he "assumes" to be already validly established. It is on the basis of these laws, moreover, that his practical activities proceed, are ordered and directed; the perfection or imperfection of the completed work will be judged accord-

[5] *Prolegomena,* p. 8.

ing to them. Yet the artist, as a rule, is not he who is a student of principles. He does not create and evaluate according to principles which he has first troubled himself to establish as valid. "He follows creatively the inner lawfulness of his harmoniously constructed powers."[6] In spite of this, however, it is generally acknowledged that there are certain principles proper to art.

The same, Husserl believed, is true of the sciences. The mathematician, physicist, and astronomer, in order to proceed with their scientific investigations, do not require insight into the ultimate grounding of what they do, although the results possess, both for them and others, the cogency of reasonable conviction. They engage in their given tasks without any claim to have previously examined and proved valid the ultimate principles of their conclusions or the principles on which the truth of their methods rests. The scientist uses what he himself has not investigated but which experience, presumably, has shown to be "good" and "true." In this respect is found the "imperfection" of all sciences, i. e., "the lack of inner clarity and rationality which must be examined independently of the elaboration of science. In this regard even mathematics cannot claim to be the most progressive of all sciences, or even to be an exception to the rule."[7] Mathematics cannot be considered the "ideal" of all science, as is disclosed by the old and constantly recurring conflicts over the foundations of geometry as well as the matter of "current methods." As a matter of fact, experience shows that the most brilliant mathematician is often incapable of giving "the logical cogency of these methods and the limits of their correct application."[8] It is not to be denied, of course, that the positive sciences, in spite of their theoretical insufficiency, have aided us immeasurably in our struggle to prevail over nature. Neverthe-

[6] *Ibid.*, p. 9.   [7] *Ibid.*, p. 10.   [8] *Ibid.*

less, it must be remembered that they "are not crystal-clear theories in which the functions of all concepts and propositions are completely understandable, all the pre-suppositions and, indeed, the entirety of all theoretical doubts, precisely analyzed." [9]

Can science turn to metaphysics in order to have its limits, aims, and methods defined? Hardly. What does metaphysics do? It "assumes" that which is unproved, indeed "unnoticed," in the way of presuppositions; it deals, supposedly, only with "real" existence and believes, accordingly,

that there is an external world which is spread out in space and time, a Euclidian space having the mathematical character of three-dimensionality, time having the one-dimensional manifold; and that underlying all becoming is the law of casuality.[10]

Metaphysics, then, could only be a foundation of those sciences which concern themselves with "reality." But as such it is not "comprehensive." Take, for instance, the case of mathematical science, whose objects are numbers, manifolds, and the like, "which are thought to be independent of real existence, or non-existence, as real carriers of pure ideal determinations." [11] Metaphysics is impotent to deal with these, not to mention another class of investigations, namely, the field of what relates sciences to sciences. From these considerations Husserl concluded that there is obviously required a *Wissenschaft von der Wissenschaft;* by them he was brought to the question of the possibility and justification of logic as *Wissenschaftslehre,* which at the same time would be a "normative" and "practical" discipline.

9 *Ibid.*
10 *Ibid.,* p. 11. Husserl, in this connection, did not specify any modern metaphysics or metaphysical system, but mentioned Aristotle's philosophy as an example.
11 *Ibid.,* p. 11.

Science, as the word indicates, proceeds from *Wissen,* knowledge.[12] Yet it must not be construed from this that science is a "sum" of *Wissensakten.* It deals with the possibilities, the content of knowledge, not the acts of knowing themselves.

It is in knowledge, however, that we possess "truth." Now, according to Husserl, there are two ways in which knowledge is defined: in the narrower sense, it consists of "self-evidence" that a certain fact "is" or "is not," e. g., "that SP is or is not; therefore is also the self-evidence that a certain fact is probable in this or that degree." [13] But in addition to this, there is a wider concept corresponding to the *Wahrscheinlichkeitsgraden,* the degrees or grades of probability; it is sometimes a great, sometimes a narrower measure of knowledge. It is knowledge in the pregnant sense of the word: the self-evidence that "SP *is.*"

The aim of science, Husserl believed, is knowledge, for in knowledge we obtain or possess truth, e. g., truth as the "object of correct judgment." [14] But this alone is not sufficient. To science there belongs more than *"blösses Wissen,"* for there is the further question of the positing of fact, "a knowledge of the existence or nonexistence of the fact." [15] The most perfect kind of such knowledge is self-evidence. *Evidenz,* in which there is an "indubitable certainty" that X is, was described by Husserl in the following way:

The most perfect criterion of adequacy is self-evidence; it is for us an immediate revelation of truth . . . absolute knowledge of truth. Self-evidence of probability of a content "A" does not indeed ground the self-evidence of its truth, but it does ground every self-evident and comparative evaluation by which we are enabled to differentiate reasonably or unreasonably the positive or negative probability-values; or better, it grounds absolutely proved assumptions, intentions, supposi-

---

12 Husserl frequently used *Wissen* and *Erkenntnis* synonymously.
13 *Prolegomena,* p. 14.   14 *Ibid.,* p. 12.   15 *Ibid.,* p. 17.

tions. In the final analysis, all genuine and especially all scientific knowledge rests on self-evidence, and as far as self-evidence reaches, so far extends the concept of knowledge.[16]

There must then be drawn a careful distinction between the acts of knowing and the facts or contents of knowledge. The acts of knowing are a grasping, a seizing, of contents. But science is more than an aggregate of such individual seizures; indeed, it is more than a sum of different kinds of knowledge. There is an interconnection, a *system* indigenous to science. What constitutes it? It is *systematischer Zusammenhang in theoretischen Sinn,* and in this theoretical, systematic connection lies the establishment of genuine scientific knowledge and all the relations and orders belonging to it.

To the essence of science, therefore, there is inherent *die Einheit des Begründungszusammenhanges,* in which, in the case of the individual sciences, there prevails the logical argument itself, and with this also the higher complexes of argument which are commonly called "theories." The purpose of science is not "mere knowledge" as such, "but knowledge in such a measure and in such a form as to facilitate the greatest possible perfection as it corresponds to our highest theoretical aims." [17]

The *Idee* of science, then, is "system" in its purest form. To this practical end the scientist works. for science is more than an "architectonic play." It is *Systematik.* Where is this system; of what does it consist? Is it "imposed" on the various spheres which science investigates? Is it a construction of the imagination? As opposed to all such "idealistic" viewpoints, Husserl argued that system lies

in things, where we simply find them, uncover them. Science will be the means of knowing the realm of truth, and, indeed, to the greatest possible extent, of grasping that truth. But

---

[16] *Ibid.,* pp. 13–14.   [17] *Ibid.,* p. 15.

the realm of truth is not a disordered chaos—there prevails in it unity of lawfulness; hence the examination and presenting of truths must also be systematic. They must reflect their systematic connections, and at the same time serve as ladders of progress in order to be enabled to penetrate, on the basis of knowledge already given or won, into higher regions of truth.[18]

System prevails in science because the realm which it investigates is constituted of (discovered or discoverable) systematic connections.

Science progresses because it is in possession of systematic *Stufenleiter*. All knowledge, according to Husserl, rests on self-evidence; but whence this self-evidence? Clearly it is not given in "mere perception." If it were, science would never have developed. Methodological formalities would never have arisen if the intention had already been given as a consequence. The relations of logical grounding are not found, then, in perception; they are a matter of "immediate revelation." At this point Husserl inquired, How is it possible to construct "proofs" or "logical arguments" when truth is discovered in this way? And he answered that as a matter of fact, the number of self-evident truths consists of a highly limited group of primitive facts. Most of our truths, he argued, are grounded in method, not in immediate revelation; yet all methodologically grounded truths and knowledge rest on prior immediate revelation. In short, the *Stufenleiter* of science is *propositional* and hence there is required a careful examination of *Satzgedanken,* the idea or design of the "proposition." Truths of science, or revelations of system, although propositional, are nevertheless built upon certain basic, immediately self-evident truths. These fundamental, primitive revelations are em-

18 *Ibid.,* p. 15. Note the antipsychologistic tone of these statements, particularly respecting the "objectivity" of the realms of "truth," systematic connections, and lawfulness.

ployed constantly by science and rightly so, yet that does not alter the fact that there is urgent demand for a science which would examine the nature and justification of these primitive principles, their origin, their adequacy, and the manner in which they are to be judged as correct. This is the realm to be investigated by logic as *Wissenschaftslehre*. Logic in this sense would examine both the primitive "self-evident" and the propositional structure of scientific *Systematik*, and in so doing it would at the same time be investigating the bases of scientific probabilities or norms. Each individual science, as already remarked, is more than an aggregate of specific sets of information, since it has system or, rather, it *is* a system.

The same holds true for science as a whole. Science is science because there exists between particular exact sciences and their investigations this property of systematic connection. Logic is the science whose task it is to investigate this datum of the primitive self-evident which makes possible the classification of various kinds of research under the one heading "science." As such it would examine the bases of scientific truths, arguments, and procedures. Argument or proof is built upon system. And system, far from being an object of *perception*, is, according to Husserl, a matter of self-evident *insight*. *Systematik* constitutes an objective realm which is *discovered*, not invented.

In order to support these contentions, Husserl called attention to three characteristics of scientific argument or proof. First, its content has "the character of established structure." [19] Second, every argument is "completely determined according to its content and form." [20] The systematic connections of argument are not a matter of arbitrary will or chance but of reason and order, that is, *regelndes Gesetz*. Take a mathematical problem concerning a triangle, ABC, and the proposition, "An equilateral

[19] *Ibid.*, p. 17.　　　　　　　　　　　　　　[20] *Ibid.*

triangle is equiangular." Here there is executed an argument or proof which says explicitly, "Every equilateral triangle is equiangular." [21] All such proofs have the same inner constitutive indigenous character which is expressed in logical terms as "Every A is B, X is A, therefore XB." Every such form of syllogism represents a *Klassenbegriff* in which the infinite manifold of propositional connections has an "expressed constitution." From this is derived the "a priori" law "that every so-called proof which proceeds thus is really correct providing it proceeds from correct premises." [22]

Thus it is generally. Whenever we progress from previously given knowledge, the manner of (correct) argument has a certain form in common with other arguments; they all stand related to universal laws according to which each can be justified. No argument stands "isolated." None connects knowledge with knowledge without this external *Modus der Verknüpfung*.

Third, "The forms of argument are bound to knowledge-spheres." [23] Such is the case in every science, and it serves as the presupposition of comparing the particular sciences. Each science has its own sphere, limitations, and place in the general field of knowledge. But the arguments of each proceed according to certain universal laws held in common, and this means, in the mind of Husserl, according to a certain "inner constitution," because each sphere contains class concepts common to all. This order and structure prevalent in all science points not only to their independence of the sciences themselves but to the a priori character of each. Logic would examine this a priori structure and order found by the sciences, as well as investigate the manner in which they are discovered and systematized in the form of argumentative proof. To

[21] *Ibid.*, p. 18.   [22] *Ibid.*, p. 18.   [23] *Ibid.*, p. 19.

do this is to examine the very nature and justification of science itself, the *Möglichkeit einer Wissenschaft.*

It is this objectively valid "form" of argument which provides the possibility of progress in science. Science can proceed in its proofs because of the *lawfulness* resident in its content, as well as the form of arguments used to exhibit the content of its discoveries. Clearly this demonstrates the indisputable independence of the form of the sphere of knowledge of science itself. Yet a science of science would have more to do than investigate laws and forms of particular proofs. This is patent from the fact that there are arguments "outside of" science, and hence it is clear that in the constitution of science itself there is something more than a group of individual or particular proofs. This, as already seen, is a unity of connections between the arguments themselves, a unity in the gradation of truths, which form of unity itself has its high teleological meaning for the attainment of the supreme aim of all sciences: truth, to lead us to the realm of truth. Hence the importance of the problem of the form of science, its systematic unities.

At this point Husserl inquired, Is Logic "normative"?[24] All sciences, he answered, since each has certain aims, are "normative" in the traditional sense of telling us what "ought-to-be." Now one of the aims of logic is to show in what way science is science, as constituted in and for itself. In this sense, at least, logic would be normative. The essence of a normative science is to "prove" universal propositions in the interest of attaining certain ends, and its value is judged in accordance with the effectiveness with which this is done. It is clear that merely to have an end in view distinguishes no science as normative in contrast to others; every science has at least the one end of

[24] *Ibid.,* pp. 26 f.

serving human activity and needs. Moreover, each science has an "ideal" of attaining "truth" about its special
subject matter. Logic has the aim of discovering the laws
of valid demonstration and the lawfulness of correct science. According to Husserl, then, logic is no more normative than any other science. But since it examines the
conditions of right method, scientific attainment of truth
in each field, and rules of demonstrative procedure, *so
wird sie zur Kunstlehre von der Wissenschaft.*

Husserl was thus forced to the conclusion that definitions of logic as the art of judging, of drawing conclusions, of knowledge, of thinking (*l'art de penser*), are
entirely too narrow. To be sure, there is included in its
task the examination of standards and norms of thinking,
but its scope is much larger. This is evident when the
problem is considered, What is the relation between what
"ought-to-be" and what "is"? To ask this is to inquire
into the relation between normative and theoretical disciplines. Husserl prepared the way to his answer by formulating the proposition,

every normative (and accordingly, practical) discipline rests
on one or more theoretical disciplines; insofar its rules must
possess theoretical content distinguishable from the ideas constituting norms (of the Ought), whose scientific examination requires, actually, such theoretical disciplines.[25]

Hence

Laws of normative science declare *was sein soll,*
whether it "is" or, under the circumstances, "can be";
    Laws of theoretical science declare what "is."

Here the question must again be asked, What is meant
by the difference between *Seinsollen* and *Sein,* the relation
of what "ought-to-be" and what *is?* Now ordinarily the
Ought, in the narrow sense, means that which is related
to "willing," or "wishing," i. e., related to acts of voli-

[25] *Ibid.,* p. 40.

tion. But there are other kinds. Considered "in the abstract," there can be an Ought when no one is there to do anything and nothing is demanded of anyone. This Ought, in the wider sense of the word, is not based on volitional acts. As an example, there is no wishing or willing or demand made of any person in the proposition, "A soldier ought to be brave." Aside from individual cases, this can mean, "Only a courageous soldier is a 'good' soldier." [26] This is a judgment which has nothing to do with wishing or willing; it is a *Werturteil* that it is correct to expect, on the basis of evaluational examination, a soldier to be courageous. The predicates "good" and "bad" are resident in the concept of soldier: here is a positive *Wertschätzung,* the recognition of a positive value-predicate unrelated to particular soldiers and irrespective of whether it can be fulfilled at all. There is present an evaluational standard or criterion which serves as a classification of certain objects, namely, good and bad soldiers. This can be put in the form, "an A shall be B," and "an A which is not B is a bad A," or "only an A which is B is a good A." [27]

Negative expressions, on the other hand, are not mere negations of corresponding affirmative expressions. For instance, to say that a soldier should not be cowardly does not mean that it is "false" for a soldier to be cowardly, but that a cowardly soldier is also a "bad" soldier. Hence the form, "an A shall not be B" and "an A, which is B, is generally a bad A," or "only an A which is not B is a good A." [28]

The result of this for Husserl was that he believed it supported his contention that judgments about the *Sollen* say nothing about *Sein.* Nothing is said of particular existence. The generalities or universalities of the Ought are of a pure, theoretical kind, and they have the character of

[26] *Ibid.,* p. 41.   [27] *Ibid.*   [28] *Ibid.,* p. 42.

"laws" in the strict sense of the word. From these analyses
it is seen

that every normative proposition presupposes a certain kind
of evaluating (sanction, estimation) by which the concept of
a "good" and a "bad" grows regarding a certain class of objects; in accordance with it, these objects coincide into good
and bad.[29]

In short, a normative judgment requires, as basis of evaluating, a concept, which is not a matter of arbitrary *Nomi-
naldefinition;* it is only a "universal evaluation" that soldiers, according to their characteristics, can be declared as
good or bad. Moreover, this is aside from the question of
whether the particular evaluation has "objective validity"
or even whether there is a differentiation between "subjective" and "objective" goods.

   Although every *Kunstlehre* is normative, it is more
than "practical" since its task includes the theoretical fixing of norms or criteria in accordance with which the aims
to be realized will be determined and judged. For this
reason, Husserl concluded that

every normative and a fortiori, every practical discipline, presupposes one or more theoretical disciplines as basis in the
sense that it must possess a theoretical content which can be
differentiated from all acts of establishing norms which have,
as such, their natural stand in some theoretical science.[30]

The basic norm determines the unity of the discipline; it
specifies the design of the normative proposition. It
serves, moreover, as a standard or criterion of measure-
ment. When is a normative proposition "practical," i. e.,
having to do with what "is" or "is not"? When it is
grounded in a theoretical proposition. Hence "an A ought
to be B" must include the theoretical proposition, "only
an A which is B has the properties C." Here is indicated,

29 *Ibid.,* p. 43.   30 *Ibid.,* p. 47.

through and by C, the constitutive character or content of the measuring predicate "good." The new proposition is "a purely theoretical proposition"; it contains nothing more of the idea or design of a normative proposition.[31] But it must also be noted that just as soon as a theoretical proposition is used in the construction of a theory, or as a basis for the only possible inferences, *it itself becomes a normative proposition.* From this it would follow that every theoretical science employs normative propositions. If the triangle "ought" to be equilateral, then it "must" be equiangular. "Only an A which is B is good," i. e., "an A ought to be B." Nevertheless, this normative use of theoretical propositions is only secondary.[32]

Husserl, on the basis of these remarks, affirmed that the theoretical relations that abide in the normative sciences must have their logical place in certain theoretical sciences. Every normative science that deserves the name must examine scientifically the relations of the normative contents respecting basic norms; then it must study the theoretical core of these relations and, by so doing, enter the sphere of the correlative theoretical sciences. On these grounds, every normative discipline

employs the knowledge of certain theoretical non-normative truths; this it borrows from certain theoretical sciences, or wins it through the application of certain propositions derived from them, out of the constellations of instances determined through normative interests.[33]

This is especially true of *Kunstlehre.* It follows from this also that theoretical sciences play a significant role in establishing scientifically the grounding of normative sciences. Whether this role were primary or secondary would depend upon the discipline at hand.

[31] *Ibid.,* p. 48.   [32] *Ibid.,* p. 48.   [33] *Ibid.,* p. 49.

Husserl, it is clear, was thus interested primarily in the *theoretical* foundations of logic, and this interest led him into the realm of epistemology, since the central problem was that of the "objectivity" of system. Logic is normative in the sense that it has certain aims and ends; it is theoretical in that it will fill the role of a science itself in order to ascertain wherein it is justified in using principles and bases which it itself, owing to its limitations, does not find within its own province. The subject matter of logic, then, in addition to stating "truth" concerning certain objects, i. e., systematic connections, includes the objective validity of proofs and arguments employed in science. Logic has a domain entirely its own, and there is a need to separate it completely from psychology and metaphysics; in fact, from all other sciences. Moreover, it is more than a theory of the "best" or "correct" thinking. As will be seen, Husserl became increasingly persuaded that it is a science of Pure Being, of essential relationships obtaining between the perceptual and conceptual data of experience and the content of scientific investigation.[34]

As normative, it will serve as guide by supplying basic norms of good thinking. As theoretical, it will state what "is," and will supply a knowledge which makes the attainment of norms possible. Husserl's logic is thus the examination of the essential theoretical bases of both theoretical and normative science.

§ 2. *Psychologism*

Psychologism in the narrow sense can be described as the tendency to reduce the objects of logic, epistemology, value, and the like, to subjective-psychical experiences, proc-

---

[34] See chaps. iv and v, below, treating of his *Philosophie als strenge Wissenschaft* and his concept of "Pure Phenomenology" respectively.

esses, and psychological forms; to derive them from psychological factors and laws; to represent them genetically as the mere result of psychical development.[35]

By implication every reasonable being is an individual, concrete consciousness which is, or can be made to be, the object of psychological study. Everything occurring in this consciousness is to be causally explained as "psychical." The laws of logic, for instance, are mere "tendencies of thinking," the "forms" with which we actually think. This applies to everything, including religion and moral tenets. As in the case of the laws of logic, there is likewise no "objective validity" of religious and moral experiences in the sense that these experiences have verifiable objective reference. It is indeed absurd to speak of an objective world of any description since there is no world known outside that of our own psychical construction. We "know" only that which is a product of our own making, and the demand for an "external" world is superfluous in that everything is explainable by an examination of the psychical events and phenomena which comprise consciousness.

These remarks indicate what psychologism is "in gen-

35 Eisler, "Phänomenologie," *Handwörterbuch der Philosophie*, 2d ed., p. 510. For a thorough treatment of the aims, methods, and contentions of psychologism, see Liebert's "Das Problem der Geltung," *Kantstudien*, Vol. XXXII, in which it is shown, among other things, how psychologism argues that metaphysics is a branch of psychology, i. e., has its basis only in psychical events and a study of them: "every positing of a metaphysical kind rests on this, that structures of original psychological value assume the appearance of separate dispositions, subjective realities. This 'coming-to-be-a-thing' is, according to its nature, a completely primary and elementary process. As with unconscious ways, it originates in human consciousness involuntarily, and it develops itself within it with psychological necessity." According to Liebert's interpretation of psychologism, the origin of metaphysics is much more than a mere hypothesizing of certain logical and theoretical determinations. The motive of all metaphysics is "a derailment of the course of psychological events"; every metaphysical system arises from "great spiritual emotions" and is nurtured by them.

eral." The question for this consideration, however, is, How did Husserl define or think of psychologism? How he defined logic and what he conceived its task or objective to be has just been described. Since it is logic in which he was fundamentally interested, it is naturally to be expected that he examined particularly the claims of those who argue that psychology is the scientific substructure of logic or, even worse, that logic is a branch of psychology. He began his study of the psychologistic contentions by giving abundant quotations from John Stuart Mill and Thomas Bain and such German philosophers as Christoph Sigwart, Hans Lipps, and Wilhelm Wundt.[36]

Mill had said,

I conceive it to be true that Logic is not the theory of Thought as Thought, but of valid Thought; not of thinking, but of correct thinking. It is not a science distinct from, and co-ordinate with, Psychology. So far as it is a science at all, it is

---

[36] The works he referred to particularly were: Mill's *An Examination of Sir William Hamilton's Philosophy* (1878); Lipps's *Grundzüge der Logik* (1893) and "Die Aufgabe der Erkenntnistheorie," *Philosophische Monatshefte*, XVI (1880), pp. 530 f.; Sigwart's *Logik*, Vol. I, particularly pp. 184 f. It is interesting that he also named Alexius Meinong as a member of this school (*Prolegomena*, pp. 181–82). Owing to the force of Husserl's attacks, Lipps himself abandoned the psychologistic position (*Prolegomena*, p. xii). It is further of interest to note that, although Jakob Friedrich Fries (1773–1843) is considered the founder of psychologism, Husserl never mentioned him; neither is there any reference to the *Abhandlungen der Fries'schen Schule*, Vols. I, II, III, and IV, 1906–18. It will be recalled that Fries articulated three arguments: (1) principle of knowledge: the sense world comes to appearance in accordance with natural laws, and we know appearance of things through perception and concepts of the understanding; (2) principle of belief: there is a being of things in themselves, and this being lies at the ground of appearance; we believe in the eternal being of things through concepts of the understanding; (3) principle of presentiment (*Ahndung*): the sense world is appearance of thing itself, and we hold it in feeling without perception or definite concepts. Cf. his *Wissen, Glaube und Ahndung* (1805) and *Neue Kritik der Vernunft* (1907). See also Heinrich Schmidt's treatment of psychologism in *Philosophisches Wörterbuch*. All of the quotations from these men, unless otherwise specified, are from Husserl's *Prolegomena*. The term "psychologian" will be used to designate those who are confessedly (or allegedly) members of the school of psychologism.

a part, or branch, of Psychology; differing from it, on the one hand, as a part differs from the whole, and on the other, as an Art differs from a Science. Its theoretic grounds are wholly borrowed from Psychology, and include as much of that science as is required to justify the rules of the art.[37]

Lipps expressed the same viewpoint in his statement that

a sufficiently clear distinction between the two is that logic is a special discipline of psychology. . . . Logic is a psychological discipline, as certainly as knowledge comes only in the psychic life, and thinking which completes itself in it, is itself a psychical event.[38]

These avowals are so plain that there can be no question of the implications contained in such statements.

Lipps's position becomes even clearer in his treatment of the *Normalgesetze des Denkens*: we think correctly when we think things as they are. But things are "such-and-such," and "we can think them, due to the nature of our mind, in no other way but this." [39] To Lipps it is "obvious" that an object of knowledge can become such only in the thinking process. Accordingly,

the rules according to which one must proceed, in order to think correctly, are nothing other than rules according to which one must proceed in order so to think, as demanded by the peculiarity of thinking, its particular lawfulness; in brief, they are identical with the natural laws of thinking itself. Logic is the physics of thinking, or it is nothing at all.[40]

Sigwart, who was interested in the *Ethik des Denkens*, likewise held that propositions are nothing but *"Funktionsgesetze"* or *"fundamentale Bewegungsformen unseres Denkens"*; it is nothing short of "fiction" to believe

37 John Stuart Mill, *An Examination of Sir William Hamilton's Philosophy*, pp. 461–62.
38 *Grundzüge der Logik*, p. 3.
39 "Die Aufgabe der Erkenntnistheorie," *Philosophische Monatshefte*, XVI, 530 f.
40 Lipps, *Die Aufgabe der Erkenntnistheorie*.

that "a judgment can be true aside from an intelligence thinking this judgment." [41]

These arguments, then, represented to Husserl typical articulations of the psychologistic school, which he himself summarized in the following manner.

If we inquire into the justification of these viewpoints, there presents itself a highly plausible argument which appears from the beginning to decide this question. Regardless of how logical *Kunstlehre* is defined—whether as the art of thinking, judging, concluding, knowledge, proving, knowing, of the direction of the understanding in the pursuit of truth, in the evaluation of grounds of proof, etc.—we always find psychical activity or products specified as objects of practical regulation. Since the technical treatment of a thing presupposes knowledge of its qualities, so here it is likewise the case, where psychological matters are especially dealt with. The scientific examination of rules, the subject to be treated, will obviously lead to the scientific examination of these qualities: the theoretical foundation for the construction of a logical art is given by psychology, and particularly psychology of knowledge.

In every instance this occurs in the content of logical literature. Of what are they speaking? Concepts, judgments, conclusions, deductions, inductions, definitions, classifications, etc.; everything is psychology, only chosen and ordered according to normative and practical standpoints. It is possible to limit pure logic so narrowly that one cannot keep away from the psychological. It is already involved in concepts which are constitutive for logical laws, e. g. truth and falsity, affirmation and denial, universality and particularity, cause and effect, etc.[42]

According to Husserl, the real question, however, is whether the essential, theoretical foundations of normative logic lie in psychology. If this were true, the question would arise, Which theoretical sciences lend the essential

[41] *Logik* I, 126. Husserl might agree with this latter statement, but would see no reason to infer that the "truth" of the judgment was dependent upon an intelligence "thinking" the judgment. "Thinking" would represent for Husserl a "discovery" not an *invention* of "truth."

[42] *Prolegomena*, p. 52.

foundations of a *Wissenschaftslehre?* But underlying this is the more fundamental question,

Is it correct that theoretical truths which we find treated in the scope of both traditional and more recent logic, and above all the essential fundamentals belonging to them, possess their theoretical standing among the already specialized and independently developed sciences?[43]

This, of course, brings Husserl to the problem at hand, i. e., the relation of logic and psychology, since the latter believes that "the essentially theoretical fundamentals lie in psychology; in its sphere belong the propositions, according to their theoretical content, which give to logic its characteristic stamp."[44]

Yet Husserl contended that logic itself spelled the doom of psychologism. Marvin Farber indicates in the following way the problem as it concerned Husserl.

With regard to the question concerning the origin of mathematical ideas or the psychologically determined development of practical methods, psychological analysis seemed clear and instructive to Husserl. But when the transition was made from the psychological connections of thought to the logical unity of the content of thought, no suitable continuity and clarity could be obtained. Husserl was further disturbed by the doubt he had regarding the compatibility between the objectivity of mathematics and of all science with a psychological foundation of logic. . . . It is the thesis of the *LU* that there is a fundamental class of entities that cannot be reduced to, or viewed as, such "real" facts; . . . the logical sphere is an ideal sphere; . . . logical objects are ideal objects which are not reducible to non-ideal entities, or to "real" ones.[45]

In 1894 Husserl had said,

Especially I believe myself able to affirm that no theory of judgment can do justice to the facts which does not support

43 *Ibid.,* pp. 50–51.
44 *Ibid.,* p. 51.
45 Farber, "Phenomenology as a Method and as a Philosophical Discipline," p. 12.

itself upon a deeper study of descriptive and genetic relations obtaining between perceptions and ideas.[46]

In his "Bericht über deutsche Schriften zur Logik aus dem Jahre 1894" (1897),[47] Husserl was seriously questioning the implications of this and other contentions to be found in his previous writings. In *Prolegomena* he emphatically denied their validity. No longer did he feel himself "able to affirm" that all problems of mathematics, logic, and epistemology could be solved by delving into their psychological foundations. No longer was he so certain that in order to understand what is thought it is imperative to appeal to a science that exalts itself as alone capable of discovering and defining the laws, contents, and objective elements of thinking.

Husserl the logician, still imbued with a zeal for mathematical precision, had long been pondering carefully the nature of psychology itself, and came to view it as a "science of fact" with "experience" as its starting-point. No matter how psychology is defined—as the science of psychical phenomena, as the science of facts and consciousness, or as the science of facts of inner experience—it is still a *Tatsachenwissenschaft* and as such it is a science based upon (sense) experience. Consequently, although their validity is not to be denied, the "laws" of psychology remain nothing more than vague *Verallgemeinerungen der Erfahrung*—generalizations of experience.[48] Psychology, in short, is empirical. If this be true, psychologistic logic, as avowedly based upon the laws and findings of psychology as a science, is alike empirical and this, on Husserlian grounds, deprives it of any valid claim to be an exact science. But careful examination, he believed, would disclose

[46] "Psychologische Studien zur elementaren Logik." Illemann, *Husserls vorphänomenologische Philosophie*, p. 32.

[47] *Archiv für systematische Philosophie*, III, 216–44.

[48] Husserl used the term "vague" as the anonym of "exact."

(at least) three serious consequences of a logic supporting itself upon empirical psychology.

First, "only vague laws can be based upon vague theoretical foundations."[49] If the laws of psychology lack exactness, so must any logic built upon them. Yet, since laws of logic are amenable to exact statement, clearly they could not be grounded on vague generalizations such as comprise laws of psychology.

Second, it would be useless to try to waive the first argument, since, according to psychology itself, no natural law is known a priori. "The only way to ground and to justify such a law is through induction from the special facts of experience."[50] Induction has nothing to do with "validity" of laws, but with their more or less "probability." The law itself is not *insightfully* valid. Consequently, all logical laws that are psychologistically established still remain "mere probabilities"; by the nature of the case they are not "exact." Yet, since it is generally acknowledged that the laws of "pure logic" are a priori valid, it is clear that the laws universally accepted as genuine cannot be won by psychologistic methods.

Finally (third), if logical laws had their epistemological source in psychologistic facts, they would be "normative applications" of psychological facts and consequently would have a psychological content in a double sense: "they would have to be laws of the psychical while at the same time supposing and including the existence of the psychical."[51] Husserl believed he could demonstrate the untenability of this assumption in the following way. No logical law implies a "matter-of-fact," the existence of ideas or judgments, or any other data of knowledge. No logical law, considered in its true sense, is a law of the facts of psychical life, therefore not for ideas (i. e., experience of ideas) or for judgments (i. e., experience of judgments),

[49] *Prolegomena*, p. 61.   [50] *Ibid.*, p. 62.   [51] *Ibid.*, p. 69.

or for any other psychical experiences. Empirical laws have their own factual content *eo ipso;* as such they are not only laws *about* facts but they imply the existence of facts. Without this material reference they would claim only the status of probability. Thus all laws of exact sciences (psychology included) are genuine laws, yet considered from the standpoint of knowledge, "they still remain 'idealizing fictions,' although fictions *cum fundamento in re.*" [52]

The significant consequence of Husserl's discussion so far is not only that all knowledge begins with experience, but that here he first began to explicate one of the most fundamental concepts of his (later) phenomenology, viz: there are in general *two kinds of experience,* "real" and "ideal." Laws relating to "real" facts are known in special (sensory) experiences; "ideal" laws obtaining in and governing ideal "facts" in the ideal world are known in ideal experiences. In the ideal sphere belong, for instance, "pure logical laws" and the laws of *Mathesis pura.* Their "origin" is not found in or derived from "induction" since they have nothing to do with "existential contents." All laws of such ideal nature are *einsichtig* and speak "fully and completely" for themselves. They are not mere *Wahrscheinlichkeitsbehauptungen.*

Failure to differentiate between the ideal realm and the real world and the ways of knowing each accounts, at least in part, for the inadequacy of psychologism. For instance, the law of gravitation is not the same kind of *law* as the logical law, "if A is a valid truth, then not-A is false." [53] Nor are the two laws "known" in the same way. This insight into the fundamental difference between the real and the ideal marked one of the first important steps in the course of Husserl's progress.

In *Prolegomena* is found Husserl's vigorous protest

[52] *Ibid.,* p. 72.   [53] *Ibid.,* p. 76.

against what he considered to be three "prejudices" of psychologism.[54] First, "the rules for the regulation of the psychical are obviously psychologically founded. Therefore it is clear that the normative laws of knowledge must be grounded in the psychology of knowledge."[55] Both assertions contained in this prejudice are, in the mind of Husserl, erroneous, since "logical laws, considered in and for themselves, are in no way normative propositions in the sense of precepts, i. e., they are not propositions whose content can prescribe *how* judging shall take place."[56] The difficulty could have been avoided by the psychologians had they differentiated between (1) "laws which serve for regulating the knowing activity" and (2) "rules which contain the thinking about this regulating itself and which declare themselves as universally binding." [57] Psychologism, in short, failed to see the difference between thinking and the content of thinking and consequently it falsely made the latter the object of its investigations while under the illusion that it was examining thinking itself.

Second, when speaking of such matters as concepts and propositions, inferences and proofs, truth and probability, and cause and effect, the psychologian apparently thinks only of *psychical* phenomena and products. Inferences "are the grounds of judgments by means of judgments, and this grounding consists of nothing less than psychical activity."[58] This would apply to pure logical and methodological propositions alike. Considering mathematics and logic to be kindred sciences, Husserl was moved to inquire, Is mathematics also to be designated as a branch of psychology? According to psychologism it would be. But perhaps it can be shown that mathematics and logic do not deal with the same domain of objects with which psychology is concerned.

---

[54] *Ibid.*, pp. 154 f.   [55] *Ibid.*, p. 154.   [56] *Ibid.*, p. 155.
[57] *Ibid.*   [58] *Ibid.*, p. 167.

Husserl granted, of course, that there are no sums without adding, no products without multiplying, and no quantities without numbering. "All arithmetically operational products point to certain psychical acts of arithmetical operating, and only in reflection can it become 'exhibited' what a quantity or sum or product, etc., is." [59] But in spite of this "psychological origin" of arithmetical concepts, it would be incorrect to infer that mathematical laws themselves are psychological in the sense that the "truth" of mathematics came into being or depended upon "thinking" them; or that truth would vanish if no one were thinking of the laws. What, then, is the explanation of the psychologian's confusion? There is, according to Husserl, only one answer. Psychology, as an empirical science of psychical facts, is concerned with numbering and with arithmetical operations as "events," i. e., as temporal, sequential, psychical acts. But in arithmetic there is a sphere of ideal species, 1, 2, 3. . . . These are individual ideal facts without any temporal character at all. Sum, quantity, and product are not accidental "here and there" results of adding, counting, and multiplying. If this be true, it is clear that they must be differentiated from the *concepts* in which they are represented. The number "five" does not depend upon anyone counting up to five or even "thinking" it. All numbers are ultimately (possible) objects of theoretical acts; in arithmetization "ideal form-species" are primarily *intended*. Such species have their concrete particular instance in individual "enumerating acts." [60] This form is an "absolute *one*," not a "mere aspect" of some psychical experience. Clearly as such it is to be considered neither as "factual" nor as the object of any empirical science such as psychology. Acts of numbering "come and go," whereas "ideal species" remain "the same."

[59] *Ibid.*, p. 170.   [60] *Ibid.*, p. 171.

The same is true of pure logic, where there must likewise be made a fundamental distinction between "the subjective-anthropological unity of knowledge and the objective-ideal unity of the contents of knowledge."[61] Let us suppose that the psychologian affirms judgments to be *Fürwahrhaltungen*, that which contains the true. What is alleged by this? That one is speaking of certain "conscious experiences." But the (Husserlian "genuine") logician understands by this that "judgment means the same as proposition, and proposition understood not as a grammatical, but an ideal unity of meaning."[62] In this manner a distinction is made between judging activity and the "forms" of such which serve as pure logical laws. Categorical, hypothetical, disjunctive, and existential judgments are not titles in pure logic for classes of judgments, but signify ideal propositional forms (*ideale Satzformen*). And the same is true of "forms of inference." In logical analysis the *proposition,* taken as a unity, is the object. The logician is concerned not with judging, but judgments; not with inferring, but inferences. For instance, "God is just" is a categorical proposition containing the subjective concept, "God." For logic this is not a mere psychical experience. The concern here is not with an experience or concept of this or that individual; much less is it a psychical act involving the word "God." There is here articulated a proposition, "God is just," which is one, a unity, regardless of the manifold experiences of God, as well as the "concept" of God which is again one in a way impossible, considered in its parts. In line with this argument, Husserl held that the logician "means by the expression 'this judgment' not 'this act of judging' but 'this objective proposition.'"[63] With the latter the science of psychology has nothing whatever to do.

Psychology, to be sure, can have judging as its object

61 *Ibid.,* pp. 173–74.   62 *Ibid.,* pp. 175 f.   63 *Ibid.,* p. 176.

of study, but not the (ideal) *content* of such activity. The principle, "of two contradictory propositions, one is true and the other is false," is not a law of judging, but a law determining the content of a judgment (*Urteilsinhalte*).[64] There are here involved "ideal meanings" which have come to be called "propositions."

Pure logic and arithmetic, as sciences of ideal entities of certain species (or from what is *a priori* grounded in the ideal essences of these species) are differentiated from psychology in this respect: psychology is the science of the particular entities of certain empirical classes.[65]

From this it should be clear that

the differentiation between the researches of psychology, which employ termini or class-termini of psychical experiences, and the objective or ideal investigations, in which the same termini represent ideal species and classes, is not merely subjective or relative; it constitutes the differentiation of essentially different sciences.[66]

Husserl formulated the third prejudice as follows: "All truth lies in judgment. But we recognize a judgment as true only in the case of its self-evidence."[67] According to this prejudice, there is reflected "a well-known psychical character of inner experience, a peculiar feeling which guarantees the truth of the judgment to which it is related."[68] If it were once granted—so runs the argument of the psychologian—that logic was the science whose function it is to lead us to truth, logical laws would "obviously" be "laws of psychology," which would be propositions designed to enlighten us about "the psychological conditions upon which the existence or absence of this 'feeling of self-evidence' is dependent."[69] Included in these

[64] *Ibid.*   [65] *Ibid.*, p. 177.   [66] *Ibid.*
[67] *Ibid.*, pp. 180 f. Husserl cited Mill, Sigwart, and Wundt as particularly guilty of this prejudice.
[68] *Ibid.*, p. 180.
[69] *Ibid.* Mill said that logic is "Philosophy of Evidence." Cf. *An Examination of Sir William Hamilton's Philosophy* (fifth ed.), pp. 473, 475,

propositions would be practical precepts which ought to guide us in realizing judgments which would be a part of this distinguishing character. And thus the psychologian would have to hold that in every case psychologically founded rules of thought would be meant when logical laws or norms were spoken of.

Husserl, as contrasted with these contentions, argued that, although "to recognize the truth and to affirm it with authority presupposes insight into truth," [70] it does not necessarily follow from this that "logic as *Kunstlehre* must investigate the psychological conditions under which self-evidence appears in judgments." [71] On the contrary, a close examination of the nature of logic discloses that "pure logical propositions have nothing whatever to say about self-evidence and its conditions." [72] Psychology, to be sure, is not to be denied the "prerogative" of studying the *psychological* conditions under which self-evidence appears in judgments, but such investigation would have to do only with the "here-and-now" experience; moreover, this would hardly demonstrate that self-evidence and its mode of appearing are "psychological." Considerations of this kind serve to call attention very forcibly to the fact that a distinction must be made between such an empirical science and logic, since the latter has as its object one of the realms of "pure" experience, or that which might be more closely determined as the *"conditions"* of the here-and-now experience. Psychology is con-

476, 478. Sigwart, accepting Mill's viewpoint, said that logic had the sole purpose of disclosing the conditions "under which appears this subjective feeling of necessity" (*Logik*, Vol. I, part 2, p. 16). Cf. Wundt, *Logik*, Vol. I, part 2, p. 91, wherein he expresses his approbation of this idea when speaking of the "normative character" of logic. See also A. Höfler's *Logik* (1890), pp. 16 f. (in collaboration with Alexius Meinong). It is in this connection that Husserl (wrongly) included Meinong as a member of the psychologistic school.

70 *Prolegomena*, p. 182.   71 *Ibid.*
72 *Ibid.*, p. 183.

cerned with "methodological" laws, with judging itself; logic deals with the contents of judgments.

What, Husserl inquired, is meant when "self-evidence" is spoken of? It is "no accidental feeling which insinuates itself into certain judgments."[73] It most certainly is not something of a psychical character appearing in so-called "true" judgments. Husserl held self-evidence to be much more the "experience" of truth. Truth is experienced as something *ideal* in a "real" act of experience; "truth is an idea (*Idee*) whose particular instance consists in the self-evident judgment of actual experience."[74] The self-evident judgment is, however, "a consciousness of the originally given."[75] And to this judgment is related the "not-evident" judgment, even as the optional conceptual positing of an object is related to its adequate perception. If this be correct, it is easily seen why Husserl must hold that

the experience of the agreement between the intention and the given itself, i. e., between the actual sense of the affirmation and the self-given facts, is self-evidence, and the ideal of this agreement is truth. The ideality of truth constitutes its objectivity.[76]

"Two plus two equals four" is an affirmation which is in no wise a matter of the present temporal experience or assertion; its "validity" is "objective": it is an assertion *"in Spezie."* To say "$2 + 2 = 4$" is merely a "matter-of-fact," a *"zufällige Tatsache"*; "$2 + 2 = 4$" is itself a discovery of an ideal, objective validity, an arithmetical relation. The expression itself does not reflect a mental process of adding $2 + 2$, but a discovery of an "ideal"

[73] *Ibid.*, p. 189.

[74] *Ibid.*, p. 190. Husserl, throughout his entire works, mentioned frequently "truth" as he understood it, but he never examined systematically the *problem* of truth and error. See chap. vi, "Five Questions Concerning Phenomenology," for a criticism of this neglect.

[75] *Ibid.*

[76] *Ibid.*, p. 191.

relation. This relation, although conceivably a "psychological" fact or reality, is in no way dependent upon mental processes for its validity or ideality.

It is obvious from the foregoing arguments of Husserl that for him a logical *Kunstlehre* presupposed, as a scientific discipline, "certain theoretical knowledge." This, he believed, becomes clear when it is remembered how such concepts as truth, proposition, predicate, object, quality, and cause and effect are employed constantly by exact science.

All science builds itself out of truths, on that which it teaches; all truth lies in propositions, all propositions contain subjects and predicates, relating themselves through them to objects or qualities; propositions as such have connection according to cause and effect, etc.[77]

These truths, which are grounded in the essential constituents of all science, and grounded as "objective and theoretical," cannot therefore be conceived as "suspended" without suspending the objective content and meaning of science itself. They obviously constitute the fundamental standard according to which the claim to be a science is judged. Is not the intention of science to give "objective truth"? Such is its aim, and it conveys its discoveries according to the laws of logic. One problem confronting the investigator, then, is, What objective validity do these laws have? Since a science proceeds in its arguments according to propositions, it must be inquired, What objective validity does a proposition have? Further, science claims "objective unity." Wherein consists such unity? Again, all science claims "empirical independence" of its truth, i. e., that its laws and discoveries, although made for the most part through "empirical investigation," are nevertheless independent of the particular facts at hand. From these observations Husserl concluded that

[77] *Ibid.*, p. 160.

scientific truths, procedures, bases, structures, and so forth cannot be considered mere "matters-of-fact"; any science investigating them would accordingly not be a science of "matters-of-fact." Recalling how Husserl depicted psychology as a *Tatsachenwissenschaft*, it is clear why, in his mind, psychology must be excluded from the possibility of being the science to investigate these scientific bases. Certainly it could never be adjudged basic to any science which proposes to do so.

Husserl contended that there are two aspects of any given science: first, its methods as dealing with certain spheres of truth; second, that every science can be considered from the standpoint of

what it teaches according to its theoretical content. That which (in ideal cases) every particular proposition affirms is a truth. But no truth is isolated in science, since it coincides with other truths in theoretical connections united through relations of cause and effect. This objective content of science, insofar as it actually meets this intention, is fully independent of the subjectivity of the examination, of the peculiarities of human nature; it is actually objective truth.[78]

It is this latter aspect which holds the interest of Husserl, and upon it he bases his contention for a necessity of a "pure logic," which, in absolute independence of all other scientific disciplines, would define those concepts which belong "constitutively" to the idea of systematic or theoretical unity; it would examine further the "theoretical connections" which are grounded in these concepts. Such a science would have

the particular characteristic that it understands the content of its laws according to its "form"; that these elements and theoretical connections, out of which it itself exists as systematic unity of truths, become governed by the laws which belong to its theoretical content.[79]

---

[78] *Ibid.*, p. 162.   [79] *Ibid.*, p. 161.

Pure logic, according to Husserl, is thus interested in the "ideal aspect" or "form" of science. It would have no interest whatever in the particular matter of particular special sciences, but "in that which relates itself to truths and theoretical connections of truths in general. Therefore its laws, which throughout are of an ideal character, must be measured by a science with regard to their objective theoretical side."[80]

To be sure, it must be admitted that ideal laws immediately become "methodological" when once employed, since they constitute "mediate evidence." It is in the "grounding-connections" that this mediate evidence grows. Its "norms" are then nothing more, nothing less, than the normative application of such ideal laws, which in turn ground themselves purely in logical categories. Here, then, is seen the significance of Husserl's logic as *Kunstlehre:* such characteristic peculiarities of logical arguments, which are the very structure of science itself,

have entirely their origin, and find therefore their complete clarification, in this, that the insight in the argument (in inferences, connections of apodictic truths, the unity of the comprehensive rational theory, and, moreover, in the unity of the argument of probability) is nothing else but consciousness of an ideal lawfulness.[81]

This "consciousness of an ideal lawfulness" Husserl called "pure logical reflection," which is directed to primitive, fundamental laws and would constitute a scientific system. Coupled with this is his argument that pure logical forms "transform themselves" into norms and rules which we should ground. Here Husserl distinguished between two kinds of norms: first, those which can be characterized as the "mere species" for arguments (empirical); then (second) there are those that "regulate" all arguments, that comprise "all apodictic connections a priori."[82] The

80 *Ibid.*, p. 162.   81 *Ibid.*, p. 163.   82 *Ibid.*, p. 163.

former relate themselves essentially to the specific "human side" of sciences. The latter, however, are of "a pure ideal nature," and discoverable only through self-evident reflection. It goes without saying that insofar as Husserl would consider logic as *Kunstlehre,* the field of normative examination would lie entirely in this ideal sphere.

§ 3. *Husserl and the "Antipsychologizers"*

As he completed his repudiation of psychologism, Husserl turned his attack upon the "antipsychologizers."

In the controversy over the psychological or objective foundation of logic I take a middle way. The anti-psychologizers principally look to ideal laws which we characterized above as purely logical; the psychologizers looked to the methodological rules which we characterized as anthropological. Consequently the two parties could come to no agreement.[83]

Husserl believed that, in their eagerness to preserve the status of ideal laws, the antipsychologizers overlooked the "theoretical" character of pure logical propositions; furthermore, they unnecessarily emphasized that "psychology has to do with natural laws, while logic deals with normative laws."[84] But the opposite of natural law is not by definition normative law. On the contrary it is *"ideal"* law, in the sense of being grounded in concepts (Ideas, pure conceptual essences).[85]

Gottlob Frege, one of the outstanding opponents of psychologism, had maintained that logic dealt with, and is based upon normative laws.[86] As contrasted with psy-

---

[83] *Ibid.,* p. 164. As antipsychologizers Husserl cited B. Erdmann, Drobish, Hamilton, Herbart, and Gottlob Frege. Cf. Husserl's references, *Prolegomena,* pp. 36 f., 55 f., and 157 f.

[84] *Ibid.*   [85] *Ibid.,* p. 165.

[86] Cf. Osborn, "The Philosophy of Edmund Husserl," pp. 43 f., for an account of Frege's attack upon Husserl. Husserl referred to Frege's *Die Grundlagen der Arithmetik* (1884) and *Die Grundgesetze der Arithmetik.* See also Natorp's antipsychologistic "Über objective und subjektive Begründung der Erkentniss," *Philosophische Monatshefte,* XXIII, 265 f. In the *Prolegomena,* p. 169 n., Husserl acknowledged his indebtedness

chology, the natural science, logic is thus to be defined only as a "normative discipline." As such "it acts on universal propositions which are timeless."[87] Those who regard logic as a purely normative science do not, however, see the crucial point, namely,

that each normative and *a fortiori* each practical discipline supposes one or more theoretical disciplines as its basis. The normative proposition, "A should be B," includes in itself the theoretical proposition, "only an A which is B has the properties C," in which C indicates the constitutive content of the predicate "good." The second proposition is purely theoretical; it contains no element of normative thought. The process is reversible, so that a proposition which runs, "only an A which is B is good," can also take the form, "A should be B."[88]

In short, every normative science must have knowledge of certain truth which itself is not normative.[89] And if normative logic must call upon something else for its bases, it cannot be accepted as final. These are the principal reasons why Husserl rejected the arguments of the antipsychologizers as untenable.

§ 4. *The Threefold Task of Logic as a Pure Science*

Not only while under the tutelage of Brentano, but after the publication of his *Philosophie der Arithmetik*

---

to the preface of the latter work and to the entirety of the former. He also retracted his old criticism of Frege's *Grundlagen*.

[87] Osborn, *op. cit.*, p. 59.   [88] *Ibid.*

[89] As indicated above, this gives rise to the first and most important question, What theoretical sciences afford the essential basis of the theory of science? It was this question, among others, that caused Husserl to draw such a sharp distinction between psychology and logic. This necessitated a further question: Is it proper that the theoretical truths which we find treated in the scope of traditional and modern logic, and particularly those belonging to its essential basis, should occupy their theoretical position within the sciences that are already delineated and independently developed? No conclusive answer to these questions is found in the *Prolegomena*. Later on he answered it in his works which developed the phenomenology unsystematically introduced in the second volume of *LU*. Cf. Osborn, *op. cit.*, 59 n.

and during the time he was wrestling with the problems surrounding the nature of logic and epistemology (1894–1900), Husserl had learned a great deal about Bolzano.[90] He became particularly impressed by his theory of logic, in which was included the idea that logic "is something more than an instrument for the drawing and verifying of conclusions."[91] On the contrary, logic is the theory of science, "the totality of all those rules according to which we must proceed in the task of the division of the whole field of truth into special sciences."[92]

Husserl himself was led to assert that "on Bolzano's work logic must build itself as a science; from him logic must learn what is necessary, that is, mathematical sharpness of differentiation, mathematical exactness in theory."[93]

In the spirit of Bolzano, then, Husserl aspired to make of pure logic the Science or Theory of science. Its chief problem would be the examination of the pure categories of meaning, the unity of foundational relations belonging to the essence of all sciences. It would reach its peak in a theory of all forms of theory; it would be the science that made all sciences plausible and possible in the sense that they would be given "internal clearness and rationality."[94] Ultimately the realization of this aim would require examinations of a metaphysical sort. The task would be to fix and to examine the "improved metaphysical presuppositions" constituting the "foundation" of all science itself. As examples of these, Husserl mentioned the "outer world," concepts of "space" and "time," the "law of causality," and so forth.[95]

---

90 Bernhard Bolzano (1781–1848) held that logic has to do with "spaceless" and "timeless" truths and propositions-in-themselves, with ideal objects intended in judgments. See his *Wissenschaftslehre*, 1837.

91 Osborn, *op. cit.*, p. 53.

92 *Ibid.*, p. 53 (from Bolzano's *Wissenschaftslehre*, I, 7).

93 *Prolegomena*, p. 226.

94 Osborn, *op. cit.*, p. 58.   95 *Prolegomena*, p. 11.

Husserl formulated the nature, scope, and problems of a pure logic in the last chapter of the *Prolegomena*.[96] Three principal tasks confront such a science. First, there is the establishment of the pure categories of meaning with which logic works. To achieve this, there must initially be fixed "the primitive concepts that 'make possible' the connection of knowledge in objective relationship, and especially the theoretical connection."[97] In this group belong such "primitive" ideas as concept, proposition, truth. Likewise there must be fixed "the elementary forms of connection which are generally constitutive for the deductive unity of propositions, e. g., the conjunctive, disjunctive, and hypothetical connection of propositions with new propositions."[98] Finally, there would be the categories of meaning, such as object, matter-of-fact, unity, multiplicity, number, relation, and connection; these comprise "the pure or formal objective categories."[99]

All these concepts must be fixed and their "origin" be studied in detail. This examination does not involve "psychological" questions, but is a matter of "the *phenomenological* origin; it is concerned with insight into the nature of such concepts and the methodological manner of fixing the unequivocal, sharply to be distinguished, word-meanings."[100] The only (phenomenological) means of accomplishing this end is to achieve the "intuitive representation" of essence in adequate "ideation."

The second task involves that group of problems concerning "the search for laws based on all classes of categorical concepts . . . having to do with the objective validity of the forms constructed upon such a basis."[101] On the one hand, this would deal with the truth or falsity of meanings "in general" and purely on the basis of their "categorical form"; on the other hand, relative to their

96 *Ibid.*, pp. 227 f.   97 *Ibid.*, p. 243.
98 *Ibid.*, p. 243.   99 *Ibid.*, p. 244.
100 *Ibid.*   101 *Ibid.*, p. 245.

objective correlates, it would deal with the "being" and "nonbeing" of objects in general, and again solely on the basis of their purely categorical form. These laws in turn compose other theories. First, there is the theory of inferences—for instance, the syllogism, which is really only *one* such theory. Conversely, from the standpoint of correlates, they give rise in the concept of multiplicity to the theory of pure multiplicity; in the concept of number to the theory of number, and so on.[102]

Once the two above-named tasks have been completed, there comes (third) "the idea of a science of the conditions of the possibility of theory." [103] Such a science would necessarily be a priori. It would be "the idea of a comprehensive science of theory which, considered in its fundamental parts, examines the essential concepts and laws belonging constitutively to the idea of theory." [104] The purpose of such a science would ultimately be to examine a priori possible theories; its consequence would be one vast system of knowledge. It would be a Theory of science and, as such, the *Grundwissenschaft*.

The last task, as mentioned above, Husserl dealt with rather sketchily in Chapters I, II, and XI of the *Prolegomena*. Its final resolution was not realized for years and reached definite completion in the *Méditations cartésiennes* (1931). The first two tasks occupied a considerable part of the second volume of *Logische Untersuchungen*.[105]

Husserl summarized the whole purpose of his investigations somewhat as follows: they will deal with the systematic connections which, "according to their essence," form the basis of theory; from the standpoint of an a priori theoretical science, his studies are concerned with "the ideal nature of science as such," in which empirical,

102 *Ibid.*, p. 246.

104 *Ibid.*

103 *Ibid.*, p. 247.

105 Cf. Osborn, *op. cit.*, p. 57 n.

anthropological considerations are "excluded." In a real sense of the word, then, the investigations are to establish the Theory of Theories, *die Wissenschaft der Wissenschaften.*[106]

What did Husserl actually accomplish in the *Prolegomena?* During the period 1894–1900, he (1) divested his thinking of all traces of psychologism, (2) changed from mathematician to logician and epistemologist, (3) fought the claims of both the psychologizers and anti-psychologizers, and finally (4) prepared the way for what he considered a "middle ground," by developing the idea of a pure logic whose principal service would be to furnish a Science of science, which would lend plausibility to and foundations for both "empirical" and "ideal" sciences. Having exempted his mind of these preliminary difficulties, he believed himself equipped for a program of positive, constructive thinking in the second volume of his *Logical Investigations.*

[106] *Prolegomena,* p. 242.

CHAPTER THREE

Husserl's

DEVELOPMENT OF PHENOMENOLOGY

I N THE INTRODUCTION to the second volume[1] of his
Logische Untersuchungen, Husserl stated explicitly
what he intended to do. Entitled, "Investigations into the
Phenomenology and Theory of Knowledge," the first
four "studies" or "examinations" are devoted to the various phases of and problems surrounding the nature of
"meaning"; the fifth and final study deals with such problems as objectivity, the intentional nature of consciousness, perception, and knowledge. Although in the remarks
to follow these studies will not be examined exactly in
the order named, the subject matter of each will be given
proper attention. For the sake of clarity, the treatment can
best be divided under two general headings, viz., (1) his
development of a pure logic and (2) his development of
epistemology. Husserl himself indicated what to expect
of his general position and procedure in the following:

"Pure" phenomenology represents a sphere of neutral investigations, in which various sciences have their roots. On the
one side it serves psychology as empirical science. In their
pure and intuitive processes, it analyzes and describes in essential universality—especially as the phenomenology of thinking and knowing—the experiences of concept, judgment, and

---

[1] Vol. II is in two parts, hereafter referred to as *LU* II and *LU* III,
respectively.

knowledge which, considered empirically as classes of real events in relation to their primitive naturalness, support the psychology of empirical investigation. Again, it includes the "sources" from which fundamental concepts and ideal laws of logic "arise," to which it must be traced back in order to establish "clarity and distinctness" necessary for the epistemological understanding of pure logic.[2]

DEVELOPMENT OF A PURE LOGIC
(QUASI-PHENOMENOLOGY)

§ 1. *The General Problem*

The first task of a pure logic would be to investigate the objects that are given in grammatical form, since all judgments, especially those which belong to the realm of science, are "exemplified" in linguistic expressions. These objects

are given, so to speak, as objects imbedded in concrete psychical experiences, which in their function of meaning or building of meaning (latterly as illustrative or evidential intuition) belong to certain grammatical expressions and construct with them a phenomenological meaning.[3]

It is left to the logician to bring out of these complexities the "act characters" in which such logical objects as ideas and judgments are realized; he must study them in "descriptive" (phenomenological) analysis. Husserl emphasized that psychical experiences are not the important objects of this investigation. As a logician he is primarily interested, not in psychological judging, that is, "the concrete psychical phenomenon," but in the *logical* judgment, "the identical statement of meaning, which is a unity as contrasted with the multiple and descriptively

---

2 *LU* II, pp. 2–3. Although Husserl used the term "pure" to describe his phenomenology in *LU*, as a matter of fact it was not until the publication of *Ideen* (1913) that he was justified in doing so, since in *LU* his thinking had not yet reached fruition.

3 *LU* II, p. 4. Husserl's formulation of the "threefold" task of a pure logic should be borne in mind (chap. ii, § 4, pp. 94 f.).

varied experiences of judgment." [4] Although, to be sure, there is a common characteristic obtaining between particular experiences and their ideal unity, the logician, instead of turning to the concrete, seeks this characteristic in the corresponding idea, in "the universal seized in the abstract." [5] On these grounds, he has no reason whatever to abandon the abstract for the concrete.

Such "phenomenological" analysis is basic to logical analysis. Although it is granted that everything logical must be given in concrete fullness, close examination discloses that in the form of concreteness it is nevertheless given "incompletely." Concepts are formulated as more or less limited verbal meanings; laws, constructed as they are upon such concepts, are likewise verbally limited affirmations. According to Husserl, logical insight does not suffer this imperfection, because we seize "the pure law with self-evidence, and know that it grounds itself in pure forms of thought." [6] On the other hand, since this "self-evidence" depends upon the meanings of words resident in the actual completion of the law-judgment, ambiguities can conceivably enter in at any stage. From this it would follow that the mere datum of logical ideas and the pure laws constituting them are not sufficient. Hence arises the very important task of bringing logical ideas, concepts, and laws to epistemological clearness and distinctness.

At this point phenomenological analysis plays its important role, since

logical concepts, as valid thought-unities, must originate in intuition; they must grow through ideational abstraction on the basis of certain experiences, and in continually growing abstraction be constantly preserved and realize themselves in their identity.[7]

---

[4] *Ibid.*   [5] *Ibid.*   [6] *Ibid.*, p. 5.
[7] *Ibid.*

Husserl was careful to emphasize that the concern here is not with "mere words" or a simple understanding of symbolic words. On the contrary, it is necessary to go to the "facts themselves," to employ the evidence contained in fully developed intuitions, that which the words truly symbolize, and to establish all meanings through determining their "irrevocable identification."

Logical acts, to be sure, do not require phenomenological analysis for completion, but since a phenomenology of logical experiences has the purpose of enlarging the descriptive understanding of psychical experiences, it could lend all fundamental logical concepts fixed meanings which would clarify the essential connection between meaning-intention (*Bedeutungsintention*) and meaning-fulfillment (*Bedeutungserfüllung*). This would result in a clarification of the relationship between "the subjective" and "the objective." Objective logical distinctions and insights would then be provided a basis of fixation.

Husserl, it must be further noted, was not here interested in "objective nature," let alone in any attempt to explain experiences of it. On the contrary, he was concentrating upon "the idea of knowledge according to its constitutive elements, and the clarification of its laws." [8] The real connections of coexistence and succession, in which "factual" cognitive acts are interwoven, were not the object of his study; he wanted, rather, to explain "the ideal meaning of specific relationships in which the objectivity of knowledge is intrinic." [9] With this would come the clarification of the forms and laws of knowledge by going back to the adequate fulfilling intuition.

In this manner Husserl stated the aim of a "phenomenology of knowledge." It is directed to the essence-structure of "pure" experiences and to the conditions of meaning inherent in them. In its "scientific" attitude there

[8] *Ibid.,* p. 21. [9] *Ibid.*

would be contained nothing whatever in the way of assertions about "real" existence; therefore there need be included no scientific, metaphysical, or (above all!) psychological statements as "premises."

Husserl's phenomenology of logical experience thus
has the purpose of establishing "an extensive descriptive
understanding (not, however, in the empirical psychological sense of the word) of those psychical experiences
and the intrinsic meanings that are necessary to give fixed
meanings to all fundamental logical concepts." [10] These
meanings, when examined for the essential connections
existing between meaning-intention and meaning-filling,
would then become epistemologically understandable
and certain.

Would such a phenomenology be "descriptive psychology"? [11] In the first edition of *Logische Untersuchungen*
Husserl, in order to enlarge upon the nature of his phenomenology, had inadvertently identified it as "descriptive psychology." By so doing, he naturally exposed himself to the criticism (what could be more odious to Husserl?) of being a "psychologizer." In the next edition he
took great care to explain that if the word psychology is
given its traditional meaning, phenomenology is most
certainly not to be classified with it.[12] Descriptive psychology, he argued, is interested in such matters as the
perception, judgments, and feelings of the "real, animal"
being, i. e., in *physical* conditions and characteristics. And
the descriptions of these apply to the events of nature and
the relations of the natural being to physical nature. Any
laws so established would have the "character of empirical universality—valid for nature." [13] Phenomenology,

10 *Ibid.*, p. 6.
11 See chap. vi, "Five Questions Concerning Phenomenology," § 4, pp.
238 f., for a more complete discussion of this problem.
12 *LU* II, pp. 17 f.
13 *Ibid.*, p. 18.

on the other hand, has no interest in the conditions of the "animal being." Rather does it speak of

perceptions, judgments, feelings, etc., *as such,* of that which belongs to them a priori, in unconditional universality, and hence of pure characteristics of a pure kind, of that which can be of "essence," even as pure arithmetic speaks of numbers, and geometry of spatial figures, on the basis of pure intuition of ideated universality.[14]

Since it would serve as the foundation of pure logical explanations, it is clear that phenomenology could not be called "psychology." Moreover, just as pure mathematics, as regards its doctrines of space and movements, is the basis of the exact sciences, so is phenomenology to be considered the basis of *genuine* psychology.[15] Just as geometric insights are valid for the spatial configurations of nature, so is "essence-insight into perceptions, will, and every other kind of such experiences naturally valid for the corresponding empirical conditions of the natural being." [16]

§ 2. *The Analysis of "Meaning"*

Thinking is articulated in affirmations which, when examined, are found to consist of expressions and certain kinds of "meaning-giving" acts.[17] Upon examining the structure of these acts, Husserl found that *logical meanings present themselves* as ideally united objects. Pure logic is concerned with these objects, or, as he called them, "ideal unities." These ideal unities have but one meaning, regardless of the circumstances under which

[14] *Ibid.,* p. 18.

[15] By "exact sciences" Husserl meant those sciences dealing with "things" with empirical configuration, movements, and so on; e. g., chemistry, physics, biology, and all disciplines that look upon themselves as branches of one or more of these (such as some types of psychology, e. g., modern genetic and physiological psychology).

[16] *LU* II, p. 19.

[17] *Ibid.,* §§ 31–32; cf. Osborn, "The Philosophy of Edmund Husserl," pp. 75 f.

they are apprehended or who utters the judgment. Phenomenologically considered, the meaning of any given
expression is thus a unity among a multiplicity and
variety.

Take for example the objective expression, "the bisectors of a triangle intersect at one point." This means
exactly what it says, nothing more, nothing less. Clearly
its meaning is in no way dependent upon him who expresses it or upon the circumstances under which the expression arises. It is simply a "judgment of fact." Is its
meaning to be found in the *act* of judging? Definitely
not, because it is an "objective," not an "occasional" expression. It is a *Geltungseinheit an sich.* As such a unity
of validity, its "truth" cannot depend upon the judging.
Were the attempt made to demonstrate that it did depend
upon the act of judging, it would be tantamount to saying that it was dependent upon thinking; this in turn
would reduce it to a mere "psychological" act. This, on
Husserlian grounds, would be intolerable, since the act of
judging is fleeting; it comes and goes. But such is not the
case with the *content* of the expression, "the bisectors of
a triangle intersect at one point." "Content" is not something which now "comes into existence" (by virtue of the
act of judging) and then "vanishes" when verbal articulation ceases. Moreover, acts of judging in each case might
be different, but the content of the judgment remains
the same. "We always recognize it as identity in intention
in self-evident acts of reflection; we do not arbitrarily
place it in the expression. We find it there." [18] Such
"objective expressions" [19] disclose insightful (*einsichtig*)

[18] *LU* II, p. 44. Husserl came to use "reflection," "abstraction," "intuition," and "ideation" interchangeably.

[19] Husserl here distinguished between objective and subjective "occasional" expressions when he gave instances of the latter as expressions of
wishes, hopes, and so forth; in short, those that concern the "I," the
speaker (*ibid.*, pp. 79 f.). Such expressions are not included in the domain
of "pure logic."

apprehension of ideal unities, ideal unities which remain valid regardless of who happens to enunciate them. As differentiated from the (subjective) psychological and grammatical form of expression, these ideal unities are properly the concern of pure logic.

As a matter of fact,

whenever pure logic deals with concepts, judgments, and conclusions, it does so exclusively with these ideal unities which we call meanings; and when we endeavor to differentiate the ideal essence of meanings from the psychological and grammatical characteristics, and when we furthermore attempt to explain the a priori relationship of adequation to the intended objectivity fundamental to this essence, we already stand in the sphere of pure logic.[20]

According to Husserl, then, "logic is the science of theoretical unity . . . the science of meaning as such." [21] The nature of all given theoretical unity is "unity of meaning"; logic is the science of theoretical unity in general.

This, according to Husserl, becomes evident from an examination of the nature of science itself. [22] Whenever science develops "systematic theories" and presents the fruits of its known truth as an "objective unity," it does not pretend to be speaking of mere subjective acts, such as judgments and ideas. Scientific expressions, such as "living power," "mass," and "integral" point not to mere

---

20 *Ibid.*, pp. 91–92.

21 *Ibid.*, p. 92. In the narrower sense, logic might be defined as the "science of meanings as such": "If, according to its nature, all given theoretical unity is unity of meaning, and if logic is the science of theoretical unity in general, it is immediately evident that logic must be the science of meanings as such, of their essential kinds and differences, including the pure laws (therefore ideal) based on them. For to those essential differences belong likewise those between objective and objectless, true and false meanings; to these laws also belong therefore the pure 'laws of thought' that express the a priori connection of the categorical form of the meanings and their objectivity, i. e., truth" (*ibid.*, pp. 92–93).

22 *Ibid.*, pp. 93 f. This is a summary restatement of Husserl's position found in *Prolegomena*. See chap. ii, § 1, pp. 14 f., "Logic as *Wissenschaftslehre*."

ideas but to objectivity, i. e., they possess, at least for the scientist, "objective meaning."

Again, the scientist constructs and builds upon "propositions." To be sure, he thereby "judges," but his propositions, not the judgments, are what he declares to be "true" or "false." These propositions, moreover, are not built of psychical acts alone, but are derived from discoveries of an objective kind. If, as frequently occurs, they are built from "concepts," these in turn are traceable to propositions based on objective discoveries.[23]

Propositions themselves are the *Bausteine* of deductions.[24] The relation of necessary conclusions, which constitutes the form of the deduction, is not "empirical" or "psychological" but is "an ideal relation of possible meaning-expressions, of propositions."[25] To say "it exists" or "it is" means "it is valid; and validity is something possessing no essential relation to empirical judging."[26] Scientific truths are "ideal" and do not depend upon the investigator or the process of being discovered for their validity.

All science, according to its objective content, is comprised of "theory," and is composed of this ideal "homogeneous stuff." It is "an ideal complex of meanings."[27] Moreover, and of greatest importance, this manifold of meanings, called by Husserl "theoretical unity of science," constitutes a unity of meaning. There is thus needed for science an investigation of its necessity, its very essence; there is required an a priori science of such categories as "meaning," "object," and "law." "Pure logic," believed Husserl, must assume this task, and as such it becomes, in the spirit of Bolzano, "the Science of science."

With these problems at hand, Husserl was confronted with the question of the nature or essence of "meaning."

23 *LU* II, p. 94.   24 *Ibid.*
25 *Ibid.*, p. 94.   26 *Ibid.*   27 *Ibid.*, p. 95.

It has been seen that Husserl must hold that the *Wesen* of meaning is not "imposed" by or found in some sort of subjective experience; it is in its "content," its "identical, intentional unity." Meaning is the identity or unity of multiplicity. What, then, did Husserl mean by "meaning"? What is "ideal unity"?

§ 3. *The Ideality of Meaning*

Meaning, according to Husserl, is of the nature of ideal unity or identity in the midst of variety. What comprises the intrinsic nature of identity? Husserl answered, "species" or "universals."[28] Meanings embody a class of concepts in the sense of "universal objects." Meanings are ideal unities, and ideal unity is identity—identity of species. Yet these objects do not have to be "somewhere" in the world or in heaven or even in "divine mind." Husserl considered any such "metaphysical hypostasization" not only as unnecessary but (logically) absurd.[29] The universal object or meaning is not real in the sense of real space-time objects, but is the correlate of the *Urteilsgeltung*, the validity of the judgment. Does this mean that it does not "exist"? Or that it has no "reality"? In the persuasion of Husserl, it *does* exist and has as much reality as any object could possibly claim. As an object, for instance, the proposition of the parallelogram of forces is just as real, taken as an object, as the city of Paris. The proposition of the parallelogram of forces indicates the apprehension of an "ideal meaning" as contrasted with the city of Paris, which is (at least potentially) a "real" object of sensory or imaginary perception. Each as an object represents a *difference of kind;* by the same token, each requires for its "being known" a correlative kind of apprehension.[30]

28 *Ibid.*, pp. 100 f.   29 *Ibid.*, p. 101.

30 The doctrine of the "intentionality" of consciousness. See § 7 of this chapter, pp. 74 f., for further consideration of this matter.

Does the ideality of meanings represent a normative ideality? [31] In answer to this Husserl argued that since the ideality of meanings is a "special instance" of the ideality of the specific, it can in no sense of the word be normative. It cannot be considered a "perfecting of the ideal" or "an actualizing of an ideal end-value. The ideal is a concrete prototype which can stand before the eyes and exist just as any real thing can." [32] Meaning is not merely a "goal" of some kind of striving; its ideality consists in the "unity in the manifold." The species itself, therefore, cannot be considered a "practical" ideal, although, to be sure, the individual instance falling under it is such a potential and eventual ideal. [33]

§ 4. *Logical Reflection*

How are such universal objects or meanings realized? By "logical reflection." What did Husserl mean by this?

Ordinarily in common discourse judgments concern not the meaning of the expression but the object itself. Although it is not constituted by the act of judging, the meaning is contained *in* the judgment, considered in the logical sense. When we formulate an expression, we make a judgment of the object in question and not a judgment about the meaning of the expression, i. e., about the judgment in the logical sense. Meanings come to us first "subjectively" in a reflective act of thought, in which we revert not only to the completed expression but perform

[31] *LU* II, pp. 101 f.   [32] *Ibid.*, p. 102.

[33] Moreover, the *concept* of meaning and meaning itself are not to be confused. In consideration of Husserl's argument, for instance, there is a vast difference between Bismarck himself and the concept of the great statesman, Bismarck. As *Logische Untersuchungen* progressed, Husserl dealt more and more with the *acts* in which meaning is given, but admitted that his epistemology could not delve deeply into the nature of meaning itself. Cf. *LU* II, p. 183: "What meaning is can be given just as immediately as are color and tone. It is impossible to define it further; it is a descriptive ultimate." The most he could say was that meaning is an "ideal unity," an "identity."

the required abstraction. This reflection or abstraction Husserl defined more closely as "ideation." It must be noted that Husserl was not here speaking of an act that occurs only under artificial conditions, for it would then be exceptional. Ideation as he used the word specifies a normal constituent of logical thinking. What this characterizes is the theoretical connection and the theoretical consideration directed to it which completes itself in progressive reflections on the content of the thinking act just completed.[34] In short, "logical reflection" *is an integral part of normal thinking.* It is that which, according to Husserl, makes possible "coherence" and "intelligibility" in ordinary intercourse with the objects of the world.

There is no connection between ideal unities which function "factually" as meaning and the means by which the mind realizes them. It cannot be said, therefore, that knowledge of all meanings has been attained or ever will be. On this point, Husserl stated that

every instance of a new concept teaches us how a meaning realizes itself which has never been realized before. Just as numbers—in the ideal sense of arithmetic—do not come and go in the act of counting, so it is with the ideal, pure unities, the concepts, propositions, truths, in short, the logical meanings.[35]

These comprise a closed, ideal realm of universal objects to which "being thought" and "expressed" are merely incidental. There are, therefore, innumerable meanings which in the ordinary, relative sense of the word are merely "possible" meanings, since they never come to expression and, because of the limited power of human knowledge, may never come to expression.

Although ideal unities are not dependent for existence upon their being verbally formulated, to become "real"

34 *Ibid.,* p. 103. Later, in the *Ideen,* "ideation," "logical thinking," "reflection," and so forth became "intuition."
35 *LU* II, p. 105.

(objectified) they must be *expressed* as meanings. Inversely, an expression to be valid must realize the ideal unity (as well as express it) in logical ideation. This logical thinking or ideation is a "fact," the same as is psychological thinking. Each has its own content and each represents a definite kind of apprehension.

§ 5. *The Ideality of Species*

If it is borne in mind how Husserl defined logical thinking, it is clear that species or universals are not real (space-time) objects of knowledge. Neither are they "concepts" or "judgmental categories."[36] Logical reflection or abstraction is essentially different from the perception of real objects. Universal objects are therefore not the content of psychological thinking, since it has sensory objects as its content. Yet there is a certain common "phenomenal" basis between psychological and logical thinking: to both is given the same sensory content in ways of apprehension which are identical. On the other hand, there is a marked difference in the acts, for in the case of psychological thinking the phenomenon serves as a basis for an act that intends an *individual* or particular object; in the instance of logical reflection, the phenomenon is the basis for an act which intends a *universal* object. The distinction between real particulars and ideal species is therefore purely categorical and belongs not to the matter, but to the *form* of consciousness. A better understanding of Husserl's concept of universals is possible when it is remembered that the term does not designate a mere name; the key to a clear comprehension of his doctrine is found in a study of the "act-characters" of the two kinds of knowledge.[37] Such an examination

---

[36] As with such critical realists as Strong, Sellars, and Russell. See chap. vi, "Five Questions Concerning Phenomenology," § 4, pp. 238 f., where I treat this problem at length.

[37] *LU* II, pp. 106 f.

discloses that there is a mode of consciousness which is completely distinct from ordinary perception.[38] The mode of apprehending species Husserl named "insightful ideation"; by it species are "objectified." [39] The discovery of act-characters and their nature marks the beginning of the clarification of meaning and indicates that there is a "phenomenology" as well as psychology of abstraction or logical thinking. For Husserl this meant that he was interested exclusively "in the content of the experiences of meaning and filling and, indeed, those which can be defined as essential contents." [40] The "universality" of psychological function is nothing less than the universality which belongs to the intentional content of logical experiences, whether it is spoken of objectively or ideally. It belongs to meanings and to the filling of meanings. The aim of phenomenological epistemology remains, then, as already emphasized, the examination and clarification of meaning and the means whereby such meaning is objectified.

All meaning, argued Husserl,

serves as a unity in thinking, and under varied circumstances judgments can be made with evidence of it in the same way. Take any given meaning: it can be the identical subject of various predicates, the identical relational point in a multiplicity of relations; as identical it is itself again the object in relation to a manifold of new meanings, even as other objects which are not themselves meanings, such as horses, stones, psychical acts, etc.[41]

How is it that meaning can be handled as an identity? For the sole reason, as pointed out above, that it *is* an

38 Perception and intuition (*Anschauung*) are sometimes confusedly used interchangeably by Husserl. For the purpose of clarity, henceforth "perception" will be designated "sensory perception," in contradistinction to intuition or ideation, the "apprehension of species or universals." A further discussion of these terms will be found under the heading, "Sensory Perception and Ideal Ideation," in this Chapter, § 6, pp. 69 f.
39 *LU* II, p. 107.   40 *Ibid.*, p. 146.   41 *Ibid.*, pp. 111–12.

identity in and for itself. Obviously Husserl is here speaking of logical thinking and reflection, and contained
within this discussion is the concept that a species "presents itself" or "comes to consciousness" as an object of
knowledge and in so doing it becomes "real" or "concrete." Moreover, in relation to the species, judgments
of the same logical form are possible, just as in relation to
individual objects. Logical concepts, or unified meanings,
are ideal objects by virtue of which they can now be conceived as universal or particular. The concept of the
Pythagorean proposition, for instance, is just as valid as
the concept, city of Berlin. Both remain identical in various discussions and intentions.

There is a definite relationship between similarity and
identity, since we find identity wherever we find similarity. It is only when we grant this identity that we can
call two things similar. In the very act of recognizing
similarity their identity is acknowledged. "Every similarity
has relation to a species which supports that which is
compared." [42] This is not a "mere" similarity, or we
would fall into an unavoidable *regressus in infinitum*.
Identity is present because of the species. We experience
and discover it. To be sure, identity does not have to be
expressed, that is, verbally articulated, or even "known,"
but it is there as ideated ("intuited") content. Identity
or meaning is to be taken as it is and is indefinable; it is
a descriptive ultimate. But similarity can be described as
"the relation of the objects which one and the same species supports." [43]

That which makes possible the declaration of similarity
between objects is thus the experience of identity or meaning. Yet identity does not reside in the particular objects
as such (considered from the standpoint of mere sensory
content). Identity is a kind of universal or species which

[42] *Ibid.*, p. 112.   [43] *Ibid.*, p. 113.

is a definite object of a particular kind of apprehension, namely, logical thinking or ideation, the knowledge of which makes coherent and intelligible experience of individual objects possible. Real objects are "objectified" in sensory perception.[44] Genuine knowledge of them is possible because of the apprehension of the universals which support them. On the basis of Husserl's argument, both the "reality" and the "ideality" of species are indisputable.

§ 6. *Sensory Perception and Ideal Ideation*

Experience has meaning. Is meaning imputed or apprehended? From the previous remarks, it could not be said it was "imputed." Following Husserl's argument, it is seen that in cognition of an object, considered from the side of the experient, there are at least two integral aspects in the knowing relation. These are the two kinds of intention, that which intends the particular, "real" object and that which intends the species, although as mentioned above both have as a basis the same sensory ground. To be sure, there is not required a *conscious* differentiation of these two on the part of the subject of the knowledge relation. The paper is known as "white" and as "paper" without the necessity of *reflecting* upon the difference between paper and whiteness or upon the nature of whiteness, let alone upon the connection between the two. The logical (ideational) differentiation makes the psychological distinction possible and self-evident without the necessity of a consciously differentiating act.[45]

These two ways of knowing Husserl called "act-characters" and meant thereby an intentional "faculty of dis-

[44] This concept will be enlarged upon in chap. v, pp. 161–76, §§ 3 and 4, "The Doctrine of Essences and Intuition" and "Intuition and Intentionality" respectively.
[45] *LU* II, p. 114.

tinction." He held that if more careful attention had been given to the act-characters of thinking and knowing in general, much of the confusion in philosophy could have been avoided. It would at least have been discovered that, as distinct from ordinary perception, there is a different mode of cognition, i. e., insightful ideation or intuition of species. It is this kind of knowing in which phenomenology as epistemology is ultimately interested. Insightful ideation is common to all thinking and has as its object essence or meaning, otherwise expressed by Husserl as "ideal unities" of thought and knowledge. Problems for the epistemologist are thus to be formulated somewhat as follows: What constitutes the meaning of that which is intended; What is the nature of that which is intended; What are its various forms and differences? The answer to these and other questions is to be found, from Husserl's standpoint, exclusively in the examination of the content of meaning and meaning-filling experiences. There is no concern, then, with "genetic functions" or relations between general and particular concepts.

Husserl's argument resolved itself into the affirmation of a *Bedeutungsbewusstein*, consciousness of meaning, and with this an *Allgemeinheitsbewusstein*, consciousness of universality. Although a study of the act-character of meaning is essential for a discovery of these kinds of consciousness, it must be emphasized that the act-character is not that upon which meaning "constitutes itself" as species. The relation between meaning and the meaning-expression is the same as that existing between the species red and the red object of perception, the object in which red "appears." While we intend red *in specie*, a red object appears to us, and in this sense we look "beyond" it. Although the red object and the redness in the object are there, "we intend much more the identical red and we intend it in a novel way of consciousness, through which, then, the species instead of the particular becomes the object."[46] Pure logic, then, differentiates phenomenologically between categorical differences of meanings, which correspond to the difference obtaining between particular and universal objects. Meanings, then, constitute the domain of pure logic.

Husserl emphasized, further, that the act in which we intend specific universals is essentially different from that in which we intend concrete particulars. As previously shown, each shares in common a certain phenomenal characteristic, namely, the same appearing concrete object, and during its appearance there is given the same sensory content in the same way of apprehension. But the same appearance carries on both sides different acts: in the case of the particular object, the appearance constitutes the conceptual foundation for an act of individual intention, i. e., for that kind of act in which we, in a mere "turning toward" what appears, intend "this thing" or "that characteristic," this part of the thing.

In the other instance, the appearance serves as a conceptual foundation for an act of a special apprehension and intending; that is, while the thing, or to be more specific, the characteristic of the thing, appears, we do not intend this characteristic as an object, this "here and now," but its content, its *Ideen*. We do not intend the redness of the house, but redness. This intending, relative to its being a basis of apprehension, is foundational. Insofar as it builds itself on the "perception" of the individual house, for instance, its redness is a "new way" of apprehension "which is constitutive for the intuitive givenness of the idea red." [47]

This universal object is the species and comes to consciousness in a manner which is wholly distinct from ordinary perception. It is alone through this faculty and by

[46] *Ibid.,* p. 107. [47] *Ibid.,* p. 109.

ideation ("logical thinking") upon its content that comparison and identification are possible. A careful examination of this mode of cognition reveals the primitive relation between the universal species and the individual object. Through this intuition a multiplicity can be grouped, compared, and identified; particulars remain distinct, yet as realized in the same species there exists between them the quality of identity. Individually they are distinct; specifically they are the same. As in the case of all fundamental logical distinctions, this is likewise "categorical." As such it belongs to the pure form of possible objectifying consciousness, and not to its matter.

DEVELOPMENT OF EPISTEMOLOGY (PHENOMENOLOGY)

Husserl had demonstrated to his satisfaction that in all sense experience there were, generally speaking, two kinds of objects of knowledge, real ("concrete") or particular, and ideal or universal, corresponding to which there are the two ways of cognition, sensory perception and ideal ideation. He had likewise shown that logical thinking, according to his definition of the term, was an integral constituent of normal thinking. This logical or ideational thinking is what lends "objectivity" to meanings. Meanings consist of species or universals, and, since they constitute the connection and coherence and intelligibility of real objects, it is clear that, since logical thinking is the way of knowing which apprehends the universals, the problem of knowledge (for Husserl) must ultimately be the nature of ideal species and the manner of our knowing them. With his transition to such problems, Husserl passed definitely from the realm of pure logic to that of epistemology and found himself confronted with new questions. What is the nature of psychical experiences in which the highest kind of meaning has its origin? What are the experiences in which the essentially different kinds of meaning arise? In short, what is the origin and foundation of the concept of meaning and its essential variations? In the light of his previous arguments, meanings should lie in meaning-intentions; what, then, would be the manner through which such meanings "come to apprehension"? It is not enough merely to say through ideation, for ideation itself has its various phases and aspects.

But before the role of meaning-intention and its relation to meaning in general could be given its fundamental phenomenological clarification, Husserl believed it essential to study first the nature of "acts." How are meanings known? "The experience of meanings should be 'acts,' and the measure of meaning in individual acts should lie not in the object but in the act experienced, and it should lie in that which makes it an 'intentional' experience 'directed' to objects." [48]

For the various kinds of objects there should here likewise correspond different kinds of acts, as thinking and perceiving; and "filling" itself should have a special relation belonging to the act-characters.

Since the word "act" is ambiguous and has been a source of constant controversy, particularly in the field of psychology, it is important, first of all, to know what is meant by the term. Husserl would show that

the concept of acts in the sense of intentional experiences comprises an important kind of unity in the sphere of experiences (comprehended in phenomenological purity), and accordingly, that the ordering of the meaning-experiences of this kind lends, in fact, a valuable characteristic to the same. [49]

Obviously this would also require the clarification of the difference between act-character and act-content; it would also include calling attention to the fundamentally dif-

[48] *Ibid.*, p. 344.
[49] *Ibid.*

ferent meanings in which "content" can be held. By delving into a phenomenology of ideas or concepts, Husserl proposed to improve upon Brentano's famous dictum, "Every act is an idea or has as its ground an idea."

After bringing to attention the traditional division between "the psychical" (considered the domain of psychology) and "the physical" (reserved exclusively for physical science), Husserl, in order to reveal wherein these two realms are not absolutely mutually exclusive, made a threefold division of the theory of consciousness. Consciousness has been defined as (1) the phenomenological characteristic of the empirical "I"; (2) the inner perception of psychical experiences; and finally (3) that which designates every kind of "psychical act" or "intentional experience."[50] After examining the first two concepts, Husserl proceeded to elaborate his own viewpoint, included in which there is found a careful consideration of Brentano's theory of consciousness.[51]

§ 7. *Consciousness as Intentional Experience*

Brentano had developed the idea of psychical phenomena, and included within this concept was a sharp differentiation between the psychical and physical. Yet Husserl believed that Brentano was guilty of failing to make a sufficiently careful analysis of the nature of psychical and physical phenomena, with the result that sometimes that which he called the "psychical" was not exactly so, and that which he defined as "physical" was frequently psychical.[52] In spite of this defect, however, Husserl held that the importance of Brentano was to be found

---

[50] *Ibid.,* p. 346.

[51] The reasons for Husserl's rejection of the first two concepts will become clear by implication in the study of his own viewpoint. Cf. Husserl's criticisms, *LU* II, pp. 346 f.

[52] *Ibid.,* pp. 363 f.

in the concept that "in perception something is perceived, in imagination something is imagined, in expression something is expressed, in love something is loved, in hate something hated, in desire something desired, and so on."[53] Furthermore, Brentano had held that every psychical phenomenon is characterized by its "relation to a content, direction to an object,"[54] which he defined as "immanent objectivity."[55] Everything "contains in itself" something as an object, although, of course, not in the same way. Out of his general scheme arose three general classifications of psychical phenomena: concepts, judgments, and emotions.

(a) *Some difficulties inherent in Brentano's theory.*— Upon consideration of Brentano's doctrine Husserl, for his purpose, considered as extremely important the concept that "there are essentially specific varieties of intentional relationships, or, in short, of intentions (which, considered descriptively, are 'acts')."[56] There is a difference between an "idea" having an "object," such as trust and doubt, hope and fear, and a judgment of something as true or false, good or bad, and so forth. Although it is not always the case, it can be said that most acts are complex experiences; if this be true, intentions are likewise complex. For instance, Husserl would show that emotional intentions build themselves upon the intentional mode of ideas or judgments.

Husserl believed, nevertheless, that the pristine intentional character of these complexes cannot be reduced to other kinds of psychical experiences; he held, moreover, that the unity of a descriptive kind of "intention" (act-character) is entirely different from those which are ground in their pure nature, and therefore precede a

53 *Ibid.*, p. 367.   54 Brentano, *PES* I, p. 115.
55 Called by scholastics "mental inexistence."   56 *LU* II, p. 368.

priori the empirical psychological facts. In brief, there are essentially different kinds and sub-kinds of intention.

He descriptively defined the intentional relation as the "inner quality" of certain experiences, as the essential quality of psychical phenomena or acts. Phenomenologically, then, psychical phenomena are simply intentional experiences or acts. Yet not all experiences are intentional, as, for instance, sensations and their complexes. This is evident when it is remembered that sensations *as such* are not "seen" or "intended," although they can be the means of exciting perception and intention. The object itself is intended. Brentano had failed to draw this careful distinction between sensations and their complexes as that which cannot be seen or intended, and the object which alone, in this connection, can be the object of perceiving and intending.

Brentano, in his dictum "that psychical phenomena are either ideas or grounded in ideas," meant that *only what has been first ideated can be judged or desired or hoped or feared*. The ambiguity of this statement lies in his failure to see the distinction between ideated content (object) and the *act* of ideating. As a matter of fact, Husserl held that he really meant the *act* of ideating, but failed to clarify it in his thinking. To avoid this difficulty, Husserl tried to abandon altogether the terms "psychical phenomena" and even "phenomena." [57] Brentano's use of the word "phenomenon" implied that *every* intentional experience is a phenomenon. Husserl, on the contrary, used the word as "appearing object" (*erscheinender Gegenstand*); he accordingly held that "every intentional experience is not only related to an object but is itself an object of a certain kind of intentional experience." [58]

[57] Not entirely with success. Beginning with *Ideen* he employed the term "phenomenon" all the time and defined it as "that-which-presents-itself." Cf. chap. v, § 1, pp. 136 f.

[58] *LU* II, p. 371.

In view of this, one thinks immediately of those experiences which in a special sense bring objects to appearance, namely, perceptions. This would mean that every psychical phenomenon is the object of inner consciousness, but Husserl has already rejected this. Moreover, it is frequently misleading to say that what is perceived, imagined, judged, wished, and so forth, "enters into" consciousness; or, inversely, that consciousness "comes to them" in relationship in some way or another, that they become "seized" in consciousness in some manner or another; or, again, that intentional experiences "contain something in themselves" as the object.

Inherent in such expressions are two principal misconceptions: (1) that there is something "real" or that there is a "real event" existing in a relationship which plays between consciousness (or the "I") and the known object; (2) that there exists a "relationship" between two of the same kind of things in consciousness which are real, i. e., the act and the intentional object, somewhat like a psychical content "indwelling" in the other.[59]

In order to escape these ambiguities, Husserl likewise abandoned the idea and term "immanent objectivity." He argued, on the contrary, that there are not "two things," the "object experienced" and the "intentional experience" which is directed to the object. Actually, there is present only a one, the intentional experience, whose essentially descriptive character is the relational intention. . . . If this experience is present, it is so *eo ipso,* which lies completed, I emphasize, in its own nature. The intentional "relation to an object" *eo ipso* is an object "intentionally present." . . . And naturally such an experience can be existent in consciousness with this its intention without the object existing at all, and perhaps not even being able to exist; the object is intended, means that intending it is the experience; but it is then merely intended and yet in truth is nothing.[60]

---

[59] *Ibid.,* p. 371.   [60] *Ibid.,* pp. 372–73.

This may be elucidated in the following manner. It is possible to ideate the god "Jupiter," which is "immanently present" and has "mental inexistence" (to use the scholastic term). There is a definite experience of ideating, yet the immanent or mental object does not belong in reality to the structure of experience. As a matter of fact, it is neither immanent nor mental, nor is it *extra mentem*. It just is not. On the other hand, if the intended object does actually exist, phenomenologically nothing is changed. The given is for consciousness essentially the same whether the ideated object "exists" or whether it is imagined, or perhaps is even "nonsensical." Phenomenologically there is the same kind of ideation when Jupiter, Bismarck, the Babylonian tower, and Cologne are ideated. Just as so-called "immanent contents" are intentional, so are "real" immanent contents not intended. They "build" the act, they make possible, as the necessary point of convergence, the intention; yet they themselves are not intended. "They are not the objects which are ideated in the act. I do not see color sensations, but colored things; I do not hear tonal sensations, but the song of the singer." [61]

By these arguments Husserl, so he believed, was able to avoid a serious difficulty inherent in Brentano's theory of immanent objectivity, namely, that only contents, not the object itself, are intended. Moreover, as opposed to Brentano, Husserl argued that what is true of the object of ideation is likewise true of all other intentional experiences. Such acts as judging, wishing, hoping and loving all have this in common: "they are ways of objective intention which we ordinarily can express in no other way than to say, the castle is perceived, imagined, ideated, judged; it is the object of this happiness or of that wish." [62]

[61] *Ibid.*, p. 374.   [62] *Ibid.*

Continuing his discussion of the difference between sensations and object, in which he showed that sensations themselves are not the object of perception, Husserl took as an example a box which is turned and moved around in every conceivable way. One and the same box is seen, no matter how it is turned or moved about, or from what perspective it is viewed. There is the same "content of consciousness"—if it is desired to call the perceived object "content of consciousness"; by turning it around there enters a *new* content of consciousness—if it is desired to call it "experienced content." Although different contents are experienced, the same object is "perceived." It follows that the experienced content itself cannot be designated as the "perceived" object. Hence it is important to observe the irrelevancy of examining the "real" existence or nonexistence of the object for the "qualitative" nature of the experiences of perception, since this is clearly an instance of the perception of this object "appearing" as "so and so," and of *that* "intended" object. Obviously, since it is *intended* to apprehend the same object in the midst of changing sensory contents, the object belongs to the sphere of *intentional* experience. We experience the consciousness of identity, and that means we apprehend that which is intended. Identity is there because it is apprehended in intentional activity. And there is clearly a difference between contents and acts, especially between sensory contents in the sensations and perceptual acts in the sense of apprehending intention, "which intention, in unity with the apprehended sensation, constitutes the full concrete act of perception."[63]

Husserl in this way came to the concept of essentially different modes of consciousness; that is, the distinctions are found in a study of the intentional relation of con-

[63] *Ibid.*, p. 383.

sciousness to its objects. The character of intention, for instance, is a specifically different kind in the case of perception, which is merely "reproductive" representation. To every logically different way in which to ideate in thought an object, there corresponds a different kind of intention. How do we know these differences? We *apprehend* them in their individual instances and bring them, by comparison, under concepts. On the other side, we can adequately apprehend out of them, through ideational abstraction, the pure species or universals residing in them, as well as the specific connections intrinsic to them. Content, then, is *experienced,* constituting consciousness as "real." "Consciousness itself is the complex of experience."[64] To intend the world is experience; the world itself is the intended object and never merely the experience of thinking.

More precisely, what did Husserl mean by "contents of consciousness"? Primarily, he differentiated between "descriptive" or "real" and "intentional" content of an act. Under the real phenomenological content of an act, he understood its *Gesamtinbegriff,* "the entirety of the partial experiences which constitute it as real."[65]

It was at this point of his studies that Husserl made what he called his "transition" from the empirical, psychological standpoint to the phenomenological, ideal standpoint. He characterized this by saying

We exclude all empirical, scientific apperceptions and positing of existence. We take the empirical experience or, otherwise expressed, that which is seen internally, according to its pure experience and as a mere exemplary support for ideations. Out of this we concentrate upon the ideative universal essence and connections of essence—the ideal species of experience, of different kinds of generality, and ideally valid

---

[64] *Ibid.,* p. 386.   [65] *Ibid.,* p. 397.

knowledge of essences which are valid, therefore, for the ideally possible experiences of the corresponding species a priori in unconditioned universality.[66]

By such a process of reasoning Husserl believed he had won insight into the realm of "pure" phenomenology, which, as a science, is wholly independent of and has nothing to do with crass sense experience, for the very reason that it does not fall within the scope of its investigation.

(b) *Intentional contents of consciousness.*—Contents in the sense of "real" is the mere application of the concept of content, in its most ordinary meaning, to intentional experiences. As opposed to this real content, the "intentional" was defined by Husserl as "the quality of intentional experiences (or acts) as such."[67] Again, under the concept of intentional content, there is a threefold distinction to be made: first, the intentional object of the act; second, its intentional matter as opposed to its intentional quality; and, finally, its intentional nature or essence. More exactly, then, the "intentional content" is the intentional *object*. For instance, when we ideate a house, it is a house. Obviously the intentional content in this sense is different from the real content. This distinction can apply not only to "outer" or external things, but in part also to those acts which relate themselves intentionally to qualitatively present experiences, as, for instance, objects of memory.

Relative to intentional content understood as the object of the act, the differentiation of "the object as it is intended" must also be made. In every act there is an object which is qualitatively ideated as "so and so," and as such it is the eventual point of various intentions, such as judging, feeling, and desiring. Then there is (second) merely

66 *Ibid.*, p. 398.   67 *Ibid.*, p. 399.

the object which is intended; by virtue of the objective unity of knowledge, it remains, however, the same object which is ideated. This is accounted for by the real condition of the act and brings it about that in all the various intentions the object is that which is intended. This is true although the intention in every kind of intentional activity might be different. Each intends the object in a different way. For instance, the Kaiser of Germany can be ideated as the Kaiser or as the son of Frederick III, and so on.

This does not completely depict, however, all the differentiations contained in Husserl's argument. There is the further and equally important distinction to be drawn between the objectivity upon which an act, taken fully and completely, directs itself, and the objects upon which the various partial acts direct themselves. Regarding the former, "every act completes itself intentionally in an objectivity belonging to it."[68] This is true both of "simple" and "compound" acts. No matter how many partial acts there are, it is always *one* act and accordingly it has its correlation in *one objectivity,* and it is this, taken in the primary sense, upon which it completes itself. Regarding partial acts, on the other hand, they direct themselves to objects. Although they can be identical with the object of the whole act, they are not generally so. While it can be said that in a certain way the whole act completes itself in objects, this is so only in a secondary sense, i. e., only insofar as its intention directs itself to it as it builds itself out of acts which primarily intend them. For example, take this compound statement: "The knife on the table." The object of the entire act is a knife; the object of the partial act is the table. This is therefore a compound act. One could say in a secondary sense that the table is the intentional object of the total nominal act. Now take

[68] *Ibid.,* p. 401.

the proposition: "The knife lies on the table." Although the knife is once again the object of judgment, it is not the primary object, since it is merely the subject of the judgment. To the whole judgment there corresponds as the complete and whole object of the judged fact that which can be ideated identically in the same way as a mere idea in a wish wished, in a question asked, in a doubt doubted, and so forth. In a wish, for instance, "the knife" is obviously not the primary object, but that the knife *"should"* lie on the table. Once again, the wish is not to be confused with the judgment, let alone the idea of the judgment. Neither the judgment nor the idea is wished. It is better, therefore, instead of using the expression, "intentional content," to speak of *intentional object*.

Having drawn and clarified the marked differentiation between "real" and "intentional" content or object, Husserl was now prepared to enter into a more detailed examination of the nature of "acts."

§ 8. *Analysis of the Structure of Acts*

Husserl first drew a distinction between the "general character" of the act, which designates it as merely ideating or judging or feeling, or the like, and its "content," which specifies the act as the idea of what is ideated, the judgment of what is judged, or the feeling felt. For instance, $2 + 2 = 4$, and "Ibsen is the principal founder of modern realism in dramatic art" are two affirmations of one kind, in the sense that each is qualified as an "assertion." That which is held in common between these two is the quality of judgment. Yet one is a judgment of this, the other is a judgment of that, and this distinction constitutes the matter of the judgment. Similarly, there are such distinctions between quality and matter in every act.[69]

[69] *Ibid.*, pp. 411 f.

(*a*) *The "matter" of the act.*—Content in the sense of matter is a compound of concrete act-experiences which can have this in common with acts of other qualities. In short, acts of different qualities can have the same content in common. For instance, the same content can now be the content of a mere idea, at another time, of a judgment, and at other times of a question, a doubt, a wish. For example, whoever ideates that there is intelligent life on Mars has the same idea as he who says, "There is intelligent life on Mars," and the same as he who inquires, "Is there intelligent life on Mars?" even as he who expresses the wish, "If there were only intelligent life on Mars." Clearly, it follows that the content in the sense of matter is a component of the concrete act-experience. Acts of different quality can, moreover, possess in common the same content.

(*b*) *The "quality" of the act.*—What does Husserl mean here by the "same content"? Obviously the *intentional objectivity* is the same in the various acts. One and the same "fact" is ideated in the idea, posited as valid in the judgment, and wished in the wish. The objectivity, however, taken in itself, is nothing. It is "transcendent" to the act. By this is meant that it is a matter of indifference in what sense and in what right its existence is spoken of, whether it is "real" or "ideal," whether it is "true" or even "possible" or "impossible"; the act, in each case, is directed toward it. If the question should arise how, as intentional objects, one could not ask these questions about it, there is, Husserl believed, only one answer:

The object is an intentional object, and this means that it is an act with a definitely characterized intention which, in this characterization, constitutes what we call the intention to this object. The relation to the object is a quality belonging to the peculiar nature of the act experienced, and the experiences which they show are called by definition intentional experiences or acts.[70]

In brief, every differentiation relative to objective relationship is a "descriptive" differentiation of corresponding intentional experiences.

However, the phenomenological nature of the act as having "the quality of being directed to objectivity" does not yet complete the description, for there can be a variety of objective relationships which are independent and fundamentally different. For instance, an objectivity can now be ideated, now judged, and so on, but all *intentionally*. "Every quality can be combined with every objective relationship," and "corresponding to this quality of the different aspects is the phenomenological content of the act."[71]

With this in mind, Husserl's concept of the "matter" of the act becomes clearer. Essentially it means that in an act which lends objectivity to the relationship in such full determination that not only is the objectivity which the act intends defined, but the *manner* is specified in which the objectivity is intended. The matter is thus the "quality" inherent in the act, which quality not only determines that the act apprehends objectivity, but it prescribes *what* it apprehends, which characteristics, relationships, and categorical forms it includes in itself. "It lies in the matter of the act that the object of the act is this and nothing else; accordingly it is the meaning of the objective apprehension which grounds the quality, or, in short, *Auffassungssin*."[72] Identical matters can thus never be of different objective relationship; but different matters can give similar objective relationships.

This means that the quality of the act is doubtless an abstract moment of the act which, removed from the

[70] *Ibid.*, pp. 412–13.   [71] *Ibid.*, p. 413.   [72] *Ibid.*, p. 416.

matter, would be absolutely unthinkable. Clearly an experience could not have the quality of judgment which did not contain a judgment of some kind of matter. Even if this were imaginable, the judgment would obviously lose the character of "intentional" experiences.

(c) The "unity" of the act.—This Husserlian depiction of the matter and the quality of the act does not, however, complete the phenomenological description of the nature of the act. Even when these two aspects are brought to unity, they do not constitute the concretely completed act, since it is conceivably possible to have two acts which can be differently described while having simultaneously the same quality and matter.

What, then, composes the unity of these essential constituents? Husserl replied, the *intentional* nature of the act. It is to be noted that if the act is "meaning-giving," its intentional nature can be spoken of as the "meaningful nature" (*bedeutungsmässigen Wesen*) of the act. "Its ideational abstraction imputes the meaning in its ideal sense."[73] It is this intentional nature that would make, for instance, the difference between the ordinary person's idea of the ice wastes of Greenland and that held by Nansen. Once again, the ideal objects "straight" and "straight line" are identical, but the concepts of them are different.

The importance of Husserl's distinction between quality and matter becomes even more evident when considering Brentano's dictum that psychical phenomena are either ideas or based on ideas. Husserl now interpreted this to mean that *in every act the intentional object is an ideated object in an act of ideation;* and that where it is not concerned from the beginning with a "mere" ideation, there is at all times an ideation with one or more further acts—or rather act-characters—so peculiarly and intimately

[73] *Ibid.,* p. 417.

interwoven that the ideated object appears thereby at the same time as judged, wished, hoped, and so forth.[74] This plural characteristic of intentional relation is effected in one strictly unifying act in such a way that one object appears only once, although in this single appearance it is the aim of complex intention. Otherwise expressed, an intentional experience wins its relation to an objectivity only because

there is present in it an act of experience of ideating which constitutes it ideationally as object. The object would be nothing for consciousness if it did not complete an ideating which thereby makes it an object, and does it in such a way that it can now become the object of feeling, desiring, etc.[75]

In the light of Husserl's observations, and using his terminology, there is found in Brentano's proposition a double meaning of "idea." In the first part of the proposition, idea is a definite kind of act; in the second, it is mere act-matter. This would mean that intentional experiences rest on ideas which are not acts but act-material, and it is this false proposition against which Husserl particularly directed his argument. The first thesis of the proposition is exemplified in multilateral acts, such as judgments, since it contains at least one idea as a basis, even as a fully articulated expression contains at least one name. Husserl's enlargement of Brentano's concept serves to dissolve such ambiguities, as well as to clarify the basic elements of cognitive experiences.

§ 9. *The Distinction between "Nominal" and "Objectifying" Acts*

Having analyzed the structure of acts in general, Husserl now drew attention to his distinguishment between nominal acts such as desiring and wishing, and objectifying acts, which are those of ideating and judging. Cor-

[74] *Ibid.*, p. 427.   [75] *Ibid.*, p. 428.

responding to this distinction, there are two different kinds of "founding" (*Fundierung*). First, there is the founding of "non-objectifying" acts (e. g., enjoying, wishing and willing) in objectifying acts (e. g., ideas and judgments) "whereby primarily an act-quality is founded in another act-quality and first, mediately, in a matter."[76]

Second, there is the founding of "objectifying" acts in other objectifying acts, whereby primarily an act-matter is founded on another act-matter (e. g., those of predicative expression in those of founding nominal acts). The condition that no matter is possible without objectifying quality must, from itself, have the consequence that where one matter is founded in another matter, also an objectifying act of the first matter is founded in just such acts of the latter matter. Consequently, there is this fact, that every act is at all times founded in nominal acts of different sources. Every founding objectified act is a nominal act, and is thereby "simple" as well as being the original source. Since, however, all other kinds of act-qualities are founded in objectifying acts, there is carried over the final founding to nominal acts from objectifying acts to all acts in general.[77]

Once Husserl had completed the analysis of acts in general and had distinguished between nominal and objectifying acts, he was brought to a series of studies which included, among other subjects, that of the levels of knowledge, and the difference and relation between sensibility and understanding.

§ 10. *The Levels of Knowledge*

Delving into the problem of "levels" of knowledge, Husserl first asked, "What is the role of perception?"[78] Take

[76] *Ibid.*, p. 48.
[77] *Ibid.*, pp. 498–99.
[78] This study marks a consideration of Part 2 of *LU* II, hereafter referred to as *LU* III. Other matters, touched upon here only by implica-

the example, "a blackbird flies up." Where is the meaning of the expression? Certainly it is not found in the perception alone. This is evident from the fact that the words and even the sense of the expression could remain the same although the perception varied or even ceased. Meaning evidently belongs to or lies in something that is held in common by the manifold acts of perceiving an object. Moreover, it is obvious that perception is not the act in which expressions of perception themselves have their meaning filled.

What part does an expression play? It simply articulates what is "given" in perception. Various kinds of expressions direct themselves to the contents of the same perception. The expression of a perception (taken objectively, "the perceived") does not belong to mere wording, but is an act itself of a certain kind. The experience of expression has "an intentional relationship to something objective."[79] Therefore there must exist between perception and articulation a mediating act which conveys meaning. Since experiential expressions have intentional relationship to some object, there is clearly involved an act to allow for this; such mediating act must serve as *meaning-giving* and makes meaning identical in the midst of various perceptions of an object.

Perception as an act determines, but does not carry meaning. There is more in expression, for instance, than mere perceiving. Reverting to the example, the *individual* blackbird is "referred to." It means *a* blackbird, *this* blackbird.

To follow Husserl's argument further: when it is said, "this paper lying before me," there is a relationship to this object, but the meaning does not lie in this. On the

---

tion, were "meaning-intuition" and "meaning-filling," and the "nature and kinds of perception."
[79] *LU* III, p. 16.

basis of perception, there builds a new act of directing, according to its nature and different from its independent act, the act of *meaning this.* In this intention alone lies the meaning, although it is granted, of course, that the perception makes possible its demonstration *in concreto.*[80] Perception is therefore the possibility for the development of the "meaning this," with its definite relationship to the object, e. g., the paper before my eyes. But, according to Husserl, perception does not constitute the meaning itself or any part of it. In short, in an "expressed perception" with a definite reference there is found "an act of indicative meaning. In this specific indication alone lies the meaning."[81] Without perception, specification would be empty; without definite differentiation and *in concreto,* it would be wholly impossible.

Husserl termed that which unites the perception and expression a "covering" (*Deckung*). Perception gives the object an expression, and the expression thinks and articulates it by means of a judgment. From this it follows that it is necessary not only to differentiate between expression and meaning of the expressed perception, but that

there lies in the perception itself no part of the meaning. The perception which gives the object, and the expression which, by means of a judgment—i. e., by means of the "thinking act" which forms the unity of the judgment—thinks and expresses, are fully to be distinguished, although in the instances before us of perception-judgments, it stands in the most intimate relationship to the covering, to the unity of the filling.[82]

Regarded statically, "this covering shows a unity of the intuitive act on the side of the objective phenomenon and of the expressing act on the side of the verbal phenomenon."[83] The "covering," in short, is the *Einheits-verhältnis:* intuitive activity is "occasioned" by percep-

80 *Ibid.,* p. 18.   81 *Ibid.*
82 *Ibid.,* p. 21.   83 Osborn, *op. cit.,* p. 96.

tion which relates all *geistig* activity to its object.[84] Regarded in a dynamic relationship between meaning and intuition, Husserl said that there is a "filling-of-consciousness," since the act of pure meaning "finds in the way of a purposive intention its fulfillment in the intuitive act."[85] Their unity is found in the meaning-intention and the more or less completely corresponding intuitions. The expression functions at first (more or less) symbolically. This means that "the intentional nature of the intuitive act (more or less perfectly) fits itself in with the meaningful nature of the expressing act."[86]

According to Husserl, then, meaning is not contained alone in "knowing," since the content of the intuitive experience is named; "in the purely symbolical understanding of a word, a meaning is completed; the word means something to us, but nothing is thereby known."[87] This is made clear by analysis of the dynamic relationship constituting the unity between intuitive and expressing acts. There is first of all the intentional meaning given for itself, then there follows the corresponding intuition. Simultaneously the (phenomenological) unity establishes itself, which now manifests itself as "consciousness-of-filling." "Knowledge of an object" and "filling of meaning intention" are the same.[88]

Out of the above analysis there appear three aspects of knowledge: (1) the object itself which is apprehended in

[84] Note the importance of this for religion and its claim of direct (unmediated) experience of Deity. Max Scheler rejected this particular aspect of Husserl's epistemology when he argued that in the realm of values the Divine is experienced "immediately" (without the necessity of mediating sensory objects). Cf. his *Formalism in der Wertethik* and *Vom Ewigen in Menschen.*

[85] *LU* III, p. 32.

[86] *Ibid.*

[87] *Ibid.,* p. 33.

[88] The act of meaning-intention, or meaning, is sometimes called "significant," or "significant act," or sometimes just "symbolic." It is the opposite of intention.

(2) perception; and (3) the act of meaning or signification. Accordingly

every perception and every imagination is a web of partial
intentions brought together in the unity of a total intention.
The latter has its correlate in the thing, while the correlates
of the partial intentions are the parts and aspects of the
thing.[89]

Consciousness, in intention, "reaches out" to the experienced object, and intention thereby fulfills itself.

Here, once again, arises the problem of the role of
sense perception. Does perception "give" the object? Certainly it "pretends" to, but as a matter of fact it really
gives only one side of it. The object itself is not really
given, i. e., it is not given as it "really is." It appears only
from the "front side," as perspectively "abridged and
shaded." If the perception were really and purely the
self-representation of the object as it pretends, since its
peculiar nature "creates itself" in this self-representation,
there would be only one special perception for each object. No argument is needed to demonstrate the invalidity
of such a claim, since there is obviously required a succession of perceptions before an object is adequately represented. On the other hand, there is no reason to believe
that the object "in itself" is completely different from that
which is realized in any given perception. Phenomenologically,

the common perception can be constructed of various aspects,
party of purely perceptual intentions, partly of merely imaginative intentions, and even partly of significant intentions;
as total act, perception seizes the object itself, although it
might be done only in the way of shading (*Abschattung*).[90]

---

[89] *LU* III, p. 41.
[90] *Ibid.*, p. 57. The word *Abschattung* was used by Husserl to indicate
the variety of acts which, taken together, constitute what he called "ordinary" perception. Such acts supply various "perspectives" or shadings.

How is it possible that a variety of perceptions belongs to the same object? An object can appear in one perception from one side, then another; it is now near, it is now far, and so forth. Yet we say the object is "there." In each of the various perceptions it is intended as the sum total of that which is known to us as a perception, and which is present in this perception. Phenomenologically, there corresponds to this variety of perceptual perspectives the continual flow of "filling" and "identifying," and the continual arranging of these perceptions "belongs to the same object." Each one is thus a combination of filled and unfilled intentions. To the former there corresponds in the object that which is given of it in "this" single perception as more or less perfect shading; to the latter, that which is not yet given of it and which therefore can come in new perceptions to actual filling presence. All the various kinds of filling syntheses are characterized by one common character, just as in the identification of the self-appearance of an object with another self-appearance of the same object. Clearly the complete self-representation of an object is a "synthesis-of-filling" of the various acts. [91]

A study of the process of filling discloses that it has the character of gradation, which leads ultimately to the "goal of absolute knowledge, of the adequate self-representation of knowledge." [92]

External perception itself supplies the "purely perspective content," i. e., what remains after all the imaginative and significant components have been extracted. It is the sensory content.

[91] Everything that can be said of perception can likewise be said of "imagination." Imagination "sees" its object from various sides; "to the synthesis of the manifold of perceptions, in which always the same object comes to self-representation, there corresponds the parallel synthesis of the manifold images, in which the same object comes to imaginary representation" (*LU* III, p. 58). Hence both perception and imagination are placed in opposition to the intention of signification. The quality of the synthesis-of-filling demonstrates (although only indirectly) the difference between intuitive and significative acts.

[92] *Ibid.*, p. 66.

Just as there can be a series of partial perceptions which is synthesized in a total perception, so with intuition. There can be a series of intuitions for each object, which series has the character of a gradation; yet every series points to an "ideal limit" or realizes such a limit in its end-term. Moreover, since it is necessary to a given intuition to belong to a certain synthesis, the series can also be regarded as "identifications." With the synthesis of each new intuition there is a growth in the fullness of knowledge, but the successive intuitions are not the fillings of those which they follow. The total synthesis in any sequence of perceptions represents, in comparison with any particular perception, such a growth in the fullness of knowledge that the imperfection of the partial representation is relatively overcome in the total representation.[93]

There are three phases in the gradation of "fullness." First, the "extent of the richness" of fullness, which varies as the object is represented with greater or less perfection, with greater or less clearness; second, the "liveliness" of the fullness, the degree of approach to the primitive similarity of the representation to the object (Hume); finally, (third) the "measure of reality," the degree of imagery contained in the fullness. In all these relations the adequate perception represents the ideal, since it has the maximum of liveliness and reality, just as the self-comprehending of the full and complete object.[94] Every objectifying act includes a representation in itself. Since, according to Husserl's restatement of Brentano's doctrine, every act is itself either an objectifying act or has such an act as its basis, the final basis of all acts is "ideas" in the sense of representation.[95]

[93] *Ibid.*, pp. 66–67.   [94] *Ibid.*, pp. 83–84.

[95] *Ibid.*, p. 94. This concept of Husserl's is obviously of primary importance for his theory of objectifying acts, since it can now be expanded to allow for their fullness. Objectifying act now has three elements: quality, matter, and fullness, or "intuitively presented" content.

Husserl considered the culmination of his theory of gradation to be in his "doctrine of adequation," since knowledge exists in various degrees. Imagination never gives the object, but an image; perception gives the object only in the sense of degrees of shading; signifying acts, the lowest of all, have no fullness whatever. Hence the consideration of the possible relations of filling-points to a conclusive goal of the gradation of filling, in which the complete and total intention has attained its filling and, indeed, not in an intermediary and partial filling, but in an ultimate and final one. The intuitive content of this conclusive idea is the absolute sum of possible fullness, for the intuitive content is the object itself as it is "in itself." Represented and representing content are identically one in this, the highest of all degrees of gradation, and where an ideational intention has created final fullness through this ideally complete perception, it has produced the *adequatio rei et intellectus*. The objectivity "is exactly the same as that which is intended as really 'present' or 'given'; no partial intention is further implied which would lack its filling." [96] *"Intellectus"* is thus, for Husserl, "the thoughtful intention, that of the meaning. And the *adequatio* is realized when the intended objectivity is given exactly as it is in the intuition, and given exactly as that which is thought and named." [97] Adequation represents, for Husserl, the ideal of knowledge.[98] In it is found a fullness which points to nothing beyond itself, since it completes all possible fullness.

Precisely what did Husserl mean by "intuitive" content? By intuitive content of the act he was not referring to the quality of the act (whether it was positing or not);

[96] *Ibid.*, p. 118.
[97] *Ibid.* Note the scholastic tinge.
[98] Could this be the clue to Husserl's resolution of the problem of "truth and error"? This is discussed in chap. vi, "Five Questions Concerning Phenomenology," § 1, pp. 207 f.

he had in mind the following two phenomenological distinctions. First, there is the "pure" intuitive content of acts, such as that "which corresponds in acts to the totality of the qualities of the objects 'coming into appearance'." [99] There is, second, the "significant content" of the act, which corresponds similarly to the totality of the other qualities. To be sure, although it is intended with it, it is itself not in the "qualities" of the appearance.

The total act of intuition possesses either the character of perception or that of imagination. Intuitive content is called, then, *"especially* perspective, or the content of perception relative to the imaginative or image-content." [100]

This intuitive content, however, is not to be confused with the perspective or the imaginative *presenting*-content, in the more specific sense of the word. Under "presenting" or intuitively representing contents, Husserl understood those contents of intuitive acts which, by virtue of purely imaginative or perspective apprehension, whose carriers they are, indicate in them definitely corresponding contents of the object. They represent in this way imaginative or perspective shadings. [101]

§ 11. *Sensory and Categorical Intuitions*

Husserl now had before him the task of determining the categorical object forms, i. e., the synthetic functions in the sphere of objective acts through which objective forms constitute themselves, through which they come to "perception," and, accordingly, to "knowledge."

As universal ideas find their filling in intuition, they build for themselves definitely new acts on perceptions and similar appearances of the same order. These acts relate themselves to the appearing object in a way quite distinct from those constituting it as perception. Otherwise

[99] *LU* III, p. 80.   [100] *Ibid.*, p. 82.   [101] *Ibid.*, p. 78.

expressed, this means that universal ideas, in finding their filling, build up new acts on the basis of perception, which acts intend their objects in a new and different way. The significant intention of this new kind of act is directed to a universal, rather than to what is merely perceptually ideated. "And where the new intention fills itself adequately through the underlying intuition, it demonstrates its objective possibility, that is, the possibility or 'reality' of the universal." [102]

To demonstrate that propositions have a certain form, Husserl took as an example, "E" is "P" (where "E" stands as a sign of a proper name), some "S" is "P", this "S" is "P," all "S" is "P," and so on.[103] Now each one of these "expressions" or "propositions" has its own meaning; yet there could not be found in perception the filling that makes the distinction. As a matter of fact, these represent the filling of categorical forms of meaning, and not the same kind of acts as are found in perception. Yet they are founded in perception and as such are obviously of a higher order or level.

There must, then, be drawn a close distinction between "sensory matter" and "categorical form" within the sphere of objectifying acts. The former constitutes itself in perception; the latter constitutes itself in founded acts. To illustrate this point, Husserl considered the concept of Being as held by Kant in the formula, "Being is not a real predicate." Husserl concurred in this and affirmed, "I see the color, not the Being of the color; I feel the smoothness, not the Being of the smoothness; I hear the tone, but not the Being of the tone." [104] Being, therefore, is nothing "inherent" in the object. It is not a part of it; it is not a quality of intensity or even a figure; it is not even a form. Being is not a characteristic which is to be conceived as *constitutive*.

102 *Ibid.*, p. 134.   103 *Ibid.*, p. 135.   104 *Ibid.*, p. 137.

Being is nothing in the object; it is not something real belonging to it internally, likewise it is not a real external characteristic and therefore is not a "characteristic" in any real sense of the word. For it is not related even to the real forms of unity which connect objects to related objects, colors to forms of colors, tones to harmony, etc. In this real form of unity are grounded the external characteristics of the objects, the right and left, the high and low, the loud and soft, etc., under which there is nothing such as IS exists.[105]

In short, since it is not a "real" predicate (Kant), Being is absolutely nothing which is perceived and, as it is not an object of sensory perception, clearly it must be apprehended in acts of a higher order.

Traditional philosophy, since the time of Locke, has entertained the fundamentally erroneous concept that meanings such as the logical categories, Being and Non-Being, unity, plurality, totality, number and series, originate in *reflection* upon certain psychical acts. This is tantamount to saying that the logical categories originate in the sphere of inner sense, of "inner perception." As against this, Husserl contended that even as Being is not any part of the external object (considered as "real"), so it is not any part of the internal thinking, including judging. "Reflection" in the traditional sense is, after all, a vague term. True it is that Being can be apprehended only in the act of judging, but that does not mean that the concept of judgment can ever be won in reflection. The concept of sensible objects cannot originate through "reflection" on the perception, because then there would result by such an act the concept, "perception"; neither does it originate through reflection on any given kind of real constituency of perception. Likewise, the concept "thing" cannot originate out of reflection on judgments or their contents. If it did, we would then have only concepts of judgments or of real constituents of judgments.

105 *Ibid.*

Obviously, on the basis of Husserl's argument, this cannot be the case. If it were, it would mean that there would have to be experienced now perceptions, now judgments; but to be experienced is not (necessarily) to be *objectified*. According to the Lockian doctrine of reflection, however, that upon which we reflected would, by virtue of that fact alone, become objective!

It is not in reflection on judgments or even on the filling of judgments, but *in the filling of judgment itself* that the origin of the concepts "thing" and "being" (in the sense of the copula) really lies; "not in these acts as object, but in the objects of these acts, do we find the foundational abstraction for the realization of these concepts." [106]

These arguments are valid, according to Husserl, for all categorical forms, that is, for all categories. A "totality," for instance, is given only in an actual grasping-of-connection (*Zusammenbegreifen*), and that means in an act which has the form of conjunctive combination, A and B and C . . . Clearly "the concept of totality does not grow through reflection on this act, but rather in the giving act. We have much more than what it gives, the totality which it brings to appearance *in concreto*." [107]

Husserl was now even more prepared, on the basis of these considerations, to call explicit attention to two kinds of apprehension. There is perception in a narrow sense, which "is related only to particular and therefore temporal existence";[108] there is also categorical intuition, in which "universal objects are perceived (*eingesehen*, 'seen' in evidence) ." [109]

It can be said of every kind of perception and intuition that the object is apprehended either directly or indi-

[106] *Ibid.*, p. 141.   [107] *Ibid.*, p. 142.   [108] *Ibid.*, p. 144.
[109] *Ibid.* This is a continuation and elaboration of the doctrine of universals as "ideal unities." Husserl had touched upon the idea of intuition when discussing "ideation."

rectly. There must be made, then, a close distinction between real or ideal objects relative to direct apprehension.
"Sensible or real objects can be characterized, namely, as
objects of the lowest grade of possible perception, the categorical or ideal objects of those of higher grades.[110] By
sensible perception, Husserl meant that an object is directly apprehended, or is itself present, and this object
constitutes itself in the act of perception in a *simple* manner. This kind of object is immediately given and given in
a definitely objective content. The acts apprehending such
objects do not constitute themselves in relations or connections or in any other kind of membership. On the
other hand, in the other kind of (categorical) intuition,
we find that the acts are founded by "simple" perception.

Hence Husserl held that simple acts of perception
function as the ground-act of new acts, which might be
included or only posited and which show in their new
ways of consciousness at once a new consciousness of objectivity, the *original essential positing,* the *consciousness
of objectivity.* These acts, furthermore, constitute new
objectivity, and in this phase there appears in the founding acts alone that which is real and given, which had not
been given before, and which, furthermore, could not
have been given before. This new objectivity is grounded
in the old, and has, in the ground-act's appearing, "objective relationship."

If the function of simple acts of perception is that of
grounding or founding, what is that of the higher acts of
intuition? In the simple acts, the categorical element is
founded, the element of that which is intuited in knowing. In them the assertive thinking finds, where it functions as expression, its filling. Accordingly there is the
possibility of complex acts of such a kind, which include
and are grounded in simple perceptions and simple imagi-

[110] *Ibid.*, p. 145.

nations; moreover, on the founded intuitions new bases can be constituted and can build up a whole series of founding. Significant intentions, according to such founding, also form themselves into lower and higher grades and, indeed, there can be a mixture through such founding of significant and intuitive acts.

In sensible perception there appears to us the "external" thing "in one glance." Hence the sphere of the sensory is determined by simple perception. "It does not require the apparatus of founding or founded acts." [111] The phenomenological content of simple perception-acts always displays a simple unity of intention in the midst of a complexity.

As contrasted with the sensory perception, which gives sensible concreteness, it is necessary to call attention to that group of acts "through which are given concretely determined facts, collections, and disjunctions, as complex 'thought objects,' as 'objects of a higher order,' which include within themselves their founding objects as real." [112] These acts can also give "generalizations" and indefinite individual comprehensions, whose objects, although they are of a higher level, do not include in themselves their founding objects.

What of identity? Unity is the unity of identification. Is identification found in perception? Is it a sensory content? Is it something inherent in the object? Not according to Husserl's theory. It is the representative content of a "new perception" which is founded in the articulated individual perceptions. The act of identification is, in fact, "a new consciousness of objectivity which brings to us a new 'object,' an object which can be 'apprehended itself,' or 'given' only in a founded act of this kind." [113]

Included in the definition of sensible or real objects, as those objects of simple perception, is the concept of

[111] *Ibid.*, p. 148.　　[112] *Ibid.*, p. 147.　　[113] *Ibid.*, p. 151.

"real part," especially the concept of real characteristic or element and real form. Every part of a real object is a "real" constituent; that is to say, any real piece or form or phase of a "real object" remains "real." The whole object is given explicitly; every one of its parts is given implicitly, for "the totality of objects which can be given explicitly or implicitly in simple perceptions constitutes the widest conceivable sphere of sensible objects." [114]

Husserl said, further, that the sensory object can be apprehended in different ways, although, of course, first in a simple way. In fact, it is this possibility that characterizes the object as "sensory." By this he meant that sensory perception can apprehend any given individual part of the object or the object as an individual whole. What, then, are the relations obtaining between the parts and the whole or between two wholes? Is it merely a matter of a series of perceptions which gives us the concept of this relation? No, for as a matter of fact, when so considered, we have new objects which constitute parts of a relation, and this relating *requires a new kind of act.*

In enlarging upon this concept, Husserl distinguished between "simple synthetic" acts, and "complex relating" acts. The distinction is however purely a functional one, and refers more particularly to the phenomenological distinction relative to intentional matter. The function of synthetic thinking has a new categorical function, for in it synthetic intention is directed to objects simultaneously with the founding perceptions. The sensory content of the object remains unchanged; the object does not have new qualities. Remaining the same, it appears in a new way. This synthetic intention plays an important role for categorical connection, the role of a member of a relation, especially that of subject-object.

Following this argument, so carefully articulated, that

114 *Ibid.,* pp. 151–52.

the relation between objects is known through relating
acts and not because the objects of the founding acts enter
into the intention of the founding act, Husserl was led to
contend that there is another group of categorical acts in
which the objects of the founding act do not enter into
the intention of the founded acts. Herein lies the sphere
of "universal intuition," which, Husserl acknowledged,
would mean to some just as much as the expression,
"wooden iron." [115]

What is the nature of these categorical acts? On the
basis of primary intuition, there begins abstraction (intuition), and accordingly there enters a new kind of categorical act-character in which there appears a new kind of
objectivity which can come only in such founded acts as
are given really or in imagination. By abstraction Husserl
did not mean here a mere emphasis on some phase of a
sensory object, but "ideating abstraction, in which there
comes to actual givenness not an independent element, but
its 'idea' (*Idee*), its universal, to consciousness." [116]

In this act of abstraction the universal itself is "given."
It is not "attained" by reflection, it is not an act of signification, but *wir erfassen es, wir erschauen es,* we seize it,
we intuit it. Husserl is here speaking of intuition, of the
insightful "perception" of the universal in its highest
sense. Since the universal is given in an act of abstraction
(remembering his phenomenological definition of that
term), it is not to be looked upon as the mere understanding of a general or universal name. The consciousness of universality builds itself upon the basis of intuition and the imagination conforming to it. The idea or
species "red," the idea of a triangle—all is itself apprehended; it is "seen" in a new and particular way. Because
of its immediacy, there is no other word which Husserl
could use to define this new act; and even though it is

[115] *Ibid.*, p. 162.   [116] *Ibid.*

grounded in perception, it has all the essentials of intuition. Knowledge as a "unity-of-filling" completes itself not on the basis of mere simple acts, but on the ground of categorical acts and that which corresponds to them, the fullness of which is found in and completed by intuitive ideation.

In one sense, intuitions correspond to expressed meanings in that every categorical act of intuition has its quality, its (intentional) matter of *Auffassungssinn,* and its representation. This differentiation does not reduce itself to the same as that which was seen in the analysis of founding acts. The quality of a "total act" can be entirely different from that of a ground-act, since the ground-act can be qualified in different ways as, for instance, the idea of a relation between an object which is held fictitious and another one which is held to be "real." Furthermore, not only has every founding act a matter, but the founded act itself brings its own matter, and accordingly the proposition is valid that "this new matter is founded in that which comes anew in the matter of the grounded act." [117]

Finally, the new act has its peculiar representation, since with new matter new representations come. It is the representation of the new which comes in categorical intuition of that which is the new objective content. To use Husserl's own words,

the same psychical momenta which are given sensibly in inner perception (consequently functioning as sensible representations) can constitute a categorical form in a founded act of the character of a categorical perception or imagination; thereby they carry a categorical representation of a totally different kind.[118]

Continuing this line of argument, Husserl drew a distinction in the sphere of sensibility between content of reflection and "primary" contents. In the former we have

117 *Ibid.,* p. 166.   118 *Ibid.,* p. 179.

those contents which themselves are act-characters or are grounded in act-characters. In the primary content, on the other hand, we find those contents in which all the contents of reflection are founded immediately or mediately. To this distinction between purely sensible and purely categorical objects of intuition there corresponds, therefore, a differentiation of representing contents. The contents of reflection can function exclusively as pure categorical representations. Husserl said that the concept of category can thus be defined as "embracing all the objective forms in itself, that is, those forms which arise from the forms of apprehension and not from the matter of apprehension." [119]

Further on he says that the distinction between form and matter is, after all, "merely relative and functional." [120] Considered in the absolute sense, a founding sensibility yields the matter for the acts of categorical form which are built upon it. Viewed in a relative sense, the objects of the founding acts generally constitute the matter, that is, "relative to the newly developed categorical forms in the founded acts." [121] It is to be noted, however, that there is nothing radical in this functional classification of form and matter.

§ 12. *The Final Positive Results of Husserl's Logical Investigations*

Upon viewing the results of his epistemological investigations,[122] Husserl believed that he had reached at least four important conclusions:

1. The opposition between intuition and signification. Mere thinking, in the sense of mere significant intending, is to be markedly differentiated from intuition as perception or imagination.

---

119 *Ibid.*, p. 180.
121 *Ibid.*

120 *Ibid.*, p. 182.
122 *Ibid.*, pp. 201 f.

2. The opposition between sensory and categorical intuition. There is a great difference between sensory perception, that is, intuition in the common, simple sense of the word, and categorical intuition considered in the widest sense of the word. The founding acts which characterize the same are valid now as the "thinking" which intellectualizes sensory perception.

3. The opposition between adequate and inadequate intuition, or, more generally, between adequate and inadequate ideas. In inadequate ideas, we *think* merely that something is so (it "appears" so), whereas in adequate ideas we see "the fact itself" and intuit it in its full selfhood.

4. The opposition between particular intuition (commonly termed "sense perception") and universal intuitions. This distinction, according to Husserl, marks a new concept of intuition. It is opposed, for instance, to "mere generalization," and with this, to the categorical acts which "imply" generalizations and, needless to say, to those significating parts of these acts. Accordingly, intuition as now conceived gives the particularity; thinking reaches out to the universal and completes itself through concepts. Ordinarily this opposition is spoken of as between "intuition and concept."

Husserl was persuaded that if Kant had drawn such distinctions, e. g., that which exists between perception and intuition, considered from the standpoint of category, many difficulties would have been avoided in traditional philosophy. For example, Kant did not see the great demarcation between intuition and signification, and consequently he had no clear insight into the difference between adequate and inadequate adaptation of meaning to intuition. Moreover, he drew no distinction between concepts as universal verbal meanings and concepts as "species" of universal concepts. Once again, he did not see concepts as universal objects, as the intentional correlates of universal ideas.

In brief, Kant was so interested in "rescuing" mathematics, natural science, and metaphysics from only he knew what that he did not see the need of delving into the relevant problems of knowledge, into the whole sphere of acts in which pre-logical objectifying and logical thinking complete themselves. Moreover, he overlooked entirely problems surrounding primitive logical concepts and laws, and more particularly those concerning their "phenomenological" origin. He failed to notice how little an explanation of analytical thinking could be won from a study of analytical propositions.

Finally, the source of all the ambiguities and unnecessary problems surrounding the Kantian *Vernunftkritik* is to be found in this: he never made clear the peculiarity of pure "ideation," of the adequate intuition of conceptual essence, and essential laws of universality; consequently, his philosophy was devoid of a genuine concept of the a priori. Therefore he could never have the objective which is possible only to a strictly scientific critique of reason, namely, that of examining the pure, essential laws which regulate acts as intentional experiences according to all their modi of objectifying meaning-giving and the filling-constitution of "true Being." It was the conviction of Husserl that it is alone by a true insight into such *Wesensgesetze* that a genuine understanding of the *"Möglichkeit der Erkenntnis"* may be achieved.

PART TWO

TRANSITION TO PURE
PHENOMENOLOGY

CHAPTER FOUR

TRANSITION

BEFORE THE PUBLICATION of his *Logische Untersuchungen* at the turn of the century, Husserl had already turned his attention from mathematics to logic; during this process it had become increasingly certain that he would some day be constrained to leave the field of logic for that of epistemology. As seen in the last chapter, this transition had actually been made before his investigations were finally brought to completion. In the interim between the publication of *Logische Untersuchungen* and the appearance, in 1913, of his *Ideen zu einer reinen Phänomenologie und phänomenologischen Philosophie*, Husserl issued only one significant publication, "Philosophie als strenge Wissenschaft." [1] In this article, which later proved to be a center of much controversy, it was disclosed, among other things, exactly what had been going on in Husserl's mind during the preparation of *Logische Untersuchungen* and since its publication.

[1] *Logos*, I (1910), 289 f. During the first decade after the turn of the century, Husserl, of course, was actively engaged in teaching and creative work. In 1928 Martin Heidegger edited and published some of Husserl's lectures during this period under the title "Vorlesungen zur Phänomenologie des innern Zeitbewusstseins." These lectures comprise chiefly an enlargement of the basic concepts found in *LU* III, with especial emphasis upon the consciousness of time (both "immanent" and "objective") as intentional experience. It also contains a critical examination of Brentano's concept of the "origin of time" (pp. 374 f.). The "Vorlesungen" first appeared in *Jahrbuch für Philosophie und phänomenologische Forschung*, IX, 1928. Since these lectures represent Husserl's earlier thinking and contain no radically new ideas that cannot be found in *Logische Untersuchungen* and *Ideen*, no use has been made of them in this study.

More particularly did it become evident what his attitude was coming to be toward all "naturalistic" philosophy, including experimental and genetic psychology, positivism, pragmatism, scientism, and any other school or
system which chooses to argue that there is only one kind
of experience and defines it as "natural" or "empirical."

In "Philosophy as Strict Science" Husserl began his
survey of current philosophy by asking, Who or what is
responsible for the *Unwissenschaftlichkeit der Philosophie?* He answered, The guilt rests squarely on the
shoulders of philosophy itself.[2] Although it has always
claimed to aim at "pure and absolute knowledge," philosophy has failed to achieve this ideal because it has
tried to emulate exact ("natural") science. This, Husserl
believed, was an unfortunate beginning because (1) such
emulation was in itself unworthy and undignified, and
because (2) science has methods and specific problems
peculiarly its own which philosophy has no business to
try to appropriate.

Even if it were possible, should philosophy imitate science? Husserl again answered an emphatic "no," since by
its very nature science is necessarily restricted to certain
fields and, moreover, is "imperfect" in the sense that
it is "continually developing" from one concept to
another.[3] Science, in this sense, is "progressive." It does
not pretend to be a *Weltanschauungslehre.* Philosophy
does. Yet, paradoxically, it has striven for the same objectives and has tried to use the same methods of a field
of investigation which makes no such pretense and, by
so doing, has needlessly set for itself limitations which do

[2] It must be borne in mind that Husserl was writing about philosophy
before 1910, and particularly German philosophy. Nevertheless many of
his criticisms and arguments are equally applicable today, e. g., those
directed at philosophy's disposition to lean upon the exact sciences (new
and critical realism, personalism, and so forth).

[3] Husserl (apparently) assumed that this was beneath the dignity of
philosophy!

not properly belong to it. More lamentable than this, however, is the fact that philosophy, by adopting such a procedure, has actually retarded its own progress. Since it has not been able to establish its specific methods and objectives, it has not developed even to the extent which science has. As a consequence, by attempting to follow in the footsteps of exact science, which is admittedly imperfect and in the midst of a continual flux, philosophy has found itself hardly able to make any real contribution to "clear thinking." Does this mean that it has nothing to learn from science? Not at all. On the contrary, it should follow the example of science at least in respect to formulating its proper problems, articulating its own objectives, and establishing its peculiar methods. But Husserl contended that as long as it depends upon science to lead the way it cannot do this since philosophy, by definition, is outside the domain of science.

What, then, should philosophy do? It must first take stock of itself by examining the conditions of a strict science, thereby bringing them to decisive clarity in order to have something upon which to build itself again. In short, there needs to be an examination of "true beginnings, decisive formulation of problems, and right methods." [4] The Greeks, and particularly Plato, were aware of this necessity; Descartes, in his rebellion against scholasticism, showed the way which philosophy should take, particularly as regards method, and his influence is traceable in the great philosophies of the seventeenth and eighteenth centuries, up to and including Kant's *Vernunftkritik*. Then what happened? "Romantic Philosophy" departed from the way of true philosophy as Descartes had pictured it. Its reaction against eighteenth-century *Naturalismus* and its unavoidable skepticism did nothing

4 "Philosophie als strenge Wissenschaft," *Logos*, I (1910), p. 292.

but add to the general confusion. The Romanticists actually fostered a falsification of what constitutes strict philosophy. Hegel himself, Husserl believed, had contributed to this degeneration with his doctrine of the "relative justification" of every philosophy for its time, which ultimately eventuated in a deadly, skeptical *Historizismus.*

Husserl saw in this decline of philosophy, particularly as represented in naturalism, a tragedy. Naturalism, it must be granted, is a natural consequence of the "discovery of nature," i. e., nature in the sense of "a unity of spatiotemporal existence governed according to exact laws of nature." [5] But what, after all, can be included in the naturalistic outlook? Nothing but "nature" and, above all, "physical" nature. Husserl described this position in these words:

Everything that is, is either itself physical, belonging to the unified connection of physical nature, or is perhaps psychical; in this case the psychical would be merely some sort of transformation dependent upon the physical or at best a secondary "parallel accompanying fact" (*parallele Begleitatsache*).[6]

According to positivism (Hume and Kant), physical nature, including the so-called "psychical," does not change when it becomes apprehended sensuously in the complex of sensations, in colors, tones, and impressions (*Empfindungsmonismus* and *Energetismus*). The net result of this tradition has been (1) *Naturalisierung des Bewusstseins* and (2) *Naturalisierung der Ideen,* including all absolute ideals and norms.

This can be illustrated by the example of formal logic and its principles, the so-called "laws of thought" which are called by naturalism *Naturgesetze des Denkens.*[7] The

---

[5] *Ibid.,* p. 294.   [6] *Ibid.*

[7] Husserl, as already seen, dealt with the absurdity of this viewpoint in *LU* I.

same thing has happened in axiology and ethics. Yet, Husserl argued, as a matter of fact the naturalist is in reality an idealist and an objectivist. In common with the avowed idealist he is filled with a zeal to bring all knowledge to "scientific clarity," e. g., "pure" truth, beauty, and goodness; he is vitally concerned with determining the universal essence of truth, goodness, and beauty. Since he desires to construct new theories, values, and practical norms, he is likewise a "reformer." Since he wants to "objectify" these, he is a strict idealist. The naturalist teaches, preaches, moralizes, reforms,[8] but denies the very validity itself of what he does. Like the skeptic, he preaches *expressis verbis;* he denies reason, yet uses it. He is doubly guilty, since he abjures, first, what he uses and, second, what he strives for. That is the preposterous result of trying to "naturalize" reason.

The same criticisms can be directed against positivism (including, according to Husserl, pragmatism).[9] In the last analysis, positivism acknowledges only *Erfahrungstatsachen,* and claims to be, therefore, a strict *Erfahrungswissenschaft.* As a strict science, it would be only a "positive" science. Reason would have no authority in and for itself. Its highest ideal would be to "keep pace" with the exact sciences.

The most unhappy aspect of this entire tendency has been the "naturalization" of consciousness, as found particularly in experimental psychology.[10] The psychologists of this group have too long been under the illusion that

[8] Husserl cited Häckel and Ostwald as examples of "naturalistic reformers."

[9] Husserl cited no particular pragmatist, nor did he try to substantiate his classification of pragmatism as "positivism."

[10] For an outline of psychology before the World War, see *Die experimentelle Psychologie im Jahre 1911*, August Messer, in *Jahrbuch der Philosophie*, ed. by Max Frieschien-Köhler, Berlin, 1913. In this article is found a continuance of Husserl's diatribe against *Psychologismus.* Cf. Chap. II, pp. 30–48.

logic, epistemology, esthetics, and ethics could thereby win their scientific foundation. But Husserl inquired, Since psychology has become a "factual science," can it claim to be a foundation of philosophical discipline? Can it even pretend to have achieved or discovered "pure" principles and norms and with it a pure logic and epistemology? Has it any right to believe, in the field of epistemology, that it has the instruments of establishing a pure logic in the sense of a *mathesis universalis?* Since psychology calls itself a natural science, anything which might be said of natural science in general would be equally applicable to it. But what does a study of exact science reveal?

Careful examination of natural science, according to Husserl, discloses from the outset that from its starting-point it is "naïve." It is assumed that the object of its examination, nature, is "simply there." Things are "obviously" resting, moving, changing, in endless space and endless time. We perceive it and describe it in judgments about experience. These are some of its assumptions; what is the goal of natural science? Nothing less, nothing more, than to know and describe in a strictly rigorous manner, and to establish in objective validity, that which is so obviously given. Psychology itself espouses this outlook when it follows the pattern of the exact sciences and examines nature from the psychophysical standpoint. "Psychical being," says psychology, is not a world in itself but is given as "I," or experience of the "I" (in various ways); it displays itself "experientially," as bound to certain "physical things," which we call "body." The problem of psychology would be, then, to examine scientifically and to determine objectively in its psychophysical relationship the lawfulness of psychical life. All psychological determination is *eo ipso* psychophysical, i. e., "of nature" in the scientific sense of signifying that which has spatial and temporal existence. The psychical is a *Naturtatsache*. Every psychological judgment, accordingly, must include within itself the existential positing of physical nature.

But natural science is not philosophy. By the same token, since psychology is avowedly a natural science and follows in the wake of the exact sciences, it cannot be considered philosophy, let alone a foundation of philosophical discipline.[11] This is not difficult to show.

If the naïveté with which science takes nature be remembered, and if it be likewise recalled how the assumption is made that nature is known exclusively through its methods, the first question that can be asked is, Whence the validity or invalidity of its "logical" rules and epistemological assumptions? For instance, what right has science to assume nature's "objectivity"? A moment's consideration of these and analogous problems discloses that, as a matter of fact, science is continually going "beyond" nature and the experience of it as they are both so narrowly defined by science itself. Ultimately, then, all problems revolve around the question of the relation between experience and thought. And that is a matter for philosophical consideration.

At this juncture, in order to illustrate his position in respect to science, Husserl enumerated several philosophical problems:[12] (1) How can experience be given as "consciousness of an object"? (2) How can experiences be corrected and justified through other experiences without their being considered only as subjective? (3) How can a play of experiential logical consciousness have objective validity in and for itself? (4) Is it not conceivable that the rules of consciousness are irrelevant for "things"? Finally (5), how shall natural science become "under-

11 As attempted, for instance, by M. Dessoir, O. Klemm, Wilhelm Wundt, Hermann Ebbinghaus, and others.

12 "Philosophie als strenge Wissenschaft," pp. 299 f.

standable" insofar as it presumes to posit and to know in its every step "objectively existing" nature as contrasted with the "subjective flux" of consciousness? These are problems which belong properly to the domain of epistemology, which is the discipline designed to examine those questions which have not as yet become scientifically clarified and, indeed, which could never be scientifically explained because of the limitations which exact science sets for itself. Curiously enough, science *assumes* the validity of the relation between objects, the experience of them, and the thought about them; although it works on such assumptions, it has never troubled to examine them as specific problems. It just proceeds. Yet it is not difficult to see the nonsense of a natural scientific epistemology *(einer naturwissenschaftlichen Erkenntnistheorie)*, including psychology. If, generally speaking, certain "puzzles" of natural science are in principle "immanent," so, obviously, their solution, according to premises and conclusions is in principle "transcendent." By such considerations, Husserl was forced to the conclusion that as a matter of fact the positing of nature in epistemology is "beyond science" since, although science assumes the validity of such "realities" as "thingness," "space," "time," and "causality," it is (admittedly) not its task to examine the implications of such assumptions. They constitute "thetic" positings of existence.

Moreover, regarding the problem of "existence and consciousness," is it not true that science assumes that existence is an "objective correlate" of consciousness, that it is something which is consciously "intended"? By what right? Existence, according to it, is that which is perceived, remembered, expected, identified, differentiated, believed, pictorially conceived, and so on. The basic problem would be, then, to investigate the nature of consciousness and to direct attention to a scientific *Wesens-*

erkenntnis des Bewusstseins. As Husserl expressed it, it is necessary first to examine

what consciousness in all its various forms is, in and for itself, according to its essence, and what it means; to determine by examining the different ways in which, according to the essence of these forms, it is now clear, now unclear, now present or past, now indicative or symbolic, now bad, now conceptual, now in this or that intentional modus; and so in infinite other forms is it objectively meant and signifies, accordingly, being as valid or real.[13]

All objects are "given to consciousness," every kind of consciousness is "teleologically" ordered and directed to various kinds of objects. An understanding of this requires an inquiry into the *Formen des Gegebenheitsbewusstseins.* Is that a task for positive science?

Furthermore, what is meant by "objectivity"? Science cannot tell us, since it merely "assumes" it without troubling to "explain" it. Yet what objectivity *is* can be ascertained, Husserl argued, *only by an examination of that for whom the world and its objects are objective,* namely, consciousness itself. This forces the conclusion that there is required a study of the "whole consciousness," and ultimately an investigation of the problem of what is meant by *"consciousness of."* Husserl described this problem as a *Wesensstudium des Bewusstseins,* including the meaning and objectivity of consciousness (*Bewusstseinsbedeutung* and *Bewusstseinsgegenständlichkeit*). Included in this would be a study of the ways of "givenness" of the objects of various kinds of experience. Such a study of the "intentional" nature of consciousness lies in the field of phenomenology. Husserl proposed, then, not a science in the sense of psychology, but a *Phänomenologie des Bewusstseins* as contrasted with a *Naturwissenschaft vom Bewusstsein.* It would be correct, to be sure, to say

13 *Ibid.,* pp. 300–301.

that both psychology and phenomenology are concerned
with consciousness; it must be remembered, however, that
each has its own standpoint, method and objective. Psychology has to do with *empirical* consciousness, with consciousness from the standpoint of crass psychophysical experience, of consciousness as existing in relation to
physical nature. Phenomenology does not scorn this, but,
since its objective is different, its standpoint and method
are perforce different from those of psychology; it will
deal with the realm of "pure consciousness." [14]

Modern "exact psychology"[15] is just as far from being
strict philosophy as is experimental psychology. It, too,
omits direct and pure analysis of consciousness. It does not
engage in a "systematic analysis" and description of the
forms of givenness which disclose themselves in the variety
of possible directions of immanent inspection. In short, it
has no interest in the analysis of pure consciousness.

Husserl, it should be mentioned at this point, had no
intention, by these arguments, of minimizing the value
of psychology, whether exact or experimental. Experimental psychology does have a role to play: it is that of a
"statistician," since it gathers valuable facts and rules of
a "mediate" kind. Although its value in this sense cannot be gainsaid, in the last analysis it is concerned with
psychophysical facts and rules. It does not examine, sys-

[14] By "pure consciousness" Husserl meant the Ego or *Persönlichkeit*,
the *Aktzentrum* of all the individual's interests, remembering, thinking,
acting, reacting, and so forth. As the *Kern* of all actions and reactions,
it would then be the "logical" or intuitive personality, which is in relation with the world of essences or universals which, it will be remembered, comprise the very nature of "empirical" objects themselves. Pure
consciousness would thus be the intuitive self which makes all experience
and meaning of our total world possible—as contrasted with the psychophysical organism which has to do only with the "physical" environment.
Husserl's concept of the pure Ego or consciousness will be treated at
length in chap. v, § 2, p. 141 f.

[15] "Philosophie als strenge Wissenschaft," pp. 302f. I do not know
whether it was original with him, but Husserl called exact psychology
"*Schreibtischpsychologie.*"

tematically, psychical life in and for itself. Since exact science, which serves as its model, denies the value of introspection, it, too, sees no point in examining consciousness itself.

What is the reason for these mistakes of psychology? [16] First, it deliberately ignores the different kinds (intentional characteristics) of consciousness. This is the guilt of exact psychology since, by definition, it has no interest in the "meaning" of the psychical in and for itself. Second, experimental psychology is untenable since it already assumes that which by definition no experiment could possibly accomplish, namely, an analysis of consciousness itself.[17]

What, asked Husserl, is "psychical existence"? It is more or less a complex "consciousness of." Both exact and experimental psychology ignore this, and so long as they do so they can never give a strictly scientific analysis of consciousness. Psychologists have long believed that they could win all the necessary knowledge of experience from superficial experiments; they have been under the illusion that they could discover the foundations of experience by such experiments. Accordingly, owing to the very nature of the experiments themselves, as well as their presuppositions, they are bound to and restricted by a theory of consciousness as a part of the spatial and temporal world as "nature." Avowedly "empirical," they can never be scientific in the true sense of the word, which, in the mind of Husserl, meant discovering the *essence* of consciousness and its life. Locke was partly responsible for the errors of contemporary psychology, since from him have been borrowed the ideas (1) that every conceptual

[16] *Ibid.,* pp. 304 f.
[17] Stumpf and Lipps shared this defect of experimental psychology, since they ignored Brentano's contribution of the "intentional character" of consciousness. They dismissed Brentano by falsely accusing him of being "merely" a "scholastic."

concept springs from earlier experience and (2) (its very opposite) that somehow in descriptive judgments every concept borrows the justification of its possible use from experience.[18] The basic error of this outlook is its affirmation that only what springs from "real" perceptions or memories can have justification for its validity, essentiality, and its valid applicability in individual instances.

But, Husserl inquired, How can psychology claim "exactness" when it has no scientific basis or methodology? No more than a physics would have which did not possess (at least) such everyday concepts as "heavy," "warm," and "mass." Yet modern psychology would avow that it does not want to be a science of the soul, but of psychical phenomena. If this is true, then it must describe and determine these phenomena in conceptual strictness. But exact psychology cannot do this, since it has not developed a method peculiarly its own. The heart of the whole problem, then, is found in the question of how to bring confused experience to scientific clarity and how to establish its objective validity in judgments about experience. And so long as "exact" psychology assumes the natural standpoint, it cannot meet this requirement. It has not examined the meaning of psychological experience, as it is in and for itself; it has no method with which to resolve the problem even if it saw it. Yet that is the central problem.

What of empirical psychology? Its plight is just as bad, if not worse. Since its origin in the eighteenth century, it has adopted the method of the physical (chemical) sciences.[19] Believing as it did that the object of its investigation was nothing but a "constituent part" of physical nature and assuming that all natural sciences have one and the same method, it, too, adopted the method of the

18 "Philosophie als strenge Wissenschaft," p. 307.
19 *Ibid.*, pp. 309 f.

natural sciences. Metaphysics adopted the false imitation of geometry and later the physical method; psychology was equally guilty. It is worthy of attention that the fathers of experimental exact psychology were physiologists and physicists, all with the same outlook, namely, that natural science "proceeds from the vague subjectivity of things in naïve sensuous appearance to objective things with exact objective qualities." [20] By the same token, psychology has the same vagueness and naïveté regarding objectively valid determinations. The limitations of this method are at least three. (1) What of the objective determination of the givenness of experience? (2) What, more closely examined, is meant by scientific objectivity and determination of objectivity? (3) Is it not true that the function of the experimental method depends upon the particular meaning of givenness and that, ultimately, this resolves itself into the relevant consciousness of experience? Natural science, so long as it tries to make consciousness a space-time "thing" is helpless to deal with these matters.

How does natural science actually differentiate between physical and psychical nature? As a matter of fact, it argues somewhat as follows:

The spatiotemporal corporeal world is alone nature in the pregnant sense. Every other individual existence, the psychical, is nature in a secondary sense; this determines the essential difference between the method of natural science and that of psychology. In principle, corporeal existence is alone experienceable, and experienceable in a multiplicity of direct experiences, i. e., perceptions which are experienced as individually identical. That is why, if the perceptions of different "subjects" are divided, the perceptions are experienced by many subjects as individually identical and described as intersubjectively the same. The same things, events, etc., all stand before our eyes and can become determined by us all

20 *Ibid.*, p. 130. Husserl did not name any of the "fathers."

according to their "nature." Its "nature" says, however, "subjective appearances" are exhibiting themselves in experience
in a multiplicity of changing ways; they nevertheless stand as
temporal unities, and remain so, or changing characteristics
are there, and they stand as interconnected in the all-connect-
ing relationship of one corporeal world with one space, one
time. They are what they are only in this unity. Only as contained in the causal connection to or relationship with one
another do they retain their individual identity (substance)
as carriers of "real qualities." All corporeally real qualities
are causal. Every real existence stands under the laws of
possible changes, and these laws govern the identical, the
thing, not in and for itself, but the thing in its unified, real,
possible connection with one nature. Everything has its nature
(as the quintessence of that which it is, it is the identical)
because it is the convergence of causalities in the midst of
the one comprehensive nature. Real (corporeal) qualities are
a title for possibilities of change of the identical indicated by
lawful causality; hence, regarding that which it is, it is determinable only through recourse to these laws. Thingness,
however, is given as a unity of immediate experience, as a
unity of manifold sensuous appearances. The empirically perceivable unchanging, changing, and that which is dependent
upon change, yield first of all to knowledge its direction, and
simultaneously function for it as a "vague medium" in which
the truly objective physical nature displays itself and through
which, accordingly, thinking (as scientific thinking about experience) determines and constructs the true.[21]

What, then, would be a "thing" of experience? According to natural science, we know only what is brought to
us in "sensuously causal connections." Nothing is known
of the thing as it is in and for itself. Consequently, on
grounds of such prejudice, the thing is merely "pretend-
ing" that it is being experienced, since it is known only
as a group of "secondary qualities." But these qualities,
by definition, are adventitious to the thing-in-itself. Husserl held that "secondary qualities" is not only an am-

21 *Ibid.*, pp. 310–11.

biguous expression but "is a bad theory of good experience." [22]

When he turned to the world of the psychical, Husserl believed he could show that matters became even more confused.[23] Presumably science will limit itself to "psychical phenomena," which the new psychology has called its proper sphere. From the outset, all consideration of the soul and the "I" will be omitted. From the standpoint of objectivity we have already been forbidden perception of things; in the world of psychical phenomena the matter of objectivity is not dismissed, *its possibility simply does not exist!* Psychical existence is reducible to "monads" that have no windows and can be known only in "empathy." Yet it is to be noticed that, as contrasted with physical existence, the psychical is not a unity which would be experienceable in several special perceptions as individually identical. This follows from psychology's contention that psychical existence is not the object of perception. As contrasted with the physical realm, at this point science holds that there is no difference (in psychical existence) between "appearance" and "existence." Hence if nature is an existence which appears only in ("real") phenomena, appearances themselves are not themselves an existence. There is only "one nature" which appears in the phenomena of things. From this it is to be concluded, on grounds of positive science, that so-called psychical phenomena *remain* "phenomena" and not nature. It follows from this, moreover, that *the psychical is foreign to the one nature which natural science assumes* and is willing to acknowledge as "existing." Hence, psychology does not deal with something which has its own nature or individual characteristics, but only with phenomenal aberrations of the one nature with which science in general deals.

[22] *Ibid.*, p. 311.　　　　　　[23] *Ibid.*, pp. 311 f.

When it is remembered that, on "scientific" arguments, a phenomenon is not a "substantial" unity, that it has no real characteristics of its own, and, moreover, that it enjoys no real changes or causality (all this from the standpoint of the natural sciences), Husserl's point is well taken. Science avers that a thing is what it is and remains always in its identity. Nature is eternal. What actually belongs "in reality" to a thing as such, in its real characteristics or modifications, can be determined objectively with validity and always in a series of new experiences. Such is the case as science sees it. On the other hand, psychical existence is only a "phenomenon." But a phenomenon is now here and then not here; it comes and goes, and enjoys no identity of its own. It is thus obvious that on grounds of natural science the psychical can never be objectively validated, studied, or analyzed. It is impossible to examine that which by definition is not. A psychology grounded in natural science has nothing to investigate!

Husserl formulated the twofold consequence of such viewpoints in this manner. First, owing to its self-imposed limitations, nature cannot be known as it is by science; and, second, since psychology adopts the scientific standpoint, it can never know what the psychical is. But must the dictum of science be accepted as final? Husserl did not believe so. Psychical life is not an object of experience in the sense of appearance (empirical "phenomenon"), as science would have us believe. On the contrary, it is *"Erlebnis,"* and experience in reflection, appearing as itself, through itself, in an absolute flux. The psychical has its own unity in consciousness: it has nothing whatever to do with "nature," i. e., space and time. Psychical life, as Husserl saw it, is a twofold, unlimited flux of phenomena, with a thoroughgoing intentional direction, with its timeless, immanent "time" which no chronometer can measure.

How, then, can the psychical be made an object of investigation? "In immanent inspection," Husserl answered,

the flux of phenomena comes to view; we proceed from phenomenon to phenomenon (each a unity in flux and conceived in flowing) and never to anything other than phenomena. Not until immanent inspection and real experience come to synthesis, do perceived phenomenon and experienced thing enter into a connection. Through the medium of the thing-experience and such experience of connection there enters simultaneously empathy as a kind of mediate perceiving of the psychical, characterized within itself as looking into a second monadic connection.[24]

The psychical, then, can be made an object of investigation. But to what extent and what can be said of it? Husserl was persuaded that an examination will be "meaningful" only insofar as it is permissible to speak of experiences, i. e., experiences of the psychical. He accordingly rejected any concept which held that the psychical must be "naturalized." Phenomena must be taken as they exhibit themselves; they must be accepted as that which flows in consciousness, intention, appearing; which has the present or the past; which has phantasy or signification; which is empty or full. Consciousness has different standpoints which can be subsumed under the one title, "consciousness of." It has a meaning all its own, and intends a certain objectivity which Husserl called "immanent objectivity," or, in other words, "the intended as such," and intended in this or that *Modus des Vermeinens*.[25]

Husserl thus disavowed any faith in the natural standpoint, as articulated by the exact sciences, and in so doing he rejected any possible falsification on psychical existence as "mere appearance." Psychical life is something in and for itself. It has its own content, its own flux of experiences. "Pure" consciousness is to be known not by the methods of exact or experimental psychology, both of which are built upon the premises of the natural sciences and have as their field a nature which is forever closed to us as it is in and for itself. Psychical life is to be studied by the method of immanent inspection.

But how is it possible so to examine psychical life? It is not "objective" in the scientific sense of the word, i. e., an object of sensuous experience; it is even incapable of scientific intersubjective validation. What is there left, what is there to grasp as an objective unity? It must be remembered that Husserl was interested only in the "pure phenomenological" sphere of experience when he answered that if "phenomena as such are not nature, so must they have an essence which can be adequately seized in immediate perception."[26] If psychology had acknowledged such a possibility of apprehending in "immediate perception" the essence of phenomena, it could have shaped a method of its own and avoided most of the mistakes traceable to its naturalistic bias.

Husserl's method is *essence-insight* or "intuition of essense." What is this *Wesensschauung?* He held that it is no more mysterious than sense perception. Consider the example of color: when it is intuitively brought to clarity and givenness, we see that its givenness is an essence. To "apprehend immediately" means to "intuit."[27] And an intuition is "pure" in the sense of not being related to the transitory, but in grasping an essence, which is *ein absolut Gegebenes*. Intuition has as its object neither psychical

[26] "Philosophie als strenge Wissenschaft," p. 314. Note here the influence of Wilhelm Dilthey.

[27] In *LU* intuition was called "ideation" and "logical reflection," whereby Husserl actually meant a series of intuitions. Intuition, ideation, *Wesenserkenntnis*, and *Wesensschauung* now came to be used by Husserl to mean the same thing.

nor physical phenomena; intuition has its seat in pure
consciousness and has essences as its peculiar data. For
instance, consciousness draws a distinction between color
and tone. It is that which makes possible this differentiation, the seizure of essences, which constitutes intuition. Clearly, this "certain something" is not the contents and appearances of sense perception; nor is the
difference between color and tone found in the psychical
relationship with objects. What, then, is it? Husserl answered, the difference is found in the kind of experience.
As a matter of fact, every psychological title of our experiences, such as perception and will, requires and presupposes an analysis of consciousness or an examination
of essences and the manner in which they are apprehended. Husserl in this manner opened the way to a study
of a new kind of experience.

Essence-insight, although not "empirical," is none the
less an "experience" in the same sense as perception,
memory, and will. Moreover, it is none the less "empirical" in the sense of being "factual" and having a
particular kind of "existence" as object. "Insight seizes
the essence as essence-existence and posits in no way empirical existence. Accordingly, knowledge of essence is not
knowledge of fact. It does not include any assertions of
individual existential contents." [28] To be sure, the starting-
point of essence-insight, for instance, the essence of perception, of memory, or judgment, can be a perception of
a perception, of a memory, of a judgment; but it can also
be a mere, although none the less clear, phantasy which
would presuppose no seizure or experience of "existence."
Essence can also be vaguely thought about, even falsely
thought about; that has nothing whatever to do with the
content of the essence-experience. Experience of essence
does not have to be rooted in empirical experience.

28 "Philosophie als strenge Wissenschaft," p. 316.

Why did Hume end in skepticism?[29] Because he limited all experience to sense impressions and spoke of our ideas as "constructed" out of these impressions. Small wonder that he ended in skepticism. Husserl was persuaded that if Hume had escaped the prejudice that sensory experience constituted the sole sphere of the intentionality of consciousness, he would have been brought to a careful analysis of pure consciousness and its objects; he would have seen that consciousness is capable of pure experience. In this way he would have become the founder of a positive theory of reason. He would have been spared the befuddlement which arose when confronted with the problem of the multiplicity of perceptions and appearances and the identity of the object which is brought to appearance. The whole phenomenological realm of essences would have been opened to him, and he would have seen identity as an object of a particular kind of experience. That a perception is a perception of such-and-such colored and formed object is, on Husserlian grounds, a matter of its essence and not of its modes of appearing. But Hume closed his eyes to this when he dogmatically assumed only one kind of experience and perforce had to conclude that the world is only our idea and that we can never be sure of the correspondence of the idea, which is constructed out of impressions, to the thing itself.[30]

"The particular is not essence; it 'has' an essence which is expressible of it with evident validity."[31] It should be clear from this that phenomenology as a science of essences could never be classified as psychological "intro-

29 *Ibid.*, p. 317.

30 And so, in fact, did Kant. For a more detailed discussion of Kantianism, see chap. vi, "Five Questions Concerning Phenomenology," § 3, pp. 229–37.

31 "Philosophie als strenge Wissenschaft," p. 318. This statement has a direct bearing on the problem of "fact and essence" (see chap. v, § 5, pp. 177–204) and my treatment of the problem of error in chap. vi, § 1, pp. 207–23.

spection." [32] As a matter of fact, on phenomenological grounds, all that is commonly called knowledge of the psychical presupposes *Wesenserkenntnis des Psychischen,* and it is vain to hope that the essence of such characteristics of consciousness as memory, judgment, and will could ever be discovered through psychophysical experiments and that strict scientific concepts could be built upon them. The fundamental error of modern psychology is that it has not adopted the phenomenological method.[33] Psychologists, on the contrary, have tried to dismiss phenomenology by stigmatizing it as "scholastic metaphysics." What did Husserl mean when he said that psychology needed a "systematic phenomenology" upon which to build itself? Simply that it ought to engage in an examination of the *Wesensgestaltungen des Bewusstseins* and its immanent correlates and to establish them in systematic connections by pure intuitive ideation, in which will be yielded the norms for the scientific meaning and content of concepts of every kind of phenomenon. Out of this would emerge, furthermore, those concepts which empirical psychology uses when considering psychical existence. It follows from this that ultimately every valid epistemology must rest on phenomenology, or the science of pure consciousness. Husserl believed that if this were once

[32] As was done after the publication of *LU.* See his introduction to *LU* I, where he dealt with the false accusation that phenomenology is only descriptive psychology; also see "Bericht über deutsche Schriften zur Logik, 1895–98," *Archiv für systematische Philosophie,* IX (1903), 397–400.

[33] At this point it is well to dispel a common misunderstanding of Husserl. He has been accused of unmitigated conceit when he declared that the natural sciences, including psychology, erred because they did not adopt the "phenomenological method." As a matter of fact, Husserl in these pronouncements never meant that philosophy and science were hopelessly lost unless they followed in his footsteps. What he was arguing was that science and philosophy, particularly since Hume and Kant, has blinded themselves to a realm of experience because of their prejudices. By "phenomenological method," then, he meant *only* a method and not his particular philosophy or system.

accepted, there would grow a phenomenology not only of theoretical but axiological and practical experiences as well.

What, then, does the "Philosophy as Strict Science" disclose of Husserl's thinking during the interim between the publication of *Logische Untersuchungen* and the first decade of the century? In his *Logical Investigations,* he had abandoned the field of mathematics for that of logic and epistemology. In the article just analysed it is revealed that he was interested explicitly in epistemological problems, a field, unhappily, which he never left.

It is noteworthy that Husserl was wise enough to see that so long as philosophy leaned upon the natural sciences it could not fulfill its true destiny as an autonomous science. Since Kant, philosophy had unfortunately restricted itself in method and objective, namely, to be a handmaiden of the exact sciences. Aside from the fact that this is a forfeiture of its true mission, the cultural world has suffered, since philosophers have thereby closed their eyes to a realm of experience which exact science, by definition, could never penetrate. Descartes, in his rebellion against scholasticism, had shown the way of a true philosopher; since Kant, that way has been obscured. Positively stated, the tragedy has been twofold: the restriction of all experiences to the senses and, with it, the naturalization of consciousness. This tragedy could have been averted if philosophy had followed in the footsteps of Descartes and not in those of Hume and Kant. Regarding science itself, Husserl held that it behooved philosophy to investigate the presuppositions and premises which are naïvely assumed to be so "self-evident." When such an inquiry is launched, it is immediately discovered that science, far from being self-sufficient and all-comprehensive, is, on the contrary, guilty of assuming the validity of that which, by definition, owing to its self-imposed limitations, comes not of itself or its investigations, but from an experience far richer than that which it is willing to acknowledge. It is that realm of experience which philosophy should espouse as its own. It is the realm of pure consciousness and its eidetic objects.

Husserl, however, was not satisfied with merely unmasking the defects of science and philosophy. He offered a new method for philosophy and prefigured the nature of his future thinking by introducing terms and concepts which were to be found in all his ensuing writings.

What, then, would be the method which Husserl proposed that philosophy should employ? Negatively stated, the first thing it must do is extricate itself from the toils of the natural sciences; positively, it should come to a full awareness that it has its own realm of investigation, which can be examined only by intuitive reasoning (ideational thinking). Such philosophical reflection is the only instrument for probing the realm of pure consciousness and of studying its contents. The realm of essences, as a matter of fact, constitutes the very structure of the so-called natural world. From this it would follow, on Husserl's arguments, that any method designed to study it would be, properly speaking, the "foundational" science. For this reason, Husserl did not hesitate to declare phenomenology as a method to be basic to a science of sciences.

Intuition, as Husserl used the term, thus has a twofold significance. First, it is a special kind of experience, a form of cognition common to all "natural" experiences of the everyday world and possessing its own content; second, it is a method, the only proper method, of investigating the world of reality as it exists in and for itself.

The world, then, as contrasted with traditional philosophy since the time of Kant, *can* be known as it is in and for itself, since, as a matter of fact, it is basically a world of essences. This world of essences is known by pure consciousness without reference to or employment of the psychophysical constitution known as "body." When Husserl spoke of essences, he affirmed that pure consciousness had an (objective) content of experience peculiar to it alone.

If what Husserl contended for in this transitional article had the slightest vestige of truth, it is clear that philosophy can and must emancipate itself from the natural sciences and indeed that it will be "free" only when it takes such a step. There might be need for a philosophy of science; there is greater need for a philosophy without science. Philosophy as strict science is possible only when it has its own methods and its own realm with which it is occupied.

Can philosophy supply a *Weltanschauung?* Husserl said that if it cannot, we will never have one. But philosophy can never give us a worldview until it is more than a critique of the sciences. Science is admittedly impersonal, but the wisdom of the ages declares: *Persönlichkeit wendet sich an Persönlichkeit.* The true philosopher will not only try to be "scientific," that is, will not only attempt to remain conversant with the progressive achievements of each exact science or to pursue truth at all costs. He will also have a "scientific method" peculiarly his own, which is not of the nature of the exact sciences. Moreover, a philosophy which would pretend to be a *Weltanschauungsphilosophie* must include within its purview the richer experiences of life, such as the religious, esthetic, and ethical. In short, it must include the entirety of racial and individual experience. When philosophy has this as its objective, it ineluctably, although unconsciously, takes unto itself the phenomenological method; that is, it acknowledges a realm of experience which can be known only in ideational reflection or intuition. Indeed, Husserl was so convinced that this was the task of genuine philosophy that he devoted the rest of his life to this objective. He thereby finally entered the portals of pure "phenomenology."

CHAPTER FIVE

PURE PHENOMENOLOGY

AFTER A LITTLE MORE than a decade of intensive study, Husserl's *Ideen zu einer reinen Phänomenologie und phänomenologische Philosophie* appeared in 1913.[1] As soon as one begins to read this epochal work, one is struck not only by the introduction and radical usage of such new terms as "phenomenon," "reductions," and "*Eidos*," but by the evidence that Husserl had finally arrived at philosophic maturity. In *Ideen* Husserl is no longer groping. He is stating his case.

As *Ideen* is closely examined it becomes increasingly apparent, among other things, that a careful distinction must be drawn between phenomenology as "method" and phenomenology as "epistemology." For this reason, in what is to follow, after a preliminary discussion of his definition of phenomenon, there will be given a treatment of phenomenology as method; the remainder of the chapter will be devoted to his development of *Erkenntnistheorie,* including such important concepts as doctrine of essence and intuition, intuition and intentionality, and finally, fact and essence. Although Husserl himself did not follow this order, it is believed that such a procedure will serve to clarify the cardinal points of the final stages of his philosophy, as found in all the publications between 1913 and 1932.

---

[1] After this publication there appeared two other important works: "Formale und transzendentale Logik" (1929) and *Méditations cartésiennes* (1931).

§ 1. *The Concept of Phenomenon*

It need hardly be said that one of the principal causes of current misunderstanding of Husserl's phenomenology is found in a failure to study closely his use of the word "phenomenon." Perhaps Husserl himself is responsible for this, since he seems to assume that the reader will learn by implication what he means by the term. At any rate, his usage must be sharply differentiated not only from that of psychology, in which it usually means "contents" of consciousness, impressed somehow by the "external" world; above all, it must be emphasized that all phenomenologists use it in a way diametrically opposed to traditional and Kantian *"Erscheinung."* Husserl adopted the Greek usage signifying "that which displays itself." It is something which presents or "exhibits" itself to the experient. The epistemological significance of this is obvious, and the implications are of paramount importance.

With this basic definition of phenomenon, and bearing in mind what has been said in previous chapters, it is understandable that, underlying Husserl's *Ideen,* there will be found the fundamental purpose of demonstrating a direct experience of such self-revealing objects by the pure Ego. This would mean, moreover, that phenomena can be brought under closer scrutiny and subjected to a special kind of investigation. For this reason Husserl wanted to develop a distinctive method by which to examine them, and, as with all truly scientific methods, this method would do so "in isolation" from everything else. It would be the means of divorcing a phenomenon from every kind of existential and systematic connection, for the purpose of ascertaining what makes a thing exactly what it is and not something else. The culmination of his phenomenology is thus twofold: on the one hand, everyday experience is of a certain *Washeit* which comprises the character of a thing in such a way that even when the thing itself is removed, ceases to "exist," or is completely forgotten, its nature will yet remain to be studied; on the other, a method would be developed whereby what remains could be scrutinized. What, for instance, is the "redness" of the red rose? Husserl, of course, called it phenomenon, but, as will transpire, since there are many kinds of experience which refer to no "sensa," there must likewise be, on Husserlian grounds, a corresponding variety of kinds of phenomena. For example, there are "axiological experiences," "mathematical truths," "religious experiences," and so forth. These may not be as commonplace as ordinary perceptual experience, yet they are none the less important because of their rarity and they too must be taken into account by any thoroughgoing epistemology (although he left a great deal for others to do).

Husserl's principal concern was first and always with meaning, so it can now be said that the inquiry in *Ideen* (and the publications to follow) dealt ultimately with the question, What constitutes the meaning—or meanings—of all experiences? He answered (in brief): every experience has some meaning peculiar to it alone, because its object consists of certain phenomenological properties belonging peculiarly to it; this phenomenological nature of objects and experience has nothing whatever to do with what is in "space" and "time," because it is "eidetic," of the nature of essences. Clearly, then, his interest would revolve around what remained after all contingency and existential characteristics had been removed. This he called the essentiality or "essence-nature" of all the objects of every kind of experience. In this way Husserl assumed the responsibility of developing a method which would be independent of all "systematic" or theoretical connections, that is, it would have nothing to do with "exact" or "positive," empirical sciences. Take, for instance, the matter of sense qualities. The physicist would (probably) describe them as "vibrations" of some sort or another; the psychologist would (probably) affirm that they are to be reduced to some kind of "sensations." [2] Husserl rejected such so-called scientific descriptions and explanations and believed it not only possible but necessary to develop a phenomenological, scientific method which would study the true nature of sensa, e. g., colors and tones, "as such," as they are, regardless of their empirical manifestations or relations, and, moreover, without any reference to such relations themselves. This should make it clear why he considered himself justified in not employing concepts and instruments designed to investigate "existential" objects and experiences. Many have interpreted this as a Husserlian derogation from the value of the special sciences. This, however, as shown previously, is nonsense. He was simply required by the nature of the task he assumed to deny their utility for his purpose.

If such an investigation proved possible, something fundamental would lie before us, since, as "that which displays itself," a phenomenon obviously represents nothing but itself. This would hold true even though, as Husserl developed his theory, phenomena as such constitute the very meaning and significance of the "real" things of nature, the objects of sense experience. He went even further than this in his concept that phenomena *as objects of study* can be "seen" or intuited and judgments passed upon them wholly without reference to that for which or for whom they comprised meaning. In the last analysis, as will be shown, phenomena are *essences* and represent the sphere of objective Being "existing" in its own right, independent alike of the objects of nature and the experient.

2 I am indebted to Lanz's "The New Phenomenology," for an elucidation of Husserl's concept of phenomenon.

It is appropriate at this point to call attention to phenomenology's anti-Kantianism, at least in respect of its emphatic rejection of any and all so-called "unknowability" theories.[3] Phenomena, on the contrary, are very definitely knowable because they are the objects of a distinct kind of experience, namely, *Wesenschau,* intuition. As contrasted with all epistemologies rooted in the Kantian tradition, the essential Being of the world (considered in the broadest sense of the word) can be known. In fact, essential Being is known in every experience insofar as it can be said to have or to "impart" meaning.[4] This aspect of the Husserlian concept of phenomenon can hardly be emphasized too much since it really designates what has been called in traditional philosophy "noumenon," if this word is rightly understood to mean that certain "X" which is the true "essentiality" of the world, albeit (according to Kantian tradition) inexperienceable and perforce admittedly unknowable. According to Husserl phenomenon is the object of immediate experience and thereby a datum of (*geistig*) cognition. In the persuasion of Husserl Kant's principal error was falling victim to the prejudice that the only objects of experience and cognition can be those of a sensational character. Husserl, as far back as his *Logische Untersuchungen,* had dispossessed his thinking of this preconception, in favor of the doctrine of many kinds of experience. That is how he came to transform the use of phenomenon to the datum of a singular mode of cognition.

[3] See chap. vi, "Five Questions Concerning Phenomenology," § 3, pp. 229–37, for a more extensive treatment of Kantianism and phenomenology. Cf. also my comparison (*ibid.,* § 4) of phenomenology and critical realism, in which it is shown how phenomenology views the latter as Kantian, since it also holds the "conceptual" or "judgmental" nature of knowledge, and with it the unknowability of "reality."

[4] Husserl readily admitted, of course, that there may be realms of essence as yet unknown and certainly that there are others not yet completely known.

Even though phenomenon is that which exhibits itself as a constituent of experiencing consciousness, it must not be construed that Husserl conceived of it as a *construction* of consciousness. Phenomena as essences are the contents of pure consciousness, and to this extent they become part of the consciousness to which they are presenting themselves. His problem, of course, is to describe satisfactorily how phenomena can at once comprise the qualia of perceptual objects and be contents of consciousness. Important to remember, however, in this regard is that, in common with most current realisms, it is nonsense to speak of anything which is not somehow experienced or known in some form of consciousness. To this extent Husserl was anti-idealistic and saw no reason for sharing the Kantian distrust of experience or for mourning over the inaccessibility of the *Ding-an-sich*. In agreement with idealism, there is a thing-in-itself; as opposed to it, it is an actual (or potential) object of (intuitive) experience.

§ 2. *Method: The Phenomenological Reductions and the Realm of Pure Consciousness*

Husserl left no doubt about his intentions when he stated explicitly that his purpose was "to establish phenomenology itself as an eidetic science, as the theory of the essentiality of the transcendentally purified consciousness." [5] The method used to accomplish his purpose he called "reduction," or, more properly, reductions. A brief consideration of his treatment of this subject will disclose many basic concepts of his phenomenology.

It has already been remarked how Husserl designated objects, i. e., objects of ordinary experience, as constituted of "essences." Objects are of a "phenomenal" character, but as contrasted with the general usage of the

[5] *Ideen*, p. 114.

term this means that they are of an "essential" character, of the nature of essences, and, furthermore, are objects of a definite kind of experience, intuition.

The contention that every known object has the characteristic of experienceability is, in the eyes of Husserl, of greatest importance. This is clear when it is remembered that essences are declared to be experienceable, as well as "that what things are . . . they are as things of experience. Experience alone prescribes their meaning, and indeed when the concern is with factual things it is actual experience in its definitely ordered, empirical connections which does the prescribing." [6] If this be true, it is nothing short of *ein Unsinn* to hold that something could be known which is not experienced. The inexperienceable (not the inexperienced) simply does not exist. Every object, whether it be factual, actual, natural, imaginary, essential, or what, is at least a *potential* object of some kind of experience.

To hold that experienceability is characteristic of every known object is tantamount, on grounds of phenomenology, to declaring that, whenever it is experienced, it is, by virtue of that fact, in a certain relation to consciousness and its Ego. Husserl held to this, although he did not deny that every object has "being" in and for itself. Yet even this is not necessarily to argue that the object has no relationship to consciousness and its Ego. In the last analysis, "the thing is the thing of the world about me—including the thing that is not seen, and the really possible thing not experienced but experienceable or perhaps-experienceable." [7] Experienceability, then, does not betoken

[6] *Ibid.*, p. 88. By "prescribe" Husserl did not mean "to impute," but "to order," "to dictate."

[7] *Ibid.*, p. 89. Note Husserl's "realism." This will be elaborated more fully in chap. vi, "Five Questions Concerning Phenomenology," § 4, pp. 238–79.

merely an empty logical possibility, but contains the concept that a "known" object has, and must always have, its motive in the system of experience. To be known is to be experienced; to be experienced means nothing less than to be in relation to consciousness and its Ego.

Yet merely to affirm experienceability is not enough to describe the phenomenological position. Broadly speaking, phenomenology argues for two kinds of experience: natural and eidetic (of the nature of *Eidos*). For purposes of expediency, all content of knowledge can be divided into "natural" objects (e. g., trees, men, and all animate and inanimate objects) and their intrinsic phenomenal essentiality. Moreover, correlative to each kind of knowledge there is a certain kind of experience and cognition, e. g., sense experience and perception which involves the psychophysical organism. As contrasted with this, the experience of essences is *immediate,* and knowledge resulting therefrom is different "in kind" from that of the natural world. The realm of essences is intuited, and although, to be sure, transcendental essences are given through empirical connections, this is not to argue that intuitive experience, in every instance, is of the nature of or involves the psychophysical organism. In brief, eidetic knowledge has its proper conditions, as well as its singular mode of cognition and its exclusive realm of objects. It is this realm and the Ego to which it stands in relation in which Husserl's phenomenology as method is ultimately interested. To achieve this objective requires the employment of the phenomenological reduction, included in which is to be found the "doctrine of attitudes" which deals with the necessary state of mind required to facilitate its performance.

It follows from these observations that for Husserl there is a marked difference between the "natural standpoint" and the "phenomenological attitude." Husserl described the former somewhat as follows.[8] The first outlook upon life that we have is from the standpoint of "natural" human beings: creatures that will, judge, feel, and imagine "from the natural standpoint." Considered from such a perspective, what does the world actually consist of? I am aware of a world that is "spread out in space endlessly and in time becoming and become without end. I am aware of it, and that means above all I discover it immediately, intuitively; I experience it." [9] Corporeal things are simply spatially distributed before me, and they are apprehended through the variety of sensory perception as an "intuitive" content. Spatial things, temporal events, and their relations are just simply "there" for me.

Included in the world about us are animals, inanimate objects, and fellow human beings, all of which are "present" as realities in my field of perception. I "assume" them to be there; I "know" them as being there, whether or not I am "in relation" to them. My world is "present" to and for me. Yet it is not necessary that all these objects be present precisely in my field of perception, since for me real objects are simply there, definite, more or less familiar, agreeing with what is actually perceived without being themselves perceived or even intuitively present. And from this standpoint I know that awareness of this world about me is not a matter of "conceptualizing," and I likewise discover that it changes into a "clearly present" world when attention is bestowed upon it.

Moreover, I am a part of this "world." I am the one aware of its as a world, yet it is not exclusively my own; I am a part of "all the world" extended infinitely in space and boundless in time. In this way, when consciously awake, "I find myself at all times and without my ever being able to change it, set in relation to a world which

8 *Ideen*, pp. 48 f.   9 *Ibid.*, p. 48.

remains one and the same although in constant change. It is continually 'present for me,' and I myself am a member of it." [10] Yet, it must be remarked, this is not only a world of "facts and affairs," but likewise a "world of values, a world of goods, a practical world." [11]

A moment's reflection shows my consciousness as standing related to all this. When I go further and reflect upon myself, it is found that "I am present to myself as someone who perceives, represents, thinks, feels, desires, and so forth; and herein, *for the most part*, I find myself related in present experience to the fact-world constantly before me." [12] But to reflect further. I am not always related to the "fact-world" alone (and this is extremely important) : I can busy myself with numbers and the laws which they represent, and this arithmetical world is there *for* my consciousness (not because of my consciousness) only so long as I intend it or assume the "mathematical" attitude. As contrasted with this, the natural world is always "there," and so long as I have its objects as *cogitata* I am in the natural standpoint.

Husserl did not hold this to be so much a "theory" of consciousness and its relation to the natural world as an attempt to describe the elementary, ordinary common-sense outlook on the world. It is the standpoint we as human beings have in our normal intercourse with a variety of objects and beings in that world. In brief, we accept initially this spaciotemporal world as always "out there" both for us and every other creature in it. From this "original" viewpoint the thought never occurs that the world and its objects are in any way "dependent" for their existence upon us as perceivers or knowers or experients, but rather do we assume our dependence upon the world itself in so far as it both restricts and enables our actions and plans. This, then, is the natural stand-

10 *Ibid.*, p. 50.   11 *Ibid.*   12 *Ibid.*, p. 51.

point: I and a community of other I's live in a spacio-temporal world containing other kinds of objects, both animate and inanimate. This is not a result of "theorizing" or drawing deductions. The experient "naturally" assumes it; it is an assumed and potentially expressible thesis.

Although Husserl was admittedly inspired by the Cartesian method, he did not employ Descarte's "universal doubt," which would entail an attempt to doubt everything "with the purpose of setting up an absolutely indubitable sphere of being." [13] To be sure, the attempt to doubt anything and everything is indeed "within the realm of our perfect freedom," yet Husserl showed that to begin to doubt means "to doubt 'Being' (*Sein*) of some sort." [14] It must be noted, however, that this attempt

does not affect the form of Being itself. He who doubts, for instance, whether an object, whose Being he does not doubt, is constituted in such and such a way, *doubts the way it is constituted* (*das So-beschafften-sein*). This way of speaking of doubting can obviously be transferred to the *attempt* at doubting. Further, it is clear that we cannot doubt the Being of anything, and in the same act of consciousness (under the unifying form of simultaneity) bring what is substantive to this Being under the terms of the natural thesis, and so confer upon it the character of "being actually there" (*"vor-handen"*); . . . We cannot at once doubt and hold for certain one and the same quality of Being. It is likewise clear that the attempt to doubt any object of consciousness in respect to its being actually there *necessarily conditions a certain suspension* of the thesis.[15]

This possibility represents the starting-point of phenomenology, and the "certain suspension of the thesis" is the first aspect or step of the phenomenological reduction to pure consciousness and its content. It is noteworthy that

[13] Farber, "Phenomenology as a Method and as a Philosophical Discipline," p. 107.
[14] *Ideen*, p. 54.　　　　　　　　　　　　　　　[15] *Ibid.*

there is no abandonment of the thesis, nothing is ne-
gated, no "thesis and antithesis" is involved: it is merely
"set out of action," "disconnected," or "bracketed"
(eingeklammert) as an investigatory expediency. This
bracketing is of utmost importance to the phenomenological position, and its possible employment is in no
way limited to the mere attempt to doubt, since it can
be used in other contexts. "In relation to every thesis,
and wholly uncoerced, we can use this peculiar ἐποχή, a
certain abstention from judgment."[16] The judgment
simpliciter is modified into a "bracketed judgment." It
is clear, then, that Husserl did not mean by "doubt" an
act of consciousness which merely brings the Being of
something into question; on the contrary he meant the
"eliminating" of that something from the focus of attention, "pushing it aside" for the moment in order to make
the way clear for concentrating upon something else. The
first step of the reduction is thus the employment of the
"perfect freedom" to do this.

As indicated above, phenomenology as a method involves a reduction to "pure consciousness" with its "correlates of consciousness," and on the other side its "pure
Ego." This would leave "absolute consciousness" as the
residuum after nullifying the world. Consciousness itself, according to Husserl, "has a Being of its own," and
to penetrate into this Being means nothing less than to
open up the whole "phenomenological" region. In other
words, it is possible both to scrutinize the contents (essences) of pure consciousness and to observe the world to
which it is properly and exclusively related. From this it
is clear that perception consists of much more than mere
"sense data"; it has "a zone of background intuitions . . .
and this is also a conscious experience . . . a consciousness OF . . ."[17] He elaborated this by holding that every

16 Ibid., p. 55.   17 Ibid., p. 62.

experience "has *its own essence open to intuitive apprehension,* a 'content' which can be considered in its sin-
gularity in and for itself." [18]

Since Husserl's ultimate objective was an investigation of pure consciousness and its correlative realm of
eidetic Being, the question now arises how these may be
observed and made an object of study. With a consideration of this problem, the positive importance of the phenomenological reductions is uncovered.

The whole world, all its objects, and the "I" as a psychophysical organism and empirical object must be "set
aside," "put out of play," *bracketed* for the purpose of
gaining an intuitive vision of the pure sphere of "transcendental subjectivity," the region of transcendental essences that constitute the content of pure consciousness.
To "see" this transcendental region implies on Husserlian
grounds that it has the character of experienceability. In
order to be an object of any kind of knowledge, this realm
"is necessarily *experienceable,* and not merely by an Ego
conjured into being as an empty logical possibility but
by an actual Ego, as the demonstrable unity of its experience-relations." [19] This means that in principle it is
experienceable by *every* Ego.

Pure consciousness then has its own world of essences,
which in turn constitute the "essential Being" of the
world as ordinarily seen from the natural standpoint. To
attain to a study of the contents of this pure consciousness would accordingly mean to have in view ultimate and
essential Being. Yet, it need hardly be said, this achievement is not facile and requires the gradual elimination
of every vestige of the natural outlook on the world; the
reductions must first be completed. Insofar as "doubt"
played a part in this it would be a methodological instru-

18 *Ibid.,* p. 61.
19 *Ibid.,* p. 90.

ment, the use of the freedom possessed by everyone to thrust aside for the moment any and all considerations concerning the "factual" or real world with which he busies himself while in the natural standpoint.

Yet bracketing the real world does not suffice. Husserl not only stated repeatedly that pure consciousness and its Ego have their realm of pure Being and peculiar essence-content, but argued that even in the world of essences there is a certain realm which also must be "eliminated." Of consciousness itself he affirmed that it exists in its own right, in that "the Being of consciousness, of every stream of experience generally, though it would indeed be modified by a nullifying of the thing-world, would not be affected thereby in its own proper existence." [20] If this means anything at all, it is that pure consciousness has a nature entirely its own; it is more than any part of or even totality of its experiences, concepts, cogitations, and so forth. Above all this is an affirmation that no real thing, i. e., none that consciously presents and manifests itself through appearances, is necessary for the Being of consciousness itself—consciousness understood in the widest sense as the "stream of experience."

In the second volume of *Logische Untersuchungen* Husserl had taken the first step of what he was later to define as the reduction by differentiating between natural and eidetic realms. In these investigations he had established, at least to his own satisfaction, that the eidetic region exists in its own right; it is not psychological, it is not physical, it is not psychophysical. But that was as far as he went. Now, in the *Ideen,* he took the further step of distinguishing between "immanent" and "transcendent" essences. This task was more difficult, since it involved considering the formations of pure consciousness itself, as well as the essences of individual events which transcend

[20] *Ibid.,* p. 91.

consciousness. This involved an examination, therefore, of essences of that which only " 'reveals' itself in formations of consciousness, 'constituting' itself, for instance, consciously through sensory appearances." [21]

Pure consciousness and its realm of pure experience are essentially independent of all existence of the type of a world or nature and, needless to say, they have no need of these in order "to be." To Husserl it was "perfectly obvious" that the existence and nature of what is natural could not condition the existence or Being of consciousness, since it arises as the *correlate* of consciousness. In the final analysis, it *is* (an object of knowledge) only insofar as it constitutes itself within the ordered connections and organizations of consciousness.

After suspending all particular, concrete realities, Husserl passed to other varieties of the "transcendent," and this step affected the series of "universal" objects, or essences. Since essences are not to be really found in pure consciousness, they are, in a certain way, transcendent to it. On the other hand, it is impossible to disconnect transcendents indefinitely, since such a suspension, although it would leave pure consciousness as residuum, would make a science of pure consciousness impossible.[22]

Husserl (perhaps unwisely) would have nothing of "ontologies," whether material or formal—although he readily affirmed that to every sphere of individual Being which can be set off as a region ("Being" considered in its widest logical meaning) there actually, of necessity, belongs an ontology. For instance, to physical nature there is an ontology of nature, to animality there belongs an ontology of animality. All such material ontologies must, however, be dissociated from phenomenological discipline. Opposed to these is "formal" ontology, considered in uni-

[21] *Ibid.*, p. 117.
[22] Husserl never explained why this would be the case.

son with the formal logic of thought-meanings, and belonging to it the quasi-region, "objects-in-general."

To be sure, there is a use for formal logic, or, as Husserl called it, "formal ontology," since it deals with universals. Its value, however, is not for philosophy but for the exact sciences and their purposes. Every special investigator in the various fields of science must use "objects-in-general," such as properties, concepts, propositions, and inferences. Now since phenomenology uses concepts, propositions, inferences, and the like, it would seem that it, too, would be required to have a formal ontology. Yet when phenomenology is understood as Husserl intended it to be, as a pure descriptive discipline "which studies the whole field of pure transcendental consciousness in the light of pure intuition," [23] it is clear that formal logic must also be placed in "brackets," and therewith all the disciplines of formal mathesis, such as algebra, theory of numbers, and theory of manifolds. This of course is to assume that the inquiry of phenomenology into pure consciousness sets itself no other task than that of making those descriptive analyses which can be resolved into pure intuition. Once this is granted, however, it is clear that the theoretical framework of mathematical disciplines, and all the theorems which develop within it, can be of no service whatever. Husserl was not interested in the formation of concepts and judgments proceeding "constructively"; neither did he value systems of mediated deduction, including the formal theory of deductive systems generally, such as mathematics. They cannot serve as instruments of phenomenological research.

Husserl, as already noted, had the express intention of establishing phenomenology as an "eidetic" science, i. e., as the doctrine of the "essential nature" of the transcen-

<hr/>

[23] *Ideen*, p. 113.

dentally purified consciousness. Yet he also argued that not everything can be bracketed, and it is most clear that above all "the essential domain of the phenomenologically purified consciousness itself" cannot be disconnected.[24] This consciousness Husserl called "a priori," and he meant thereby consciousness "in its purity," which concerns itself with the transcendental realm (in contradistinction to the "natural").

Hence even in the realm of essences there must be drawn a sharp distinction between the "transcendental" and the "immanent." The latter may be defined as "those which within the particular events of a stream of consciousness, and nowhere else, possess particularized influx-conditioned experiences of some sort or another."[25] Clearly, all essences do not belong in this classification. Just as there is a distinction among "particular" objectivities between immanent and transcendental, so is there a similar differentiation in the realm of essences. Husserl cited as transcendent essences "thing," "spatial shape," "movement," "color of a thing," "man," "human feeling," "psychical experience," "quality of character," and "person." Now obviously, if Husserl desired to construct a phenomenology as "a pure descriptive doctrine of the essential nature of the immanent formations of consciousness of the events which, within the limitations of the phenomenological suspension, can be seized within the stream of experiences,"[26] it was necessary to *exclude* from this restricted field everything that is transcendentally particular, including transcendent essences. Their logical position is rather in the "theory" of the essential nature of the relevant transcendental objectivity. No disciplines preoccupied with such transcendent-eidetic regions could contribute any premises at all, and this includes all "ontologies" belonging to such domains.

[24] *Ibid.*   [25] *Ibid.*, p. 114.   [26] *Ibid.*

In the same manner as phenomenology disconnects the "real nature" of physical science and the empirical natural sciences, it must now go one step further and bracket those eidetic sciences whose objects of study belong essentially to the physical objectivity of nature as such. Geometry, kinematics, and physics are included within the bracket. Similarly, since all empirical sciences dealing with the nature of animals, and all mental sciences concerning human beings in personal and social relationships, and the subjects of history, including all the cultural institutions belonging to men are suspended, so likewise is it inevitable that every eidetic science corresponding to these objectivities will likewise be suspended. Briefly, Husserl was not interested in "nature" or any objectivity belonging to it; by the same token he would employ no science which dealt with nature or any part of it. Pure consciousness and its experiences have as content not nature, but essences. Yet some of those essences, the transcendental or universals, are, from one standpoint, a "part" of nature, since they "lend" any and all meaning to "natural objectivities" which they might be declared as having. There remains, then, nothing to do except to suspend them and to deal only with the immanent essences which are a part of the *stream of pure consciousness* and which, in the final analysis, give to the world and all therein—both natural *and* transcendent— their proper meaning.

Immanent Being is therefore without doubt absolute in this sense, that in principle *nulla "re" indiget ad existendum.* On the other hand, the world of the transcendent *"res"* is related unreservedly to consciousness, yet certainly not to logical conceptions but to what is "actual." [27] Clearly, Husserl was here arguing that the transcendent, owing to our constitution as human beings, was neces-

[27] *Ibid.,* p. 92.

sarily given through certain empirical connections. It is given directly and with increasing completeness to perceptual continua harmoniously developed and, through certain methodic thought-forms grounded in experience, it reaches ever more fully and immediately theoretic determinations of increasing transparency and unceasing progressiveness.[28]

Husserl went on to argue that in the sense of "inward" experience, consciousness and real being are not two coordinate forms of Being entering somehow, and upon certain occasions, into relation or connection. When "objective" or "subjective" is spoken of, it is actually in terms of empty logical categories and does not reflect the true constitution of "pure" consciousness and its content.

The whole spaciotemporal world, to which man and the human Ego claim to be born as subordinate singular realities, is, according to its own meaning, mere *intentional* existence, which therefore has the mere secondary, relative sense of "existence for a consciousness." To put it another way: it is an existence which consciousness in its own experiences *posits,* and in principle is intuitable and determinable only as the identity common to the motivated appearance-manifolds; over and beyond this, it is just nothing at all.[29] On the other hand, considering consciousness in its "purity," it must be reckoned as a self-contained system of Being, as a system of absolute Being, into which nothing can penetrate and from which nothing can escape since its whole region is already "there." Pure consciousness has no spaciotemporal exterior and cannot be "inside" a spaciotemporal system. As such it cannot experience causality for anything or exert causality upon anything, since it is presupposed that causality bears a normal sense of "natural" causality as a relation of dependence between "realities."

[28] *Ibid.*   [29] *Ibid.*, p. 93.

It is clear from this that Husserl deliberately inverted the meaning of Being. What for us is ordinarily accepted as "primary" Being is really *secondary* for him, since it is what it is only in relation to the primary. Hence "reality" essentially lacks independence, it is not absolute, it has no "absolute essence." According to phenomenology, "it has the essentiality of something which in principle is only intentional, only known, consciously represented as an appearance." [30]

Reverting once more to the reduction, and granting, at least for the moment, Husserl's contentions, it is apparent that on phenomenological grounds a new philosophical standpoint is possible. To bracket the whole field of psychophysical reality, including all of its theoretic standpoints, is to find remaining the whole field of absolute consciousness. Instead of living naïvely in commonplace sense experience and subjecting it to theoretic inquiries, it is possible for philosophy to perform the phenomenological reduction. Otherwise stated: instead of merely carrying out those acts proper to the nature-constituting consciousness, with its transcendental theses, and allowing ourselves to be led by motives that operate therein to still other transcendental theses, and so forth, the phenomenological reduction places even these outside of action, takes no part in them. Apprehension and theoretic inquiry are directed to pure consciousness in its own absolute Being, which Husserl called "the stream of experience." It is this which remains over as the phenomenological residuum, and the whole world ("nature") has been suspended—the whole world including things, living creatures, men, ourselves included. But nothing has been "lost." On the contrary, the whole of absolute Being has been won, absolute Being, which, properly understood, "conceals" within itself what has been tradi-

[30] *Ibid.*, p. 94. Here is seen a hint of Husserl's "idealism."

tionally described as transcendental. The basic field of phenomenology is that level whose datum is the infinite field of absolute (eidetic) experiences. "Reality" is suspended and Being is apprehended: *das Grundfeld der Phänomenologie* is in this way uncovered.

Husserl constantly referred to pure consciousness "and its Ego." In his mind, as already seen, phenomenological reflection upon experience discloses that there are in sensory perception at least the two elements of sense data and eidetic meaning. The world of meaning, accordingly, does not admit of spaciotemporal classification, i. e., that which makes "reality" what it is, is itself not of the nature of reality. There is a realm of meaning, a region of Eidos, and these essences constitute the world and all that is in it as "such and such," and not "something else." This realm consists of "objects" which are experienced and known by *geistig* intuition.

That which is in constant relation with this eidetic realm Husserl called the Ego and its "pure consciousness." Since it alone is capable of seizing the meaning of events and objects, which means nothing less than that it alone can intuit, the Ego is always active, even when its experience is concerned with objects and events that are ostensibly only in the spatial and temporal world. The objects of sensory perception "have" meaning by reason of the Ego's constant experience of that which composes all and every meaning of the "natural" world, its essences. At this point the justification of the methodological reductions becomes apparent: to formulate systematically the meaning of the world it is necessary to observe and to study those objects which prescribe the *contents* of that which makes all experience of that world possible, namely, the Ego and its pure consciousness. Natural knowledge begins with sensuous experience and remains within the limits of such experience; the psychophysical organism has the role of a means of contact between the Ego and the real world. But this empirical experience "can be transformed into essential insight (ideation) ; . . . the object of such insight is then the corresponding pure essence or *Eidos*." [31]

It is clear that by "pure" Ego Husserl meant the personality as completely purged of all psychophysical reference and content. It is "the I to which I am present." [32] Once the whole world of nature (including the self as an empirical subject) is "bracketed," there is left the pure consciousness of the Ego which can be described "in complete isolation from everything else." [33] This pure consciousness has the pure Ego "as its unifying factor. Every stream of consciousness . . . has its own Ego that transcends the very stream in which it is functionally immanent." [34]

Clearly the Ego, as the condition of all experiences, is the presupposition of knowing the world. Or, to put it in another way, my experiences presuppose the existence of myself, my person, and as such it is I who make possible my experiences. This is not to suggest, however, that phenomenology would contend in the manner of some idealists that "my" existence is the *only* factor involved, or that other Egos and their community of objects both in

31 *Ibid.*, p. 10. At this point it is well to emphasize that a careful differentiation must be drawn between the experience (or "knowing") of essences and "knowledge" of them. All knowledge of essence presupposes the experience of essence, but the experience of essence does not necessarily include or even imply a knowledge of it. Essence-experience is common to all, indeed necessary insofar as the world is known as having any meaning; concomitant with sensory perception there is always experience of the eidetic realm, which lends significance to the data of perception. Yet (scientific) *knowledge* of that realm is an entirely different matter. In the one case it is merely a matter of intuiting; in the latter instance phenomenology would make the data of intuition the object of a special study.

32 *Encyclopaedia Britannica*, 14th ed., XVII, 699.

33 *Ibid.*, p. 701.

34 *Ibid.*, p. 700.

the natural and ideal realms are "dependent" upon my existence or the experience-relations within which I find myself. Once again, as against some kinds of realism, phenomenology in no wise holds that the object somehow is "constituted" of a "relationship" between an unknown "something" and an ethereal "I". On the contrary, both the I and its experiences, and the objects of experience are given a metaphysical status of equal importance.

The word "pure" thus betokens a differentiation between personality and the "self" as a psychophysical organism, which can be made an object of psychological study. Were this understood more fully, Husserl could never be stigmatized as a psychologist, since psychology deals principally with psychical reality, with concrete mental processes, and psychical "facts." Husserl, in contrast with this, is concerned with "pure meanings in their logical interrelations, . . . with pure ideal contents only." [35] Psychology is a science of ("real") experience and deals with the components and elements of that experience insofar as the psychophysical organism plays a role. But phenomenology is concerned with essential Being and meaning, with the essences of all experience, and has as its object the study of the Ego and its pure experiences.

In what manner did Husserl try to substantiate his arguments for the existence and nature of the Ego? Experience of every description presupposes an experient as well as an object experienced; cognition, a knower and an object known; to be sure, logical "proof" may not be forthcoming here, but Husserl was rarely concerned with the proofs of formal logic. He argued, in part, that if reflective apprehension

is directed to my experience, I apprehend an absolute self whose existence is in principle undeniable; that is, the insight that it does not exist is in principle impossible; it would

<hr/>

[35] Gibson, "The Problem of Real and Ideal in Phenomenology of Husserl," *Mind*, XXXIV (1935), 311 f.

be a contradiction to contend it as possible that such a given experience were in fact *not* existing. The stream of experience which is mine—that of the one who is thinking—may be to ever so great an extent uncomprehended, unknown alike in its past and future reaches, yet as soon as I look towards the flowing life in its real present and with it grasp myself as the pure subject of this life . . . I affirm plainly and inevitably: I AM, this life is, I live: *cogito;* . . . each of us carries in himself the guarantee of his absolute existence as a fundamental possibility. . . . There is no contradiction in the possibility that every alien consciousness, which I posit in experienced empathy, does not exist. But my empathy and *my* consciousness are originally and absolutely given, not only essentially but existentially.[36]

There is nothing except the Ego and its experiences that can be made the object of immanent perception; there is nothing so "certain" as the Ego and its stream of experience.

Although it is perfectly clear from what has been said that Husserl never questioned the independent existence of the natural and ideal worlds, he held that this evidence of the Ego is, above all, in no way subject to doubt. To be sure the world, since it is of a "contingent" nature, does not contain the certainty of existence (for the Ego) that the Ego itself, for which the world is there, does. As contrasted with its knowledge of the contingent and even the eidetic world, the knowledge of its own existence brings with it a necessity so indisputable as to make all attempts at denial seem nothing less than *unsinnig*. As a matter of fact, the world itself "is not subject to doubt in the sense that there are rational grounds which can be brought against the tremendous force of unanimous experience, but in the sense that a doubt is thinkable, and this because the possibility of nonexistence is in principle never excluded." [37]

[36] *Ideen,* p. 85. This problem is discussed further in chap. vi, "Five Questions Concerning Phenomenology," § 5, pp. 279–99.
[37] *Ideen,* p. 87.

The net results of Husserl's elaboration of the reductions as a method can be summarized as follows:

First, there are, broadly speaking, two realms of experience, the natural and the eidetic. Experience of the second lends all significance and meaning which the first might be said to possess. The natural world is what it is because of the realm of essences constituting it.

Second, corresponding to these two worlds are two kinds of experience, sensory and essential. Every object, whether it be "natural" or eidetic, is known because of its experienceability. Sense experience, in and for itself, is inadequate and imperfect and, without the concomitant intuitive experience of essences, it would be meaningless. On phenomenological grounds, therefore, it is untenable to speak of unknown or inexperienceable realms. [38]

Third, all eidetic knowledge is "connected with" sense experience. Essences are apprehended in "spiritual" (*geistig*) intuition, yet this is possible only *in and through* sense experience. The "pure" experiences of pure consciousness and its Ego must not be interpreted as meaning that essences are intuited or experienceable wholly independently of sense experience and its objectivities.

Fourth, for purposes of methodological expediency a distinction must be drawn between immanent and transcendent essences, since the latter refers to those essences dealing with the objectivities of experience, and the former alludes to the essences of inner perception or intuition within the sphere of pure consciousness and its proper "Being."

Fifth, even as nature and all its objectives are bracketed,

[38] Husserl persisted in his refusal to consider the problem that experience does not always have universality and necessity. He refused to consider that there is a difference between the statements "direct experience gives no universalities" and "direct experience is not sufficient to ground the validity of universal theses" (cf. Bannes, *Versuch einer Darstellung und Beurteilung der Grundlagen der Philosophie Edmund Husserls*, pp. 50 f.).

so are all sciences dealing with them, including any science of essences which are definable as "transcendent."

Sixth, that which remains as residuum, pure consciousness and its pure experiences, is the field of phenomenology as a science. This residuum consists of the realm of immanent essences.

Finally (seventh), the Ego, with its pure consciousness and experiences, is the core of all experience, since it is its relationship with essences that yields to experience its essentiality or "meaning."

§ 3. *The Doctrine of Essences and Intuition*

It is evident from the foregoing that Husserl made no denial of the existential sensuous world, that world "out there" which we as human beings unquestionably take to be independent of us, whether or not we are there to experience it. Yet once he granted the "independent" existence of the "factual" world he was ineluctably committed to the responsibility of explaining, on phenomenological grounds, its "nature" or "constitution." Such considerations, it is now clear, comprise the problem of essences and intuition.[39]

Husserl was of course emphatic in his objection to the contention that the "factual" is the only world.[40] It is usually meant by such a position that, even granting the possible existence of any other kind of world or realm, *it is neither experienceable nor knowable,* since all knowledge, conditioned as it is by our peculiarly constituted psychophysical "make-up" or constitution, is and must ever remain restricted to the "natural" world. This is tantamount to holding that there is only one standpoint, and that is the "natural standpoint." In short, according to this "empirical" outlook, the only world known is that which is

39 The problem of "fact" and essence will be treated more extensively in § 5, pp. 177–204, of this chapter.

40 *Ideen*, pp. 33 f., "Naturalistic Misconceptions."

experienced by the senses. It would obviously follow from this that every science would accordingly be a science of sense experience, a science of "fact"; there would be only "natural science." Such is the theme of the philosophy commonly known as "empiricism," or, to be more specific, the naturalistic empiricism so familiar to the readers of such men as Herbert Spencer, Julian Huxley, and Bertrand Russell, to mention but a few.[41]

According to Husserl, empiricism rightly holds that all knowledge springs from experience, but wrongly contends for sense experience alone. This would mean, for instance, that all universalities, necessities, principles, and rigidness are somehow known (or perhaps, as with most idealists, "imputed"?) subsequent to some kind of experience of sense objects and their spaciotemporal relations. Clearly, Husserl must deny this. While treating the naturalistic attitude, Husserl expressed the conviction that

Genuine science and the genuine absence of prejudice peculiar to it demand, as a foundation of all proofs, judgments which as such are immediately valid, drawing their validity from originally given intuitions. These, once again, are categorized as prescribed by the *meaning* of the judgments, or the proper essentiality of the objects and the contents of judgments.[42]

Husserl meant nothing less than this. The principles and propositions which positive science employs on the *"assumption"* of their strict self-evidence are actually not to be found in the empirical world to which science so tenaciously clings and acclaims as the only world; neither are they to be conceived as "derived from" or "arrived at"

[41] And, he might have added, the theme of American and British neo-realism and critical realism. Cf. my treatment of this in chap. vi, "Five Questions Concerning Phenomenology," § 4, pp. 238–79.

[42] *Ideen*, p. 36. It must be remembered that Husserl was writing in the decade following the turn of the century, when science was more "naturalistic" that it is at present. Yet in many respects his depiction of the prejudices of science, and his criticisms thereof, are as valid today as then.

by deduction or induction. To be sure, they are *instruments* of work which science uses, but, according to Husserl, instruments not of its own making or discovery *as exact science*. Restricting itself by definition to the sense world, the components of which are always in a state of change, clearly science could never lay claim to deriving from that very world itself such non-sensible essentials as the principles of the syllogism and the principles underlying the modes of inference, universalities, and necessities. An examination of the field of science and its materials discloses that these instruments simply are not there. If this be true, they must be discovered in, or drawn from, *another* realm which is none the less experienceable merely because it is not "natural." They all constitute a self-givenness intuitively apprehended "prior to any theorizing," and without which empirical sciences would be helpless to proceed. If this is true there is needed a science to investigate and substantiate the validity of all these "scientific instruments." The special sciences need a Science of science.

From the standpoint of phenomenology it would be nothing less than suicidal for the positive sciences to deny the existence and knowledge of this other realm of essentials, universalities, meanings, and necessities; in other words, were any given empirical science to decline these and try to stand alone, it would be helpless to explain its systematic connections and exactness. In short, it must admit that essentiality is likewise "out there" and "in" that world. Yet, although "within" the world, it is distinct from it. It is distinct as enjoying essential and qualitative difference, distinct as yielding itself in an experience not to be categorized as sensory. It is because of knowledge of this realm that the world and all therein have "sense" (*Sinn*) and meaning (*Bedeutung*).

What, after all, is "contingency"? Husserl argued that

all contingency, the "object" of "direct experience," is correlative to a necessity. The character of essentiality belongs to it; it is related to necessary universality.[43] As being especially constituted, every object "contains its own proper mode of Being, its own supply of essential predicables which must belong to it." [44] Since direct experience yields not generalities, but only particular elements, there is, in every sense perception, and at the same time, *essential insight*, the object of which is the pure essence or *Eidos*. Every *sensum* has its *Eidos*.

More specifically, what did Husserl mean by essence? He said that fact and essence are different and defined fact as "accidental." Although it is "such and such," a factually real thing has spaciotemporal existence. But essence is not of the nature of space and time. In *Logische Untersuchungen*, essence was called "Idea"; in *Ideen*, it is called "Eidos." [45] "Idea" is defined as "ideal unity," the "universal," of which the concrete is an instance. These ideal unities embody a realm in and for themselves and are seized in correlative acts of ideation. Stated in logical terms, in *Logische Untersuchungen*, what is now called *Eidos* meant the "species" or "concept" which has no temporality or spatiality. It is a unity which supplies identity to the manifold of actualities and factual concepts.

In *Ideen*, Husserl was careful to draw an even sharper distinction between "fact" and "essence." [46] If contingency is correlative to a necessity and yet has the character of essential necessity, the reason must be that it is in relation to essential universality. The implication is inescapable that "it belongs to the meaning of everything contingent that it should have essentiality and therewith an *Eidos* to be apprehended in its purity; and this *Eidos* stands under

[43] *Ibid.*, p. 9.
[45] *Ideen*, p. 6.
[44] *Ibid.*
[46] *Ibid.*, pp. 7 f.

essential truths of varying degrees of universality." [47] An individual object is something "unique," i. e., it is constituted "thus and thus"; as "in and for itself" it has its own proper mode of existence, "its peculiar constitution of essential predicables which must qualify it *qua* 'Being as it is in itself.'" [48] Moreover, whatever belongs to the essence of the particular could likewise belong to any other particular; hence it is the widest generalities of essential Being that delimit "regions" or "categories" of all concrete particulars.

It is clear, then, that Husserl used "essence" to indicate the intimate selfhood of an individual object, since it qualifies its *whatness (Washeit)*. If this concept of Husserl's be granted, it must be further held that every particular "concrete" perception contains "within itself" essential insight or ideation. The object of such insight would be, then, "the corresponding pure essence or *Eidos*, be it the highest category or one of its particularizations, right down to the fully concrete." [49] Even as in perception there is a variety of clearness and distinctness, so with essence-insight. There can be imperfect or inadequate ideation; there can be a "one-sidedness" of intuition.[50]

Eidos is an object of a novel type of "perception," and the correlative ideational intuition has the character of a dator act, and this implies that even as the datum of particular or empirical perception is a specific sensory object, so is the datum of essential intuition a pure essence. Essential intuition thus is no less "prepositional" than empirical perception. Ideation is the consciousness *of* something, of an "object," of something toward which the glance of

47 *Ibid.,* p. 9.
48 *Ibid.*
49 *Ibid.,* p. 10. "Essence-insight," "essential insight," "ideation" and "intuition" are interchangeable terms.
50 This problem is considered at length in chap. vi, "Five Questions Concerning Phenomenology," § 1, pp. 207-23, "The Problem of Error."

the Ego is directed, a something which is "self-given." As such it can be "presented" in other acts, vaguely or distinctly "thought," made the object of true and false "predications." Such is the case with every "object" in the necessarily extended sense proper to formal logic. But possibly the most important thing to emphasize in this connection is that Husserl's intuition is a fundamentally unique and novel kind of prepositional apprehension possessing its proper object.

Did Husserl mean by pure intuition that essences can be ideated with reference only to themselves? Emphatically not. To be sure, they can be seized in their purity, although it lies undoubtedly in the "intrinsic nature" of essential intuition that it must rest on what is a chief factor of individual perception, namely, the striving for this, the "visible presence" or particular (sensuous) facts.[51] This does not mean, on the other hand, that its nature or object "presupposes" any apprehension of sense objects or any recognition of their reality. Consequently,

it is certain that no essential intuition is possible without the free possibility of turning the glance to a "corresponding" particularization and of shaping an exemplar; just as, contrariwise, no particular perception is possible without the free possibility of executing an act of ideation, and thereby directing the glance upon the corresponding essence which exemplifies itself in something individually perceptible.[52]

Yet this does not alter the fact that there is a sharp difference between gross sense perception and eidetic intuition; in addition there are "the corresponding essential relations between 'existence' (here clearly used in the

[51] This, as will be seen later in this chapter (§ 5), may still be a moot question. Sometimes Husserl held that intuitive activity is possible only when evoked by experience of sensuous objects. At other times he argued for intuition of essences without the necessity of "sense experience" (e. g., in mathematics and syllogistic logic). This problem will be treated at length at the end of this chapter.

[52] *Ideen,* p. 12.

sense of particular object) and 'essence,' between fact and Eidos." [53]

Husserl emphasized, further, that there are intuitions of a merely "imaginative" order, i. e., those that can be the data of mere fancy, just as the pure essence can be exemplified intuitively in the data of experience, data of perception, memory, and so forth. This means that we can live through fictitious acts of everyday life, and that we can bring spatial shapes of one sort or another to such experiences as social events and melodies. Here, it is clear, there is ideation of pure essences in manifold variety, such as spatial shape "in general" and melody "as such." Obviously, these do not have to be given in actual "sense" experience. From this it would follow that "the positing of essences and above all the intuitive apprehension included does not imply the positing of any particular existence whatsoever. Pure essential truths do not embrace the slightest assertions about facts." [54] Hence from these *alone* not even the smallest truths concerning the "fact"— world can be inferred. Since to "think" or "express" a fact it is necessary to ground it in experience, so thought concerning pure essence needs for its grounding and support the conditioning insight into the essence of "things."

In geometrical propositions, for example, there are judgments made about essences which are "unmixed" with positing of anything "particular," although, to be sure, there is judgment about the particular which is an "instance" of essential Being and in accordance with the rubric "in general." In geometry there is judgment about the straight line and angle "in general" or, as such, about triangles in general, and so on. It is clear, furthermore, that the geometrician *assumes* that such universal judgments have the character of essential generality. Husserl speaks of pure, rigorous, unconditioned universality. It is

[53] *Ibid.*   [54] *Ibid.*, p. 13.

this, he believed, that makes it possible for eidetic judgments, judging, and propositions to be declared to possess "essential necessity." From this he argued that "essential generality" and "essential necessity" are strict
correlates.

When speaking of the experience of essence and its
validity, Husserl formulated his "principle of all principles" as follows:

that every primordial given intuition is an authoritative source
of knowledge, that everything which originally presents itself
in "intuition" (as it were in its bodily reality) is simply to be
accepted as what it discloses itself to be, although only within
the limits in which it then presents itself.[55]

Without doubt he meant by this that knowledge is not
limited to objects brought to our attention through sense
perception, and, moreover, that as the objects must be accepted "as they present themselves" in simple perception,
so in intuition essences are not constructions of imagination, or logical concepts alone, but are objects of a
definite kind of experience. Essence is thus the "whatness"
of an object, the very *qualia* themselves, on the basis
of which a knowledge of all recognition, differentiation,
and classification of our world of perceptual and ideal
objects is made possible. Yet, as the ultimate of everything, in the final analysis essence escapes all attempts
to squeeze it into the confines of a narrow, logical definition.

It might be asked, what is the relation between the doctrine of essence and the phenomenological Ego? To this
must be replied that only the pure Ego—the *Personalität*
considered apart from any psychophysical reference—can
experience the realm of essences; only the Ego can intuit.
Once Husserl had established this to his satisfaction, he believed it followed that in order to know this realm it is

[55] *Ibid.*, pp. 43–44.

necessary to study the contents of the Ego's consciousness, since the objects of the eidetic realm are the contents of pure consciousness. Essences are "appropriated" by the Ego in its intuitive activity, and to know the Ego's world of objects would be to know essences themselves. Just as intuition of essences, in ordinary intercourse with the "natural" world, yields basic knowledge of the world itself, so would a study designed to examine the contents of the Ego's consciousness result in a "deeper understanding" of the essential nature of the natural world.

In the light of these remarks, it should now be clear that when it was said that, to delve further into the realm of essences, the natural standpoint must be abandoned, it was meant that this is required for a *deeper* knowledge of essences. That the Ego unconsciously, or rather inadvertently and necessarily, intuits essences in its ordinary commerce with the empirical world does not mean that there is "knowledge" of its essentialities. For instance, when I look about me and see things as "red" or "white," or situations and other beings as "good" or "bad," and so forth, I am, to be sure, "being aware of," or cognizing their essences. This would not mean, however, that such mere awareness yielded genuine knowledge of essences themselves, any more than awareness of the sidereal bodies guarantees astronomical knowledge. In other words, in every experience there is always awareness of some meaning or meanings without having knowledge of what it is or what makes possible that meaning, let alone the manner in which it is apprehended. To make such an inquiry, in fact, is the first step toward genuine knowledge. In order really to "know" essences scientifically it is required first to intend them, "go after them," even though they have already been the object of intuition, albeit the experient has been unaware of his intuitive activity. It must be inquired of the object or situation, What makes you what you are, and not something else? And curiously enough, to answer this the (sense) object itself, as well as all other like objects, must unreservedly be abandoned. Hence, although awareness of meaning is common to all, knowledge of its significance is an entirely different matter, involving as it does further phenomenological insight into the realm of essences.

§ 4. *Intuition and Intentionality*

It is to be regretted that Husserl did not formulate systematically a brief and clear definition of intuition. At times it is referred to as *"Schau,"* now as *Einsicht,* then as *"unmittelbare Sehen."* In *Prolegomena*[56] he had said that "scientific knowledge" is *Erkenntnis aus dem Grunde* and elaborated this as "to have insight into" essences. In this way the logical justification of a theory is established, and intuitive insight thus gives not only the theory itself but its justification. The logical justification of a theory requires and is based on intuitive insight into its *Notwendigkeit.* In *Logische Untersuchungen* he carried this idea over to the problem of constructing a pure logic; in *Ideen* he used it to build an eidetic science.

A science of essence must, then, have its final grounding act in the intuition of essences. The term intuition, it is clear, does not refer to the psychological phenomenon or object of mental experience, but to *Wesenserlebnisse,* those acts of consciousness in which essences become "presented." There is with Husserl, when speaking of method, continual allusion to pure science as requiring a foundation built upon judgments which are immediately valid and which draw their objective validity directly "from originally given intuitions." Noetic standards, which every science uses, can be fixed only through eidetic insight, and that again means "revealed in and through the

---

[56] Page 231.

originally given intuitions and fixed through judgments that are faithfully commensurate with the data intuitively given." [57] Hence sensory perception of experience is not sufficient; immediate "seeing" as the original dator of consciousness of any kind whatsoever is the *ultimate* source of justification for all rational statements. Therefore, although in *Logische Untersuchungen* intuition meant the act of ideation, the presupposition of the possibility of all knowledge, in *Ideen* it now becomes the foundational act of eidetic sciences as well. Ideation *as a method* is the *Schau* of "phenomenologically reduced" essences; or, in other words, it is an act whose role is to direct itself to the realm of essence. Yet more important than Husserl's usage of intuition as a methodological instrument is his concept of the role it plays in the experiences of everyday life. When examined in this light there is found an indissoluble connection between his doctrine of intuition and that of intentionality.

Husserl, as already remarked, adopted from Franz Brentano the idea that consciousness is "intentional." Consider the case of sense perception. During perceiving activity the contents of perception are in constant flux, and the stream of consciousness is in continual flow; yet the object is said somehow to remain the "same." But how is it possible to affirm this under these conditions? Husserl answered, because its meaning, its *Sinn* is there for the Ego. The tree is a tree, even though it is "perceived" inadequately, partially; the tree is perceived in certain of its aspects only. The "other side" of the tree is not "seen" in one and the same act. Now what is meant when it is said we are "conscious" of the object declared to be a tree? Merely that it is (sensuously) "perceived"? Hardly. The truth of the matter is, *its meaning is seized.* It is noteworthy, moreover, that in the act of perceiving itself

[57] *Ideen*, p. 36.

there is no question of the object being "real" or "not real." A tree in a picture, for instance, is "enjoyed" and is "real" so far as meaning is concerned. A mere perception *as such* could never constitute genuine experience in the sense of telling the experient something of the object perceived, for it would lack meaning. Accompanying it must be that "something else" which Husserl believed to be the content of pure consciousness, the object for the Ego which has its own stream of cogitations with its *cogitata*. Since it is not of the sensuous, the world of the Ego is an ideal world.

How is access to this world possible? Or, better still, how is this world *experienceable?* Husserl replied, because of the *intentional* character of experience; and he understood by intentionality "the peculiarity of experiences 'to be conscious *of* something.' " [58] An intentional experience has *"Beziehung auf Gegenständliches,"* a *"Bewusstsein von etwas."* Brentano had held that "all mental life is activity," and that psychology "is the study of acts or psychological functions; it is the study of experience of acts which are psychical and which 'intend' or are directed toward material or physical objects." [59] Owing to this intentional character, consciousness is always "pointing to" objects, and thus "the different classes of consciousness, such as judgment, feeling and will, are to be distinguished by their intentional direction, i. e., by the way in which something becomes an object for them." [60]

Husserl thus appropriated the idea that for consciousness to be intentional it must point to something besides itself. As opposed to Brentano, however, he believed that merely to say that consciousness is "of something" is in-

58 *Ibid.,* p. 168.

59 Bixler, "A Phenomenological Approach to Religious Realism," in Mackintosh and others, *Religious Realism,* p. 69,

60 *Ideen,* p. 168,

sufficient, since, as a matter of fact, to be conscious of something means to be "intentionally related to something." Moreover, as further opposed to Brentano, to be intentionally related meant for Husserl much more than a mere "psychological connection" with material or physical objects. That there are such experiences is not to be doubted, but Husserl asserted that, when intentionality is spoken of, the concern is with "experiences in their pure essentiality, with pure essences, and with that which the essence 'a priori,' in unconditioned necessity, embraces." [61] Continuing in this vein, Husserl argued

that an experience is the consciousness of something: a fiction, for instance, the fiction of a certain centaur; a perception, the perception of its 'real' object; a judgment, the judgment concerning its subject-matter, etc.; this does not relate to the experience-fact within the world, especially within some given psychological context, but to the pure essence seized ideationally as pure idea. In the essence of an experience itself lies determined not only *that,* but also *whereof,* it is a consciousness, and in what determinate or indeterminate sense it is so. Likewise, in the essence of consciousness as dormant lies included the variety of actual *cogitationes,* in which it can be differentiated through the modification already referred to as "the conscious turning of attention to that which was previously unnoticed." [62]

There is involved in such intentional experience a certain "directedness" on the part of the Ego, for in every *cogito*

the subject 'directs' itself within it towards the intentional object. To the *cogito* itself belongs an immanent 'glancing-towards' ['*Blickauf*'] the object, which from the other side springs forth from the 'Ego,' and therefore can never be absent. This glancing of the Ego towards something is in conformity with the act involved, perceptive in perception, fanciful in fancy approving in approval, volitional in will, etc.[63]

61 *Ibid.,* p. 64.   62 *Ibid.,* pp. 64–65.   63 *Ibid.,* p. 65.

Taking the word in its broadest sense, not every experience has intentionality; neither is the essential object of consciousness to be identified with "merely apprehended object." Drawing this distinction between intentional and apprehended objects makes possible the phenomenological differentiation between mere "awareness" and *experience* in the strict sense of the word. The experient is always "aware" of much that occurs around him without its necessarily entering into the sphere of his conscious experiences. To be conscious of them requires first of all this "glancing toward" the object. In every wakeful *cogito* the pure Ego glances toward the object of the correlating consciousness for the time being; it directs itself toward the "thing," the "fact," the "situation," and therewith enjoys the typically varied consciousness of it. The intentional activity of the Ego initially institutes the experience of or direct contact with the essentiality of objects and events in the midst of which it finds itself. This directedness of the Ego upon the objects and events allows for the first time their becoming "meaningful." The intentional act opens up to consciousness, as it were, the stream of pure experiences of the phenomenal or eidetic realm, and when this is done, intuition plays its role; seizing as it does its object, it "sees," for the first time, objects in their true essentiality. When this is done, and only when it is done, objects become content of genuine experience. After intentional activity follows the "reception" of meaning through the unifying act of intuition. In this sense alone can it be said that the experient "constitutes" his objects. The Ego's part is to turn intentionally toward the object; this act supplies the basis of intuitive activity, through and following which experience has meaning. Thus, broadly speaking, since intuition functions *only* after intentionality has been brought into play, it can be said that intentional experiences are there as unities through the bestowal of meanings. In one sense, then, intentionality resembles a universal medium which in the last resort includes within itself all experiences.[64]

Every intentional experience has its own intended object, its proper objective meaning. "To have meaning" (be it ever so vague or variegated) is, on Husserlian grounds, unquestionably the signal characteristic of all conscious experience. But every experience *qua* experience, every perception *qua* perception, is one-sided, inadequate, incomplete. Hence, to mean anything for the Ego which is conscious of it, there is required this intentional turning-toward, this directing-its-attention-to, the eidetic content of the otherwise merely sensory objects. Perception without intuition would be meaningless; intuition without intentionality would be powerless, impossible.

It now becomes increasingly clear why the doctrine of intentionality is such a cardinal feature of Husserl's phenomenology. As a science, phenomenology is interested not only in the discovery of the why and wherefore of essential knowledge, but in its extension as well. It begins with everyday experience and ends with the same experience; but such experience is now seen in a new light. The Ego, consciousness in its supreme purity, is that which experiences the realm of meaning, and this signifies that it has *Eidos* as its content. As already remarked, the extension of essential knowledge entails a reduction to pure consciousness and its data, which in turn presupposes as a first step the "suspension" of the natural thesis. Yet, since in ordinary experience consciousness deals not only with the world as known through the psychophysical organism but is likewise related to the world of essences, so must the Ego, in order further to extend its knowledge of that realm, devote its attention to

[64] In *LU* this general function was referred to as "act-character."

essences. Just as ordinary intentional activity requires "glancing toward" the object in its essentiality, so must any and all broadening of knowledge require a further and more concentrated directedness to it. Objects thus assume a new aspect; no longer are they just spaciotemporal "things." They are seen in a new light, in the light of meaning. "Apprehension of something" is thereby transformed into a possible "comprehension of something."

Intentional activity, according to Husserl, when employed as an investigatory instrument, can even determine "beforehand" regions to be further studied. The positive aspect of such activity is redirecting attention toward a domain of "pregiven objects." There can thus be axiological and practical attitudes dealing with essences. In principle, intentionality can take place in any sort of activity so long as essences and meaning of the objects of those activities are sought. Objects can be known differently, e. g., the objects of valuing, volition, and judging. Indeed, it must be said that every kind of object requires a certain kind of attitude, or intuitive direction, in order that it may be "known" by the Ego. A mathematician and an esthete cannot have the same attitude or intend the same objects so long as each is concerned with the objects which, by definition, preoccupy him. The intentional activity of the pure Ego is required in every meaningful experience, be it "everyday" or the pursuit of that kind of knowledge which marks one as an investigator or an authority. In both, intentional activity plays the important role of making it possible for the essential realm to become opened to the Ego, to its intuitive activity, which in turn results in the "reception" of meaning, the structure and bulwark of all significant experience.

§ 5. *Fact and Essence (Tatsache and Wesen)*

In the foregoing the paramount importance of Husserl's doctrine of essence has been shown. It now remains to describe in greater detail how he conceived of essence, and such a consideration naturally leads to the question of the relation between "fact" and essence.

The problem of the relation between fact and essence is one of (ontological) metaphysics. Unfortunately, however, it is practically impossible to find a strictly *systematic* metaphysical treatment of any subject whatever in Husserl's writings, including that of the nature of essence. For instance, at times he discussed fact and essence from the standpoint of logic (*Logische Untersuchungen* and first chapter of *Ideen*) ; at others he approached it epistemologically. The best way to deal with the matter, then, is to ascertain what he said about the two from these standpoints, and then to consider some of the metaphysical implications arising from his treatment.[65] To this end, the following examination will begin by indicating more closely his concept of essence and the manner in which he drew a careful distinction between "formal" and "material" essences.

What did Husserl mean by "pure" essence? It must be noted at the outset that he would have nothing whatever to do with the concept of "substance"; neither were essences for him mere "laws." It has already been shown how Husserl had begun to conceive of essence as a "concrete totality" to which the particular object is related, not in the sense of subordination to a species, but in the way of a direct participation in qualia. Yet there is a sharp differentiation between essence and fact. Although essence is that which makes an "empirical fact" precisely what it

[65] The problem is treated further in chap. vi, "Five Questions Concerning Phenomenology," § 1, pp. 207–23; § 4, pp. 238–79.

is and not something else, it cannot, in some aspects at least, be identified with it. Empirical fact is unstable; it is in a particular time-spot and of a private spatial configuration. Empirically speaking, fact is "real." Essence, on the contrary, is "irreal," since it does not change or possess the character of instability (red is red, no matter when or where or how it manifests itself in any given unstable empirical object). Essence is thus devoid of spatiality and temporality. Its nature in no way depends upon when it appears, any more than it would depend upon where or in what it made its appearance. This is another way of saying that essence "persists" independently of the empirical facts which it constitutes and, moreover, that it can be "detached" from the particular fact without thereby losing in any sense of the word its proper Being. Empirical facts are thus "grounded" in essences, which "present themselves" as integral parts of such facts.

It is clear from this that essences could in no manner be identified with or even compared to Kantian "a priori" forms.[66] As will shortly be seen, Husserl was very careful to demonstrate that all essences are not formal, and it is equally clear that on Husserlian grounds they are not limited to sense perception and its "categories."

The constitutive role of essences, as depicted above, led Husserl to contend that such characteristics bespoke the "universality" of essences. It has been shown how, in *Logische Untersuchungen,* whose central problem was that of meaning, he finally formulated the concept of intuition (ideation, logical reflection) of species, universals, or essences. The universality of essence is disclosed when it is remembered that its manifestations are always the same, no matter when or where they comprise an empirical fact for what it is. Essences are *Allgemeinheiten.*

[66] Or critical realism's "categorial forms."

In *Logische Untersuchungen* he began, and in *Ideen* he completed, a novel distinction between "formal" and "material" essences.[67] Since this concept represents a radical departure from all previous and subsequent ideas of essences, it deserves particular attention.

What is formal essence? It is "completely empty" of content, in the sense that it is applicable to all other essences which are of a particular kind and which arrange themselves according to certain laws springing from formal essences themselves.[68] Formal essence is "a mere essential form" which, in its formal universality, has even the highest mathematical generalities subordinated to it and indeed prescribes laws to the formal truths which belong to it. Formal essences form a region which "is properly no region at all but the pure form of region-in-general; it has all regions with all their essential varieties of content *under* (though indeed only *formaliter*) rather than side by side with itself."[69]

From this it would follow that there is required a "formal ontology" which for Husserl was the same as formal logic. Such an ontology is the eidetic science of object-in-general, the "object" taken as "everything and all that is."[70] By logical category, then, Husserl meant categories of the logical region, "object-in-general," i. e., pure logical basic concepts.

As examples of essences of formal ontology, Husserl gave unity, multiplicity, relation, identity, equality, group (collection), number, whole and part, genus and species, substantive meaning (fact), property, and so forth.[71]

67 I acknowledge my indebtedness to Gurvitch's *Les Tendances actuelles de la philosophie allemande*, Section I, for a clarification of various phenomenological problems, and particularly Husserl's distinction between "formal" and "material" essences.

68 *Ideen*, p. 198.   69 *Ibid.*, pp. 21–22.   70 *Ibid.*, p. 22.

71 *Ibid.*, p. 22. Cf. *Prolegomena*, pp. 242–44; *Ideen*, pp. 19–23; *Formale und transzendentale Logik*, pp. 133 f.

What, then, are "material" essences? In the first place they are identical with all irreducible and original qualities of "the world." Most essences within our experience, accordingly, are material.

All sciences of the "natural" or "physical" world deal with and require knowledge of material essences. This is another way of saying that they require ontologies of nature and that all philosophies as well as sciences of the world are in consequence "eidetic." In this connection Husserl said that it is clear that

it belongs to the *essence* of a material thing to be a *res extensa,* and consequently that geometry is an ontological discipline having to do with the essential phase of such thinghood, the essential form.[72]

Husserl showed that, historically, after geometry had taken the lead there was a greater and more rapid development of mathematical sciences (both formal and material) which served the purpose of "rationalizing the empirical." It was because of this that rational physics was enabled to make such important advances. Hence, "every factual science *(Erfahrungswissensschaft)* has essential theoretical basis in eidetic ontologies." [73]

By such considerations, Husserl arrived at the concept of an "infinite number" of pure essences; that every quality of our world is a pure essence in the sense that it is something in and for itself, depending upon nothing whatever, and most emphatically not the experient, for its constitution. These material essences are as "pure" as those of unity, relation, and identity. As examples of material essences he gave society, man, nature, race, perceptual qualities, and consciousness.

In what way is it possible to distinguish between the universality of material and formal essences? The latter

72 *Ideen,* p. 20.
73 *Ibid.,* p. 19.

are not only distinguishable from the standpoint of being "empty" in content, but their import, validity, and application are universal. For instance, the essence of unity applies to all contents and all essences themselves. In contrast, the import of material essences is limited to special regions; the "field of application" is restricted in each instance to certain kinds of particulars. For example, the essence of red applies only to red objects or contents bearing redness or a red tinge. "Every concrete, empirical objectivity, together with its material essence, orders itself properly within a highest material genus, a 'region' of empirical objects." [74] For this reason, to such material pure essence there belongs a regional eidetic science. Essences, moreover, never have the character of a generic type or law. They are not "abstract generalities," but "concrete totalities" to which particulars are coördinated as integrating parts. If certain material essences can be classified as "species" (e.g., shades of red), it is possible only in relation to each other and never in relation to the empirical facts which manifest them. The harmony between material particulars and concrete essences is thus a matter of participation.

Husserl, consequently, rejected both (historical) nominalism and realism, since he saw both as ending in a *Hypostasierung des Allgemeinen*. This rejection was possible because of his development of a new theory of abstraction. Realists hypostasize the abstract as an extratemporal element, the nominalists as an empirical phenomenon of psychical life. Husserl, on the contrary, found the abstract by detaching essences from the elements which belong to them but which themselves cannot be what they are without them. As comprising the *Washeit* of something, it is concrete and not abstract. It is "abstract" only when one separates from its totality an in-

74 *Ibid.*, p. 19.

tegrating part which is not constant by itself. "The abstract designates itself as nothing more and nothing less than an unstable part, aside from a concrete universal." [75]

The ultimate difference, then, is one between dependent and independent contents of the integrating elements of a whole. The problem from the standpoint of Husserl is one of the relation between the whole and its parts.

The "whole" clearly signifies an ensemble of contents unified by a connection with a common element which founds them all. "To found" means to be posited necessarily and precisely, without which the founded part would lose its proper character. [76] Unity and totality thus come about through the Ego's act of founding. That which is commonly designated as abstract meant for Husserl nothing more than that which is dependent; it is inferior and subsumed under the absolutely concrete totality. [77]

What is a *Tatsache?* [78] Merely to say that it is a "fact" is ambiguous since, as shown above, essence is likewise a fact, if it is meant by that term "an object of (some kind of) experience." In *Logische Untersuchungen* Husserl had drawn the distinction between "Being as species" and "being as particular," corresponding to which were correlative forms of cognition. [79] In the spirit of Plato, species are transcendent to all "reality." Moreover, they are *ir-*

[75] Gurvitch, *op. cit.*, p. 41.

[76] *LU* II, pp. 261 f.

[77] Cf. *LU* II, 106 f., 121 f., 166 f., 219 f., 275, 281; regarding "founding," see *Ibid.*, pp. 261 f.; regarding "totality" and "the abstract," see *ibid.*, pp. 266, 275 f. In *Ideen*, §21, Husserl said "object" is a "title for varied though connected formations such as 'thing,' 'property,' 'relation,' 'fact,' 'group,' 'order,' etc., which are clearly not equivalent but refer back at times to a type of objectivity which has, so to say, the prerogative of being primarily original (*Urgegenständlichkeit*)."

[78] Husserl used the following synonymously: fact (*Tatsache*), matter-of-factness (*Tatsächlichkeit*), contingency (*Zufälligkeit*), thing (*Ding*), thingness (*Dinglichkeit*), individual (*Individuum*), the real, reality (*das Reale*), existence (*Existenz*), object (*Objekt, Gegenstand*). The ensuing remarks are an epistemological treatment of the problem at hand.

[79] See chap. iii, §§ 4–5, pp. 64 ff.

real, and, by virtue of this, species embrace the real "manifold" of particulars. In this way numerical identity is explained in the midst of multiple nonidentical real facts. What is the relation of species to particulars? The latter, according to Husserl, are various "instances" of ideal identical species. For example, there is the relation of the real instances of the number four to the mathematical number four. Consider the proposition, "Four is a relative prime number to seven." When this is done, there may come to mind various "groups of four," but we do not make judgments about these instances; rather is the *number* four the specific unity, the subject of the proposition "four is relative to seven." Although "this particular" four may be spoken of, *in intention* there is meant not only this or that four but *"the* four, the ideal, timeless unity." [80] This, in the eyes of Husserl, represents knowledge arising from a definite kind of experience which, as now known, he described as essence-insight. The ideal, identical, endless essence "four" is that which makes possible knowledge of and judgments about particular groupings of four. This is indicative of Husserl's mathematico-logical approach.

While speaking of the "inseparability" of fact and essence in everyday experience Husserl observed that

the acts of cognition underlying our experiencing posit the real in particular form, posit it as spaciotemporal existence, as something existing in *this* temporal spot, as that which has its own particular duration; the particular has a real content which in its essence could just as well have been present in any other temporal spot; they posit it, moreover, as something which is present at this place, in this particular physical form (or is given there united to a body of this shape), where yet the same real particular might just as well, so far as its own essence is concerned, be present at any other place, and in any other form, and might also change while yet remaining

---

[80] *LU* II, p. 141.

in fact unchanged, or change otherwise than the way in which it actually does. Particular being of every kind is, generally speaking, "contingent." It is such-and-such, but essentially it could be other than it is. Even though definite laws of nature obtain, by virtue of which specific definite consequences must follow, when certain real conditions are present, such laws exemplify only regulations that do, in fact, obtain. They nevertheless might run quite differently, and are already presupposed as pertaining *ab initio* to the essence of objects of possible experience, so that the objects thus ordered by them, considered in themselves, are contingent.[81]

The only conceivable interpretation of this is that contingency is correlative to a necessity, which necessity has the character of *eidetic* necessity and therewith a relation to essential universality. In Husserl's words, "it belongs to the meaning of every contingent existence that it should have essential Being and therewith an *Eidos* to be apprehended in all its purity; and this *Eidos* comes under essence-truths of varying degrees of universality."[82] Otherwise expressed: an individual object is possessed of a nature of such-and-such contingency; this proper mode of Being is traceable to its peculiar embodiment of essential predicables which "qualify it *qua* Being as it is in itself."[83]

The *Eidos* or pure essence can be exemplified or apprehended intuitively in the data of sensory experience, perception, memory, and so forth; it can likewise be exemplified in the contents of *Phantasie*. An essence can be seized in its primordial form by starting out from corresponding empirical intuitions; but it is likewise possible to begin from nonempirical intuitions, i. e., intuitions that do not ground themselves in sensory existence. For example, this is done in such instances as plays of fancy, melodies, social events, spatial shapes, reliving of events, and objects of will in which, through ideation or progressive intuition, there can be gained adequate insight into

[81] *Ideen,* pp 8–9.   [82] *Ibid.,* p. 9.   [83] *Ibid.*

pure essences, e. g., essences of spatial shape "in general," of melody, of shape, of social events "as such."

It follows from this that the positing of essence, with its concomitant intuitive apprehension, "does not imply the remotest positing of particular existence whatsoever; pure essence-truths do not make the slightest affirmation about facts." [84] As examples of sciences of such essential Being, Husserl pointed to pure logic, pure mathematics, pure time theory, space theory, and theory of movement.[85]

From these considerations, it is possible to indicate provisionally Husserl's concept of the distinctions between and the relation of fact and essence, as follows.

1. The particular is the "concrete," individual fact of experience;

2. Fact-experience posits essence-experience;

3. Individual objects of fact-experience are characterized by *this* spatiality and temporality (its own particular "duration");

4. Every particular could be other than what it is; it is contingent, but

5. It is what it is because its contingency is correlative to a necessity. It *has* essentiality. Individual objects or "facts" are what they are because of their essential Being, but

6. Essence is in no way "dependent upon" particular "facts";

7. Essence constitutes the identity and essentiality of numerically nonidentical facts;

8. Essence constitutes the "quality" of particular objects;

9. Essence-experience does not (necessarily) posit fact-experience;

10. Essence has an ontological status all its own.

[84] *Ibid.*, p. 57.
[85] *Ibid.*, p. 61.

Husserl's position may be elaborated in the following manner. The first question with which his position is confronted from the epistemological standpoint is, What is it that belongs to the concrete, real nature of perception itself, as *cogitatio*? It cannot (as opposed to critical realism) be the "physical" thing, for it is "radically transcendent," i. e., transcendent as opposed to the whole world of appearances. Even the latter cannot be said to belong to the real nature of perception. If the real nature of the content of perception is transcendent to perceiving itself, the problem arises, What is the relation of the transcendent to the consciousness that knows it? Husserl concluded that perception and the physical thing are in principle and "of necessity" not really and essentially one and united.[86]

To illustrate this, take as an example a table.[87] I walk around it; I change my position in space; the "bodily presence" of the table remains "out there" and it remains "one and the same" table. While I am doing this, the perception of the table continually changes, and according to Husserl this means that what I call "the table" is a continuum of changing perceptions. I close my eyes; I open them. The perceptions prior to the closing of my eyes vanish, yet the table is "the same." How can this be? Husserl answered: recollection plays a role and it is connected by the new perception through "synthetic consciousness." If what I call "the table" remains the same in a variety of perceptions, it must be concluded that the "perceived thing can be, without being perceived, without our being aware of it even as potential only . . . and perhaps even without itself changing."[88] The perception itself, not the table, is within the steady flow of (empirical)

86 *Ibid.*, p. 73. This will be enlarged further in chap. vi, "Five Questions Concerning Phenomenology," § 4, pp. 238–79.

87 *Ibid.*, p. 74.

88 *Ibid.*, p. 74. Again, Husserl's realism.

consciousness; it is in constant flux. The perceptual "now" is ever passing over into the adjacent consciousness of the "just past," and a "new now" simultaneously gleams forth, and so on.[89] Husserl thus drew no distinction between "primary" and "secondary" qualities. The perceived thing-in-general, all its parts, phases, and aspects are necessarily transcendent to perception. For instance, color is in principle not a real phase of the consciousness of color. It simply "appears," and, even while it is appearing, the appearance itself is continually changing. The same color appears in continuously varying patterns of perspective color variations. The same applies to every sensory quality, as well as to every spatial shape. The thing, then, insofar as it "consists of" such qualities, is transcendent not only to consciousness but to its perceiving. It is not required of a thing that, in order "to be," it must be perceived.

The "self-sameness" of a thing continually confirms the unity of its own nature, and the thing essentially and necessarily possessed a multiple system of continuous patterns of appearances and perspective variations, in which all objective momenta of the bodily self-given which appear in perception reveal themselves perspectively in definite continua.[90]

The object remains "one" because each determinate feature has its own system of perspective variations and, moreover, each feature

remains one and the same for the consciousness which, while grasping it, unites recollection and new perception synthetically, and this in spite of interruption in continuity during the course of actual perception.[91]

Briefly, real qualities "exhibit" themselves. To every phase of perception there necessarily belongs a definite content in the way of perspective variations of color, shape,

---

[89] *Ibid.*   [90] *Ibid.,* pp. 74–75.   [91] *Ibid.,* p. 75.

and the like. It is these perspective variations which we ordinarily call "sensa." Thus the real concrete nature of perception consists of the consciousness of one identical thing derived through the confluence into one unity of (intuitive) apprehension, a confluence grounded in the essential Being of the apprehensions unified, which unification includes the possibility of syntheses of identification. Each qualitative field or unity or region has its own essence, and the syntheses of identification are grounded, not in the "unifying mind," but *in the essence of the different unities.* Sensory data, considered functionally (phenomenologically, how else could they be considered?), "present" such aspects of the object as color, smoothness, and shape; it is a function of "exhibiting." It follows from this that sense data differ wholly, and in principle, from color, smoothness, shape; in short, from all the generic aspects which a thing can display. The perspective variation, that which belongs to the thing "as exhibited" by and through sensory data, is thus an experience and, indeed, an experience which is not spatial. For example, there is a difference between a triangle as "perspective variation" and a spatial triangle, which manifests itself through the appearances of sensory data. Clearly, there must be drawn a careful distinction between the various real phases of perception as *cogitatio* and the phases of the *cogitatum* that transcend it.

If the thing is transcendent over and against the perception of it, it would follow that it is transcendent over and against "every consciousness generally" which refers to the thing. This would imply, finally, that in absolute, unconditioned generality or necessity, a thing cannot be given as really immanent in any possible perception, or even in any possible consciousness. This necessitates Husserl's basic and essential differentiation between "Being as experience" and "Being as thing." It marks the difference (but not separation) between consciousness and reality, between immanence and transcendence.

It would follow from the phenomenological opposition between immanence and transcendence that it is accompanied by a fundamental difference "in the mode of being given." [92] Husserl must obviously draw a careful distinction between "a thing" as perceived through the perspective manifestations of all its determinate qualities and "an experience" which possesses no such perspectives. Experiences of real perspective variations and determinations he denotes as *cogitationes,* and describes them as nonspatial and nonperspectival. Since all experience is both intentional and propositional, i. e., *of* something, and since, furthermore, a spatial thing cannot be known exclusively in and by its perspective shadings, it must be further concluded, on grounds of Husserl's previous argument, that a spatial thing constitutes for consciousness an *intentional unity* which can be given only as a unity of such ways of appearing. The *cogitatio* of perception is thus seen to be the *cogitationes* of experience. The spatial content of thinghood is never known in its purity. There is required the intentional unity of experience. [93]

Husserl took great care to draw several cardinal distinctions between (1) the perception of things and (2) the intuition of experience. [94] First, there is a "certain inadequacy" in the perception of things. This is "of necessity," since in principle a thing can be given only in one of its aspects; in other words, it is given not only incompletely but imperfectly. Its givenness is limited to its perspectival presentation, and all of its perspectives can-

[92] *Ibid.,* p. 77.

[93] As opposed to Kant, Husserl thus affirmed that perception does come into contact with the "thing-in-itself." Kant had failed to see that there is a difference between perception, on the one hand, and the presentation of a symbol in the form of an image or meaning, on the other. Cf. *Ideen,* pp. 78–79.

[94] *Ideen,* pp. 80 f.

not be seen at once. The givenness of a thing consists in its "modes of appearing," whose factors are a nucleus of what is "really presented." These modes are "an outlying zone of marginal 'co-data' of an accessory kind, of a more or less vague indeterminacy." [95] This indeterminacy, furthermore, indicates new possible patterns of perception. Perspective perceptions are always passing away or being recollected or indicating new perspectives, all of which coalesce into the unity of a single perception. Hence the correlation, "thing" and "thing-perception," remains forever incomplete. Consequently, transcendent existence, whatever its genus may be, when understood as being for an Ego, can become a datum only through appearances. This means that transcendent existence can be known only as some kind, or rather some perspective, of "thing-hood."

Second, "thing" exhibits itself; experience does not so present itself. [96] This implies that the perception in experience, to use Husserl's own words, is "plain insight" into something which is given in perception as "absolute." Thinghood is given as an identity uniting modes of appearances to perspective continua. Yet this is not true in the case of experience; for instance, "feeling" has no perspectives. It is simply "absolute," to be taken as it is. It cannot be viewed now this way and now that. To be sure, I can think truly or falsely about it, "but that which stands there in the center of mental vision is there abso lutely with its qualities, its intensity, and so forth." [97] Contrast this with the tone of music, which exhibits itself through perspectives. Obviously, it is "different" when I am near it or far away, or whether I listen to it through a wall or from within the same room. In not one of these

[95] *Ibid.*, p. 80.
[96] *Ibid.*, p. 81.
[97] *Ibid.*, p. 81. Husserl took no cognizance of any theories of feeling as developed by the psychologists of his time.

ways of appearing does it claim that it gives its data "absolutely." Since this is the same with all "perceptual data," it can be concluded that that which gives itself through perspective appearances in no way yields the matter in question in an absolute form. Yet what is "immanently given," as in experience, is "an absolute" that has no aspects or varieties of perspective. Immanent experience is therefore not "functional," as is perception. The perspectively varying sensory contents, as real, belong to our experience of the perception of the thing and function therefore for something other than perspective variations. Yet they are themselves not manifested in turn through perspective variations.

Third, it is impossible, since an experience is not seen in its completeness, to say that it is grasped adequately "in its full unity." [98] Experience flows. We can reflect upon it, but it is only in this kind of retrospective remembrance that it is "retained." In this retention the whole stream of experience is a unity of experience. Hence once again, as contrasted with perception, although experience is absolute, the perception of experience is a matter of retention or reproduction on the part of the experiencing Ego. Memory of this kind is not mere recollection of past experiences and is certainly not to be identified with mere "reproduced perspective variations."

Fourth, perceptual presentations yield "gradual differences" of relative clearness or dimness. It is to be noticed, however, that such a difference in degree of perfection has nothing whatever to do with the stream of experience which constitutes "the conditions under which perspective appearances are given." [99] The conditions of appearances do not suffer the same vicissitudes as the appearances themselves.

[98] *Ibid.*, p. 82.
[99] *Ibid.*, p. 83.

Fifth, that type of Being peculiar to experience is different from that of perception, in that its insight can direct its immediate, unobstructed gaze upon every real experience "and hence enter into the living experience of an original presence." [100] Such an insight Husserl called "reflection." One of its peculiarities is that what is apprehended is characterized as something which not only is and endures during perception, but was "already there" before attention was directed to it. The meaning of the dictum "All experiences are conscious experiences" thus becomes clear. With regard to intentional experiences, it tells us that they are not only conscious *of* something and as such present when they are objects of a reflective consciousness, but that, when unreflected, they are already there as a "background" and therefore, in principle, always accessible to perception. Even though "unnoticed," they are available because they are already "consciously known in a certain sense, and that means in their case, when they appear." [101]

Sixth, an experience is perceivable only through reflection.[102] Things are apprehended as "things in the world about me"; i. e., they are perceivable. Since they belong to the world without being perceived, they are still there for the Ego. A stream of experience is private to each and every Ego, yet transcendent things are "public." Now, since transcendences can never be presented to the same Egos in exactly the same way and since there is an infinite variety of perspectives, and no two Egos can occupy the same positionality to receive such perspectives, how can it be said that transcendent things are public? There must be a possible reciprocity of understanding between Egos, if one is to identify its world of experience with that of other Egos. The basis of that understanding is that all Egos (potentially) share the Being of inward experiences,

---

100 *Ibid.*   101 *Ibid.*, p. 84.   102 *Ibid.*, p. 84.

which Being constitutes the background, the structure, of all possible transcendences. For instance, the content of perception as such, since it is a multiplicity of perspective variations, could never be experienced as the same thing by a plurality of Egos. Yet essences, the data of immanent experience, are sharable by any number of Egos, because, as is the case in perceptual data, they do not suffer spatial and temporal limitations.

Finally (seventh), every immanent perception necessarily guarantees the existence of its object.[103] Reflective perception, when directed to individual experience, apprehends an "absolute self" or Ego whose existence is undeniable; i. e., the insight that it does not exist is *in principle* impossible. The indubitability of the immanent perception of selfhood is the surest of all insights; in contrast, no perception of thinghood gives such absolute indubitability, since "existence in the form of a thing is never demanded as necessary because of its givenness; in a certain sense it is always contingent." [104] This implies that the further course of experience can conceivably force us to abandon any thesis about the thing-world apprehended in sense perception. The world of things has only a "presumptive reality." The self for whom it is there is an absolute reality, "given through a positing that is unconditioned and simply indissoluble."[105] Husserl summed up this "essential law" of necessity on the one hand and contingency, on the other, by saying that

the thesis of the world, which is "contingent" stands opposed to the thesis of pure self and its experiences, which are "of necessity" absolutely indubitable. Every corporeally given thing can also not be; no corporeally given experience can also not be: this is the essential law which defines this necessity and that contingency.[106]

---

103 *Ibid.*, p. 85. 104 *Ibid.*, p. 86.
105 *Ibid.* 106 *Ibid.*

Clearly, as said before, Husserl was not arguing that the contingent world "is not," but simply that in spite of the tremendous force of unanimous (perceptual) experiences, *a doubt is nevertheless thinkable,* since the possibility of nonbeing is in principle never excluded. The absolute Being of experiences, and at its core the pure Ego, are not, however, subject to such thinkable doubt.[107]

It was said at the beginning of this division that Husserl was investigating perception in order to discover its "content." What, then, is this content? Certainly not the "physical" object itself, since, as shown above, Husserl held that the object is "transcendent" to both perception and perceiving. The content of perception is, in part, sensory data; but what are sensory data? Once again, they are not the physical object itself, but the various phases or perspectives of the object as it "exhibits" itself. Briefly, then, sensory data would be the "exhibitions" of the object in the form of its various perspectives, such as color and shape. The object is not "contained in" sensory data or its perspectives, since perceptual content is not the object itself but consists of the object's "ways of appearing" to the Ego. These ways of presenting itself, however, do not constitute knowledge, strictly speaking, although, to be sure, the content of perception has its own being. Yet, according to Husserl, it is both transcendent and contingent, which means that it is "in principle" always subject to doubt. Yet this is not the complete description of Husserl's concept of perceptual contents.

Since he had demonstrated what he believed to be the "inadequacy" and "imperfection" of the sensational content of perception, insofar as supplying complete knowledge of the object, Husserl had to look elsewhere for the

---

107 This is one important respect in which Husserl differed from most current "realisms." (Ralph Barton Perry, E. B. Holt, Bertrand Russell, J. A. Laird, Durant Drake, and others.)

source of what might be called genuine knowledge of the object.

Transcendent *cogitata*, taken alone, are insufficient; as a matter of fact, they constitute only a part of the system of experience. What objects are, said Husserl, they are "as things of experience." [108] "Experienceability" is characteristic of every known object, and this means that every (known) object is always in relation to consciousness and its Ego, "the demonstrable unity of its system of experience." [109] What is this system of experience? It is the Being of pure consciousness. Ultimately, Husserl assumed or posited only a system of experience which he calls *"cogitationes."* What is the nature, or content, of the Being of experience? It is not the sense data of perception; it is comprised of essences.

It has been said that the thing is a "unity" of appearing perspectives. By this Husserl meant that it is a unity in a system of experiences of pure consciousness. If a thing is known truly in the apprehension of its essences, what is the object, aside from its sensory variations? It is a system of essences. If an object is what it is, as a thing of experience, or in the stream of experience alone, the Ego knows the object *as it is,* i. e., as *one* and not a multiplicity of perspective variations. It is clear that Husserl must hold, since the data of experience are contents of intuition, that *an object is its essences.* That which we call Nature is, then, the content of the system of the Ego's experiences. This system of experiences he calls "absolute Being," and it is essentially independent of everything intrinsic to the "real" world or nature; it has no need of these for its existence. [110] In short, since the perceptual, sensational variations can tell us nothing of the object in and for itself, although a thing is a unity of appearances

[108] *Ideen*, p. 88.   [109] *Ibid.*, p. 90.   [110] *Ibid.*, p. 97.

of such variations, it is clear, on phenomenological grounds at least, that "thing" or "fact" consists essentially of intuited essences seized, arranged and unified by the Ego in nonsensory eidetic activity. True knowledge of the object, then, consists in a spiritual (*geistig*) seizure of its essential content, which spiritual seizure comprises a stream of experience. Sensory data, whose function is to "present" color, shape, and so forth, differ from color and shape *simpliciter,* and that means they differ from all the generic aspects which a thing can show. *Cogitatio,* or the perspective phases of the object, are on these grounds a most insignificant part of knowledge and seem to have the function only of presenting certain spatial, "existential" aspects of the thing itself. The object as *cogitatum,* however, is the "objective side" of the system of experience and is known immediately in intuition. Experience of the object as *cogitatum* does not share any of the inadequacies and shortcomings of bare sense data.

It is this system of experience as *cogitatum* which is immanent and absolute Being. It can even be said that it is the "subjective" aspect of experience. There would then be on Husserlian grounds two kinds of Being: the contingent and transcendent content of perception, on the one hand, and the immanent and absolute content of intuition on the other. Does this mean that perceptual data can be known independently of intuitive activity? Since mere sense perception can reveal nothing of the nature of the object, it must be concluded that there is no possibility of the perspective phases of an object being known without intuitive content, for this would mean that an object can be known outside of a system of unifying and connective experience. Such a standpoint would seriously violate Husserl's axiom of the necessary experienceability of every known object. To be known is to be experienced, i. e., to be in relation to an intuitive consciousness and its Ego. If this means anything at all, it is that to be known is to have the essential characteristics seized in a nonperceptual or spiritual ideation or eidetic intuition. Ultimately, it can be said without fear of contradicting Husserl's general principles that the sense data of perception have one function only, and that is to announce the spatial and temporal "presence" of an object. *What* the object is, is grasped in a system of immediate experience. It is this system of experience, the content of pure consciousness, which phenomenology makes as its object of special investigation. Phenomenology, then, is not entirely "presuppositionless." [111] It posits first a stream of experience, and, second, a pure Ego and its consciousness.

Since every intentional experience has a noema, and with it a meaning through which it is related to the object, so, inversely, everything that we call by the name of object, meaning that which we have before us existentially, is in this respect already an object of consciousness. From this it follows that whatever the world and reality may be or may be called must be present within the limits of real and possible consciousness by corresponding meanings and positions, filled more or less with intuitive content.

Every "real" natural thing is determined in a peculiar way and, as such, figures as the correlate of possible intentional experiences. It is noematically constituted as self-identical. This self-identity is possible both in individual consciousness and to every conceivable community-consciousness. The identity of any real entity can be given and identified intersubjectively. It is the essential data with the appropriate apprehension and act-characters—all in their connected unity—that make up what we call the "empirical consciousness of thinghood." Over against the thing in its unity stands an infinite ideal manifold of no-

111 As Husserl frequently and erroneously claimed.

etic experiences of a thoroughly determinate, essential content. That is why the object can be called "the same" by a variety of conscious experiences. This identification of the object is a priori and remains the same.

Consciousness, according to Husserl, passes judgments *about* reality.[112] It inquires and doubts and gives verdicts of reason.[113] This is possible because the essential *qualia* of so-called real objects are seized. Self-identification of the real object, although it may change in spatial and temporal circumstances, is possible because of the intuition of its essential qualities. Cognition of a real object means, then, the *immediate apprehension of its essential embodiment.*

One mode of experiencing meaning is the manner of intuiting whereby we are made aware of the "meant object as such" through direct vision; this "direct vision" is the primordial object-giving mode. This noematic character of experience Husserl called "positionality," and it belongs to all cases of corporeal appearing of a thing. Positionality, then, would be the positing of the essence or essential relationships primordially given in our vision of essential Being. The mode is insight; the result is "self-evidence" on the part of the object.

What, then, is "thing"? It consists of a continuum, i. e., a connection of endless processes of continuous appearing. Although this is infinite in all directions, there remains constant the same determinable "X." An object is always inadequately perceived in the sense of "presenting itself" as real from every side in any given space-time spot. All finite objects are within the finite limits of appearance.

[112] This does not mean that cognition is "judgmental" (Drake, Sellars, and others).

[113] To what end, Husserl never explained. If intuition is exhibitive of the object, what possible role could judgment and reason play? But how can "error" be explained, if judgment and reason are absent? I examine this difficulty of Husserl's in chap. vi, "Five Questions Concerning Phenomenology," § 1, pp. 207–23.

It is this continuum of appearances and its concomitant intuition of essences that allows us to call it "an object" as a whole.

The thing in its ideal essence presents itself as *res temporalis* in the necessary form of time. Intuitive ideation shows that the thing necessarily endures. We grasp in pure intuition the idea of temporality and of all the essential phases included in it. Furthermore, the thing appears as *res extensa;* i. e., it is capable of infinitely various changes of shape. Finally, the thing is *res materialis,* or substantial unity, and as such it is the unity of causal connections endlessly varied in their possible structure. These are essential necessities. Time, space, and substantiality are "regional ideas," and prescribe the series of appearances. This implies that anything which has the character of a spatial or temporal thing is intuitable only through appearances, wherein it is given, and indeed must be given, as changing perspectively in varied yet determined ways.[114]

Intuition is possible only with objects coming under the regulated series of appearances which necessarily hold together within the unity of a single appearing object. An object consists of its essence (or several essences?) which is seized only when intuition is aroused by such essences when having substantiality, temporality, and spatiality. All so-called real *qualia* are thus, according to Husserl, essences. Sensory qualities are "sensory" only in so far as a particular frame of experience requires that essences make themselves known "spatially," "temporally," and "substantially." The thing, therefore, is composed of a unity of its own not imposed on it by the mind. Yet there is more in its constitution than is disclosed in mere perceptual experience; even perceptual appearances would be meaningless if it were not for the simultaneous intuitive activity which seizes upon the noematic, essential

114 *Ideen*, pp. 90–91.

characteristics which constitute the very structure of the
supposed sensible appearances.

Husserl's concept of "fact" and "essence" might be
illustrated by the following table:[115]

Fact or *Thing*	*Essence*
Temporality	Timelessness
Individuality	Universality
Happens but once	Lasting numerical identity
Reality (existence)	Ideality
Could be otherwise	Could not be otherwise
A posteriori	A priori
Contingency	Absolute necessity

Knowledge of	
Empirical	A priori
Assertoric	Apodictic

Husserl had shown, to his own satisfaction, wherein
consist the distinctions between the particular object and
essences. He summarized in the following way how each
is known and expressible.

As with the thing itself, every quality that belongs to the
thing's essential content and, above all, every constitutive
'form,' is an Idea (*Idee*); and this applies with equal validity
from regional universality to the lowest particularity. In
closer detail: The thing presents itself in its ideal essence as
res temporalis, in the *necessary* "form" of time. Intuitive
"ideation" (which, as insight into the "Idea" here especially
warrants its name) teaches us to know the thing as necessarily
enduring, as, regarding its duration, in principle infinitely
extensible. We seize in "pure intuition" (this ideation is the
phenomenologically clarified concept of Kant's pure intuition)
the "Idea" of temporality and all the essential phases it includes.

[115] As suggested by Celms, *Der phänomenologische Idealismus Husserls,*
p. 271.

The thing, according to its Idea is, moreover, *res extensa;* for instance, from the standpoint of its spatial relations, it is capable of innumerable, various changes of shape and, where the configuration (or its change) remains constant, it is "movable" *in infinitum.* We apprehend the "Idea" of space and all the Ideas which it embraces.

Finally, the thing is *res materialis,* it is *substantial* unity; as such it is the unity of *causal connections,* whose possible structures are infinitely varied. Likewise, with these specific, real properties, we encounter Ideas. Hence, *all* components of the Thing-idea are themselves *Ideas,* each implying the 'and so forth' of 'infinite' possibilities.[116]

Husserl thus stated his case.

But has he actually solved one of the most essential questions, namely, *What is the precise relation between the individual object and essence?* Is it not true that ultimately the problem resolves itself to this:

Is an object, for instance a rose, a *single* essence; or

Is it a combination of various essences, e. g., spatial configuration, temporality, color, and fragrance?

Husserl never resolved the problem in this way; he neither asked nor answered such specific questions. In "Philosophie als strenge Wissenschaft,"[117] he had remarked, "For the particular is indeed not essence, but it 'has' an essence which is expressible of it with evident validity." Some years later (as noted above) he argued in *Ideen* that an individual object "has its peculiar mode of Being, its own supply of essential predicables, which qualifies it *qua* 'Being as it is in itself.' "[118] Is it not true that here are two contradictory answers to the problem at hand? Husserl perennially referred to *"the"* thing; he likewise continually referred to the various "qualities" or "characteristics" *constituting* the thing. He never asked

---

116 *Ideen,* pp. 312–13.
117 *Logos,* I (1910), 318. (Cf. my treatment in the previous chapter.)
118 Page 9.

himself, Is an object *an* essence, or is an object what it is because of the totality of its "essential predicables"? To be sure, he told us *how* we know sense objects; i. e., there was never any doubt in his mind that there is something in experience besides a sensory relationship with "empirical facts." This "something," as has been shown, is *essentiality,* essential Being, a datum of intuitive insight, cognition of which discloses the *whatness* of particular objects. It is difficult, nevertheless, to ascertain whether, in his mind, "a thing" (the rose, for instance) constitutes a new "single" essence by virtue of its being a totality of various essences resident in this particular object in this particular time-spot, or whether an essence, Rose, is there. Without question, this is a serious problem inherent in his phenomenology.

It can be inferred, however, from his general discussion (see table of "Fact" and "Essence," *supra*), that an object is what it is, i. e., distinct from all other objects, because it is a totality of essences.[119] But it could likewise be concluded that such aspects as spatiality, temporality, substantiality, and color are mere "perspectives" of *essential* insight into the One Object—the Essence, Rose, Tree, Body, and so forth. The "inference" one made in the matter would very likely depend upon one's own prejudices.

In no case, however, is Husserl to be called a "nominalist." He is without doubt a member of the tradition of Realism (not to be confused with current "realisms").[120] *Dasein* is a matter of empirical knowledge; *Sosein,* the *Was* of the object, is a datum of essence-experi-

119 As will be shown later, this has a significant bearing on the problem of error. See chap. six, "Five Questions Concerning Phenomenology," § 1, pp. 207–23 f.

120 Husserl avowed that he might be "stigmatized" as a "Platonizing realist" if one should choose to do so, because he carefully distinguished "object" and "empirical object" and differentiated "reality" and "empirical reality." *Ideen,* p. 40.

ence. Essence is an "eternal," a "timeless-ness." It remains what it is whether or not it is "exemplified" in particular instances, and indeed it would remain even though they all vanished.

Perhaps this is as much as will ever be known of Husserl's resolution of the problem.

Husserl believed that in his *Ideen* he had finally shown the way to the achievement of a "pure" phenomenology; "shown the way" is used advisedly, since he himself never pretended that his philosophy constituted a complete "system." As a matter of fact, he viewed all his labors (including his *Méditations cartésiennes* of 1931) as only preliminary groundwork for those who would follow in his footsteps.[121]

The foregoing remarks in this chapter purport to give only an exposition of Husserl's final development of phenomenology and should be taken just as they are intended, viz., as a description of his basic principles rather than a delineation of the development of his argument. The laborious manner in which he arrived at his conclusions is entirely too complicated to be of much interest to anyone except the ardent student of Husserl. With this in mind, before treating of some specific problems of phenomenology, as well as some curious interpretations of it, it appears advisable to summarize as briefly and simply as possible, the basic arguments and principles of Husserl's final phenomenology. They may be formulated as follows:

1. There is an "external real world" whose "existence" and "meaning" can be "known."

2. Included in our varieties of experience are both "sense" objects (empirical "facts" or real things) and various kinds of "essential" objects (essences) (and their "connections").

121 In a letter to the author, June 17, 1933.

3. The "whatness" (or "sense qualities") of an object consists of its essences.

4. Corresponding to these, there are certain kinds of cognitive relationships (doctrine of intuition and intentionality).

5. The existence and meaning of objects are "independent" of the knowing subject and its cognitive activity.

6. Both existence and meaning yield themselves in special modes of "self-givenness."

7. Self-givenness is "received" (objects are not "constructed," "transformed," or "ordered" from a "chaotic material").

8. All consciousness is "prepositional," having both a subject and an object.

9. All contingency is "correlative" to essential Being.

10. All knowledge is based upon experience, in which objects "make themselves known" by "presenting themselves."

11. The central methodological problem of Husserl's epistemology was to investigate how objects are known by the method of "immanent inspection," since they are known only when they become resident in or contents of pure consciousness (the "phenomenological reductions").

All these must be carefully borne in mind while considering the various problems dealt with in the following, and concluding, chapter.

PART THREE

CONCLUSION

CHAPTER SIX

FIVE QUESTIONS CONCERNING PHENOMENOLOGY

THE MANY and various misunderstandings surrounding Husserl's phenomenology are doubtless due, on the one hand, to careless and prejudiced reading on the part of those outside the group, and on the other, to Husserl's tedious (it might even be said, circuitous) approach to philosophic problems. Yet even admitting Husserl's shortcomings in this regard, there are some misconceptions of phenomenology abroad for which there is neither excuse nor the slightest basis in fact. Among these, the principal ones are charges that phenomenology is (1) "scholasticism" and, from others, (2) that it is "psychology." These two false interpretations will be dealt with, the latter under the heading "Phenomenology as a Science" (§ 5). Before turning to these, however, there is the one serious "problem of error" which requires special attention, and it will be dealt with first. Then, after examining the charge of scholasticism, the question of wherein phenomenology is "anti-Kantian" will be discussed; as concluding remarks, after attention is given to the matter of whether phenomenology should be considered primarily as "science" or "epistemology," a comparison will be drawn between current realism and Husserl's phenomenology.

§1. *The Problem of Error in Husserl's Phenomenology*

The problem of error, since it has to do with cognition, is clearly one of epistemology. Phenomenological epistemology, it is now clear, has two principal aspects of experience as the object of investigation: first, to discover what is "presented to" consciousness and, second, conscious acts. More explicitly stated, this would mean that phenomenology is interested in the act of "intuiting" and the content of intuition; it examines the *Selbstgegebenheit* of all possible *Sachgebiete*. Intuition and its content, then, must serve as the center of consideration for the problem at hand.[1]

In spite of his interest in epistemology, Husserl was primarily a logician, and it is to be expected that his treatment of problems of knowledge would be principally from the standpoint of logic. As he himself says, "Knowledge is principally a name for logical truth, so characterized from the standpoint of the subject as correlate of its self-evidencing judging; but it is likewise a name for every kind of self-evidencing judging itself, and, finally, for every doxic act of reason."[2]

From this it is understandable why any examination of his treatment of the problem must begin with his logical considerations. But as will be shown, this is hardly sufficient; he not only failed to treat the problem systematically from the standpoint of logic, he refused categorically (for what reason, no one knows) to examine such a simple epistemological problem as, If the "whatness" of a sense object is comprised of its essence-structure, and we know this essentiality through intuition, and intuition is direct, how can error arise?

[1] Husserl touched upon "truth and error" in *Ideen*, pp. 282 f., particularly §§ 136, 137, 138, 139, 140, 141, 142, and "Formale und transzendentale Logik," pp. 245 f. Cf. my treatment to that found in Street Fulton's "Husserl's Significance for the Theory of Truth," to which I am greatly indebted for a clarification of how Husserl treated this problem from the standpoint of (eidetic) logic.

[2] *Ideen*, p. 291 n. "Doxic," the adjectival form of *Doxa* ("Belief") was used by Husserl to mean "of the nature, form, or characteristic, of belief." "Protodoxic" means the certitude of primary belief (*Protodoxa, Urdoxa*). Cf. Gibson, *Ideas*, p. 435.

When attention is directed to the few scattering logical references of Husserl to the question of error, it is readily seen that it is ultimately resolvable to the matter of the relation of "rationality" to primordial dator-meaning. Hence the first question, What is "primordial givenness"? It is the way in which an object discloses itself through some kind of direct mental vision, insight, or self-evidence (Husserl, as now known, used these terms interchangeably). More narrowly defined, primordial givenness refers to the *noematic* character of an object's embodiment, its state of being originally "filled" with intuitive content.[3] The embodiment, then, is "objective" and *presents itself* to consciousness, in which presentation it motivates rational positing.

When objects *simpliciter* are spoken of, there is meant as a rule real objects that truly are and belong to this or that category of Being. Whatever is affirmed, then, concerning objects . . . must be submitted, whether as meant or spoken, to "logical demonstration," "proof," direct "vision," or mediated "insight." In the logical sphere, in that of statement, "that which truly or really is" and "that which is rationally demonstrable" are, in principle, correlated; and so for all doxic modalities, ontical or positional. Obviously, the possibility of a rational demonstration here is not to be understood as empirical but as "ideal," as an essential possibility.[4]

It is important to note carefully that Husserlian "rationally demonstrable" and "rational demonstration" are *eidetic*, a matter of *Wesensmöglichkeit*.

Husserl was careful to draw the distinction between "positional experiences" in which there is acquired primordial givenness, and those, on the other hand, which do not acquire such givenness; this is a distinction be-

[3] "Noematic" is the adjectival form of "Noema," and was used by Husserl to mean the "nucleatic" character, the "nucleus" of objects considered objectively in contradistinction to the "Noetic," subjective, character of perception.

[4] *Ideen*, p. 282.

tween "perceiving," "seeing" acts, understood in the broadest sense, and "nonperceiving" acts.[5] As an example of that which has no primordial givenness, we have the "recollection" of a landscape, since it is not "perceived" in the sense of "seeing" it. Mathematical propositions likewise illustrate such a case; we can execute "with insight" the judgment "$2 + 1 = 1 + 2$"; and here the *Sachverhalt*, "the synthetic objectivity corresponding to the synthesis of judgment is primordially given, seized in a primordial way."[6]

Such "fullness-of-meaning" alone, however, is not enough, since an account must be given of the *modes* of experiencing the meaning, and the principal one, of course, is the intuitive, "whereby, through direct insight, the 'intended object as such' is known, and a particularly outstanding case is that in which the mode of direct insight is the primordial object-giving mode."[7]

The noematic setting, the character of "objective embodiment" as the primordial state of "being-filled-out," combined with pure meaning, serve as a foundation of the "noematic character" of positionality, of "corporeal appearing" of a thing. While viewing the matter from the standpoint of "rational consciousness" of every kind Husserl said

To the corporeal appearing of a thing there belongs in every instance this positionality; it is not only one with this appearing in a general way . . . it is one with it in a unique sense, it is "motivated." Consequently, the positing has its original ground of legitimacy in primordial givenness.[8]

The same is true of the positing of essence and essential connections, for they too are given in "direct vision" of essential Being, and their positing belongs to the "material" of essential Being, to the "meaning" in its mode of

---

givenness. The result of this is that insight, self-evidence generally,

is thus an entirely unique occurrence; at its "core" it is the unity of a rational positing with that which essentially motivates it, the whole situation being intelligible in terms of the noema as well as of the noesis. The reference to motivation fits excellently the connection between the (noetic) positing and the noematic meaning in its mode of fulfillment. The expression, "self-evident proposition," in its noematic meaning, is immediately intelligible.[9]

From the above it is clear that Husserl had in mind that there is more than one kind of "self-evidence." On the one hand there is the assertoric (and inadequate) vision of the transcendent particular object which, owing to its perspectival positionality, cannot be given adequately (completely) in finite consciousness; on the other, there is the apodictic insight into adequately given immanent essences and essential connections. This self-evidence, or insight, "is a positional doxic and also *adequate* dator-consciousness which 'excludes otherness.'"[10] The *kind* of evidence is determined by the kind of object in question. These observations would substantiate Husserl's arguments that only immanent or essential Being can be given adequately and completely in finite consciousness. In intuitive insight primordial meaning "coalesces" with the real object; nothing transcendent, since it includes an infinite series of *noemata,* an infinite variety of "perspectives," can, in Husserl's mind, be adequately given.

Having made these careful distinctions, and while discussing "theoretical, axiological, and practical truth," Husserl elaborated his theory of "truth" as follows.

An act of positing *(eine Setzung)* . . . has its justification when it is reasonable; the rational character is itself the character of rightness, which "belongs" to it not contingently as a fact

9 *Ibid.,* p. 284.　　　　10 *Ibid.,* p. 285.

under the accidental conditions of an empirically positing Ego, but essentially. Correlatively the proposition (*Satz*) is justified: it stands within rational consciousness instructured with the noematic character of rightness which, moreover, belongs essentially to the proposition as the qualified noematic thesis and the content of meaning. More precisely stated, there "belongs" to it a peculiar fullness which, on its own side, supplies the rational character of the thesis.[11]

All doxic (i. e., of theoretical belief) and protodoxic (i. e., those of protodoxa, *primary* belief) modalities, aside from their content and conditions of motivation and considered from the standpoint of their "rational" characters, "point back, so to speak, to one primary rational character (*Urvernunftcharakter*) which belongs to the domain of primary belief (*Urglauben*) : to the instance of primordial, and, in the final resort, to perfect self-evidence."[12]

The matter of *"Wahrheit"* is resolvable to the relation between "primary belief" and its "primary reason" in the sense that

Truth is manifestly the correlate of the perfect rational character of the protodoxa, the believing certainty. The expressions: "A protodoxic proposition, a stated meaning, for instance, is true," and "the character of perfect rationality belongs to the corresponding belief and judgment," are equivalent correlates. There is no reference here, of course, to any fact of experience or to any individual judger, although it is eidetically obvious that truth can be actually given only in an actual consciousness of the self-evident, and this is applicable also to the truth of this that-which-is-obvious (*Selbstverständlichkeit*) itself, that of the previously indicated equivalence, etc. If the protodoxic self-evidence, that of believing certainty, is lacking, then we say, with respect to its content of meaning "S is P," a doxic modality can be self-evident; for instance, the presumption that "S may be P."

----

11 *Ibid.*, p. 289. Gibson translates "Satz" as "posited meaning," "meaning as posited" (*Ideas*, p. 387).

12 *Ideen*, p. 289.

This modal self-evidence is manifestly equivalent to, and necessarily connected with, a protodoxic self-evidence of altered meaning, namely, with the self-evident position, or the truth: "That S is P is presumable (probable)"; on the other hand, likewise with the truth, "There is something to be said for the assertion that S is P;" and again: "There is something to be said for the assertion that SP is true," etc. All this indicates essential connections which require phenomenological inquiries into fundamentals.

Self-evidence, however, is in no sense a mere title for rational developments of this kind in the sphere of belief (and indeed in that of the predicative judgment only); it holds *for all thetic spheres,* and particularly for the important rational connections that run *between* them.[13]

Since Husserl held "rational" and "essential insight" to be synonymous, apparently the answer to the problem of truth and error would rest on the question of the self-evidence of essences and their connections as presented to pure consciousness; in short, whether adequate primordial givenness is "correlated" essentially with true Being. The immanent object or essence has no perspectival variations. This would mean, since essence is known in intuition alone, that "to be given adequately" is synonymous with "to be given with intuitive clarity." Does it follow from this that "to be given clearly in intuition" requires that it should be given "adequately"? Not at all, since it might not satisfy the "main intention."

The particular intuitions serving the apprehension of essence may be sufficiently clear to win a fully clear essential generality, yet not be adequate to satisfy the main intention. It is devoid of clearness on the side of closer definitions of the interwoven essences.[14]

But what is the *guarantee* that insight seizes its object with "perfect self-evidence"? Husserl employed such expressions as "clearly given" and "perfect clarity." Yet,

[13] *Ibid.,* p. 290.   [14] *Ibid.,* p. 129.

according to him, these are not "standards" for "true judgments." They are merely "some of" the characteristics of the self-evident. From the excerpt just cited it follows that although as clear, "the intuition of essence is apodictic . . . this does not as such fulfill the demands of adequacy."[15]

Husserl rejected theories of "coherence" and "correspondence," or any other concept based on psychology. He held that although the "adequate" must be "self-evident," the reverse does not follow. All this and much more he emphasized, but the fact remains that *he did not offer a positive standard* for judging with finality the "self-evidence" (or "truth") of the alleged self-evident. He acknowledged that there are "alleged" intuitions, but he gave no satisfactory answer to the question, How to distinguish between alleged and "genuine" intuitions? Certainly not "social agreement." No truth is established merely by the testimony of more than one person, even granting their "integrity." Yet he named nothing which could be called "intrinsic" to genuine insights which would make them inevitably distinguishable from alleged intuitions.

It might perhaps be suggested that insight into the primordially given is a necessary condition of consciousness of truth; this is true, but such insight, as already seen, is insufficient. It seems as though, in order to deal with the problem, it must be insisted that there are required other conditions to complete consciousness of an object; by the same token, there would be required other conditions to complete consciousness of truth *about* the object. Yet to insist upon this would violate Husserl's general outlook. Apparently recourse must be taken to rationality in the traditional sense of a judgmental "reasoning process," unless some criterion is supplied whereby it can be determined whether the intuition of a given essence or group

[15] Fulton, *op. cit.,* p. 301.

of essences is "completely adequate." But since, from Husserlian contentions, intuition is "self-evident," this, once again, would contradict Husserl's general scheme.

This is about as much as can be said, from the standpoint of "logic," of Husserl's consideration of the problem of the truth and error of eidetic insight. How, from the standpoint of epistemology, does he deal with the problem of error in everyday sense perception?

If the epistemological summary at the end of the last chapter be remembered, and it be recalled how the conclusion was reached, from the discussion of the relation of fact and essence, that "sense qualities" are ultimately the content of intuitive cognition, it is plainly to be seen that by the word "quality" Husserl's phenomenology means the eidetic *whatness* of sensory objects.[16] Every object, in addition to mere "existence," in the sense of occupying certain space at a certain moment, has a group of peculiar characteristics, a *Washeit,* which serves, on the one hand, to allow us to differentiate it from all objects and, on the other, to classify it with certain other objects (doctrine of species, universals). For instance, a peach tree and a plum tree, although each, considered singly, is different from all other possible trees, are members not only of a certain species of tree, but of "trees in general," as distinguished from such objects as dogs and mountains. Now it is this certain eidetic "X" which permits such distinction and classification, to which the phenomenologist points as the whatness of an object. Upon analysis it is seen that the fact *that* an object exists is not of great importance; *what* it is, or what we believe it to be, is, however, of paramount importance, since it serves as the basis of our actions and reactions to it. The mere recognition that objects "exist" is called by phenomenology "knowl-

16 Consideration of this aspect of the problem of error involves touching upon some of Husserl's epistemology already treated in previous chapters.

edge of factuality"; recognition of what constitutes an object as such-and-such is called "knowledge of essence." Both are viewed as unique and distinct forms of cognition, and together they comprise normal sense perception.

On grounds of phenomenology, then, we are aware of the object itself, not of mere hyletic data as something signifying an object. Is there, then, such a thing as *Erfahrungsevidenz?* Husserl avowed that there is, since

It is absolutely obvious to everyone (not only the troubled philosopher) that the thing perceived in perception is the thing itself, in its graded existence, and that if perceptions are deceptive it means that they are in contradiction with new perceptions which show with certainty what is really there in place of the illusory.[17]

Consciousness knows the object *simpliciter,* "as it is"; hence "perceptual" object is in fact the eidetic content of pure consciousness. In the case of perceptual objects, the object *simpliciter* abides for consciousness as "a self-same thing." It endures through a series of variously changing perceptual determinations, infinite in variety and in determinacy. When I see a tree, it remains a tree, no matter from what perspective I view it (or whether I view it at all). The hyletic data coming to me from one side of a tree, and those coming to another from a different perspective on the other side are, "existentially speaking," different. Yet we both speak of "the same tree" and such characteristics as greenness, fruit-bearing, and height. Phenomenology inquires, how is this possible? It is obvious that from the standpoint of "mere sensory data" *as such* we do not see the same tree, because, owing to bodily restrictions, we cannot both be at the same moment in the same perspectival location. But the phenomenologist avers that we *do* see the same tree, and we see it be-

17 *Formale und transzendentale Logik,* p. 248. Husserl, in this volume, uses "*Erfahrung,*" "*Selbstgebung,*" and "*Evidenz*" interchangeably.

cause there is a certain "primordial givenness" in the cognitive relationship which, since it is neither spatial nor temporal, yields a certain kind of knowledge of the object known as "this particular tree," to both of us, and to an infinite number of persons, at any time, under any normal conditions. It yields, moreover, what might be called its "tree-ness," and upon analysis it is discovered, indeed, that this whatness consists of much more than the sum total of its hyletic characteristics. The tree, as well as every other object, has an essence (aside from the question of whether this essence consists of the totality of multifarious essences) entirely and peculiarly its own, which classifies it as a member of the universal "tree" or whatever object it might be.

What, then, is the role of "sensations"? It is nothing more than that of announcing to the experient that a certain object "is." Yet, when they are examined in and for themselves, it is ascertained that sensations are qualitatively "neutral." They are meaningless; they say nothing *about* the object; analysis discloses that they consist of certain vibrations affecting eventually the nervous system and the cerebrum and announcing to the subject that "something is there." At this moment, says phenomenology, concomitantly with it, the Ego directs its attention to the object of this announcement, intuition is brought into play, and the object becomes, strictly speaking, "known." Husserl, in his *Méditations cartésiennes,* called this intuition of essences "self-evidence," and meant thereby "the experience of a thing and its mode of Being; our mental glance reaches the object itself." [18] The object gives itself as being or consisting of a specific nature, and this qualified embodiment, disclosed directly and immediately, reveals itself through the channel of intuition. Sensations do not do this.

[18] *Méditations cartésiennes,* p. 10.

What, then, is sense perception? It cannot consist of mere sensations; it is essentially eidetic. According to phenomenology, perceptual intuition is a form of geistig insight into the whatness, into the basic essentiality of the object. Moreover, it is "passive" in the sense that it is the means by which the object "discloses" its essentiality to the subject. We never know sensations in and for themselves, because as such they have nothing to say. The hyletic content of sense perception is never given alone. There is no such thing as a "pure" sensation which could have any possible cognitive value, nor can any conceivable combination of "pure" sensations serve as genuine data of knowledge of objects. Although analysis might show that the sensational content, insofar as it is an announcement of the existence of an object, is "temporally prior" to the intuitive content, it is, nevertheless, a minimal part of sense perception. Sensations serve only to "point to" the object, and not to speak about it. On the other hand, so far as the so-called "physical world" is concerned, intuition could never function without the "existential announcement" of sensations. Ultimately, however, since all sense experience has some kind of meaning, and meaning is not found in or contained in the sensations but in intuitive cognition, "perception" would signify the intuitive seizure of the essentiality or *Eidos* of an object. These epistemological considerations must serve as the basis of considering the problem of error in sense perception insofar as it concerns Husserl.

By definition, or at least on Husserlian grounds, intuition is not a rational activity in the sense of a reasoning, judgmental process. It has been explained how Husserl argued that it has a certain dator-content which "speaks for itself." If this is true, such content does not require "reason" to organize it into concepts of the object (Kantianism and critical realism). After all, for Husserl an object is its *Eidos* and nothing more, since every object is a qualitative object and its *qualia* are known because they reveal themselves as data of intuition. The object is not a categorical creation of the percipient.

Here, then, is the crux of the problem: rationalistic philosophy can readily solve the question by describing error, in the case of sense perception at least, as mistakes of judgment and inference on the part of the reasoning Ego. In short, error consists of ascribing to the object of perception something which does not belong to it. Truth would then be correct assignation.[19]

But phenomenology is avowedly not rationalistic in this sense. According to its basic principles, since the data of intuition present themselves and are to be accepted "as they give themselves," there would (presumably) be no reasoning required; rational activity would have no role to play in cognizing or understanding sensible objects. Sensations, since they are by definition meaningless, are neither chaotic nor orderly. That leaves only essences and the cognition of them, and the following problems:

1. Are there "defective" intuitions? or
2. Are there "partial" intuitions?

Such specific questions are never encountered in Husserl's writings. Neither are they answered by him explicitly or implicitly. Husserl's "Principle of all principles" sug-

[19] This is likewise the case with critical realism, which, since it makes knowledge judgmental and categorial, is rationalism in disguise. Cf. *Essays in Critical Realism* (Drake and others); particularly A. K. Roger's "The Problem of Error" (pp. 117 f.), in which it is said "The definition which critical realism gives of error is briefly this: When we 'know' an object, we are assigning a certain 'essence'—a character or group of characters—to some reality existing independently of the knowledge-process. And truth is the identity of this essence with the actual character of the reality referred to; so error stands for the lack of such agreement, and the ascribing of an ideal character to what we are mistaken in supposing to be real, or the ascribing to a reality of a wrong instead of a right one" (pp. 117–18). But this is nonsense because critical realism's epistemology does not permit the subject to know "reality" (the thing itself)—it is a "categorial" creation. See this chapter, § 4, pp. 238–79.

gests we are to accept without question that which is given in intuition "as it gives itself." The implication is that *there could never be any question about defective or partial intuitions,* although, as indicated above, he does speak of "alleged" and "genuine" intuitions without offering a basis for distinguishing between the two.

Finding no answer to the problem of error here, and turning to the content of intuitions, at least two questions present themselves:

1. Can an essence be "partly" intuited? This would mean, on phenomenological grounds, Can an essence disclose itself partially? Or,

2. Can an essence lie? This might seem like an absurd question, yet does not a stick, when immersed in water, (ostensibly) utter a lie when it presents itself as "bent"?

Once again, there are no suggestions of this sort in Husserl's writings, which means in substance that nothing is said of defective intuitions, or of *essences disclosing themselves partially* (an essence is a "unity") or deceitfully. In short, errors of sense perception are apparently traceable neither to the act nor to the content of intuition. Sensations are dismissed summarily by phenomenology as valueless in saying anything about the object. *Apparently,* to resolve the problem or error there is only one recourse, that of bringing in "rational activity" as a component part of perceptual cognition. But phenomenologists abhor this, since error would consist in mistaken inferences and judgments about the content of intuitive activity, which, we are told, is sufficient unto itself. This possibility, then, must be rejected.

Note that it was just said that this step must "apparently" be taken; there is, in fact, one more possibility. It is at least conceivable that in the case of error the phenomenologist could say that *the subject has not intuited all the essentiality of the object* of which he is capable.[20] (Not to be confused with the concept of essence *partially* disclosing itself). This would mean that the object had not been given "full opportunity" to disclose all of its inherent characteristics, which complete disclosure would allow it to tell the subject its true nature and identity. But is this not a matter of "adequacy"? And hence a violation of Husserl's epistemology? And how could one ever be absolutely ("self-evidently") certain that all the possibilities had been exhausted? Husserl did not tell us.

From a previous reference [21] it was shown how Husserl said that it is "obvious" to every one that in perception the "thing perceived" is "the thing itself," and how he had argued that an illusory or deceptive perception was disclosed as being so by "subsequent" perceptions. But does that solve the problem? Not in the least, for in the first place he did not consider the matter of *how* bare sense perception could be illusory at all; (second) he gave no guarantee whatever that subsequent perceptions of any given series would be "less illusory," let alone *more* "truthful," and (finally) he offered no criterion whatever for comparing the two—except *"intentionale Untersuchungen"!* Moreover, what standard could he give to warrant the belief that "subsequent" perceptions would be any more "truthful" than their antecedents? This is indicative of Husserl's reasoning when dealing with this matter. At one moment he discusses "sensory illusions" or "errors" of sense perception, then suddenly and without warning he begins to lapse into matters of logical investigations. It apparently never occurred to him that, in the case of ordinary sense perception, when one is confronted with an error, it would be impossible to engage in a lengthy

20 This is *not* Husserl's argument, but just a suggestion of a possible solution.
21 "Formale und transzendentale Logik," p. 248.

"phenomenological reduction" to arrive at the heart of the trouble in order to dispel the illusion. For instance, at one time he said, "Experience, self-evidence, gives existence and gives it itself; it is imperfect when it is imperfect experience, perfect when (according to its essence) it is perfected, i. e., expands itself in the synthesis of agreement." [22] *Evidenz* (self-evidence) here means *Selbstgebung*. But it must here be asked of Husserl, How do we know when experience, however defined, has so expanded itself in order to be "perfect"? Have you answered the problem by saying *Evidenz* has its *"Gradualitäten in der Vollkomenheit der Selbstgebung"*? [23] Not at all! That would make knowledge *additive*. Husserl, of course, would probably reply, it is a matter of *Wesensbefragung der Erfahrungen*.[24] But that, be it noted, is nothing but a matter of "phenomenological reduction."

On grounds of phenomenological epistemology, then, the whole problem of error might be summed up as follows:

1. The source of error cannot be found in sensations: they are a minimal part of sense perception, and are qualitatively "neutral." As such, they could be neither "truthful" nor "deceptive."

2. Since an object consists of its *Eidos*, the content of cognitive intuition, error of sense perception should have its root either in the act of intuiting itself or a deceptive announcement on the part of the content of intuition regarding the eidetic constitution of the object. But,

3. On Husserlian grounds, intuition does not delude or deceive.

4. Yet neither is there such a thing as a "partial" intuition or partly intuiting an essence. Moreover,

5. The content of intuitive activity, *Eidos*, is to be accepted as it gives itself, and there is no reason to be-

---

[22] *Ibid.*, p. 248.   [23] *Ibid.*, p. 253.   [24] *Ibid.*, p. 248.

lieve that essence now discloses part of itself and now all of itself.

6. According to Husserl's phenomenology, it is impossible to believe that there is required for knowledge of objects a "reasoning process" such as the Kantians assume. This precludes any possibility of tracing error to "mistaken judgments" *about* the eidetic content of sense perception.

Of course, this leaves the inquirer exactly nowhere. If it be attempted to resolve the problem on grounds of Husserl's phenomenology, it cannot be done; if reason, or some other kind of rational activity, is brought into the picture, it violates his theory of knowledge.

Does this of itself destroy credence in Husserl's theory of knowledge? [25] There are many who would say so; there are just as many who do not believe that it does. It can be pointed out, for instance, that the problem of error is only a part, indeed, according to some, a small part, of the general theory of knowledge and that, although it is important, it would be unjust to reject an entire epistemology merely because the problem of error cannot be satisfactorily solved. The phenomenologist can rightly inquire, Who, after all, has solved the problem? This is not necessarily to fall into skepticism; it is merely an admission of the obvious, first, that error does exist, and, second, that as a problem it has not been adequately solved by any system of philosophy. Further than that, apparently, it is impossible to go. But even the most ardent disciple of Husserl must admit that he failed to do justice to this problem. [26]

25 I do not know of a single phenomenologist who has tried to establish his theory of knowledge by attacking an opponent's treatment of the problem of error, a habit so characteristic of American and English philosophers, particularly the critical realists. But have *they* solved the problem?

26 For a discussion of "error" by an avowed phenomenologist, see Max Scheler, *Vom Umsturz der Werte,* II, 8 f. I have not included this for two reasons: first, it is not Husserlian, and, second, his remarks concern a

§ 2. *Phenomenology and Scholasticism*

One of the most common, yet erroneous, charges against Husserl's phenomenology is that it is nothing but a revival or further development of "scholasticism," or, more properly, of the philosophies of Aristotle and St. Thomas Aquinas. There are several reasons for this, of which the two principal are, first, his acknowledged indebtedness to Brentano (himself in great part a scholastic) and, second, his avowed interest in examining the intentionality of consciousness, *das Immanente*. This charge, as might be expected, has arisen chiefly from the naturalistic and Kantian psychologistic schools. Yet anyone at all acquainted with the development of Husserl's thought, as well as its fruition, should know that to confuse his philosophy with that of the scholastic tradition is *lächerlich*. This readily appears when several of Husserl's fundamental principles

---

Schelerian phenomenological "explanation" of the nature of illusions (deceptions) of perception and the senses, and error (*Täuschung und Irrtum*); he, too, ignored entirely the real problem, viz., the problem of error in the intuition of essences and intuitive "feeling" of values.

It is my personal opinion that error can be explained, without doing violence to Husserl's epistemology, by asserting that owing to the free intuitional activity of the Ego, the Ego can too hastily "cut off" its attention to the object and thereby close its intuitive eyes to further essence-insight. *Why* it would do so is yet another problem. This, I believe, is not a violation of Husserl's theory of intuition; it is just one of its aspects which he unfortunately missed or ignored. What I do not like about my theory, however, is its brevity—in that respect, at least, it resembles Perry's treatment too much to leave me comfortable! He says, "Subjectivity accounts for the possibility of error; but it does not itself constitute error. . . . But there is no error until fiction is mistaken for fact; and there is no truth in the correlative sense, until a content of mind is rightly taken to be fact. Error and truth arise from the practical discrepancy or harmony between subjective manifolds and the manifolds of some independent order" (Perry, *Present Philosophical Tendencies*, pp. 324–25). This, of course, is a truism; a description of what everyone knows. The *real* problem (for Perry) is how a "mind" which is nothing aside from its content—and therefore not a *substance*—can be "mistaken" about that which comprises it. Whence such dynamic activity? How is it possible to introduce for purposes of solving the problem of error, a metaphysical dualism, while pleading for an epistemological monism?

are recalled and compared with those of traditional scholasticism.

Take, for instance, the Aristotelian concept of "induction." In the *Prolegomena*,[27] while taking under consideration the psychologistic interpretations of logical principles, Husserl called explicit attention to the problem of the "infinite regress." In reference to empiricism, he averred that it denies itself the possibility of a "reasonable justification" of mediate knowledge and with this denial it deprives itself of the possibility of being a "scientifically grounded theory." To be sure, it admits the "possibility" of a logic, and indeed builds upon it; yet it proceeds to argue that the very foundation of principles upon which it proceeds can find its highest justification only through recourse to those principles themselves! Husserl was certain that this eventuates in empiricism's falling into either a vicious circle or an infinite regress, since those principles themselves need a foundation. On this point he contended that empiricism's procedure is obviously an "absurdity" since

it is self-evident that the examination of a justification based on principles can have for mediate knowledge a possible meaning only when we are capable of knowing, by insight and immediately, certain final principles upon which would rest, ultimately, every foundation. All justifiable principles of possible grounding would accordingly have to be deductively accomplished on certain ultimate, immediately evident principles, and indeed in such a way that the principles of this deduction itself must occur similarly under those principles.[28]

Although, to be sure, Husserl was here speaking against empiricism, his point that *Wesensintuition* is the only means of discovering (not "creating") the bases of logical procedures, applies equally to scholasticism, and more particularly to the Aristotelian concept of induction. Aris-

[27] Pages 84 f.   [28] *Prolegomena*, p. 85.

totelian logic had argued that, in order to avoid the infinite regress, appeal must be made to induction; it was necessary, of course, to avoid the infinite regress, otherwise the logician would be faced with the impossibility of knowledge, since no foundations would be forthcoming. This would mean there would be no "proof," and consequently there would result the "impossibility" of strict science. Accordingly, in order to justify knowledge, Aristotle had to assume "unprovable principles." This was forced upon him, since if it were assumed that knowledge was impossible on a deductive foundation only, there would be required proofs for the principles themselves; otherwise, it would be necessary to face the alternative of granting that principles, strictly speaking, could never be "known."

It has been described how Husserl inveighed against this while speaking of *Evidenz,* which is a property of intuitive activity in which principles can be and are known. It is not only the basis of deductive knowledge, but its justification as well. What, in Husserl's mind, was the source of Aristotle's difficulty? He was eventually forced to the conclusion that principles could not be known, and on this basis he proceeded to prove them *per inductionem;* this, he declared, was "another kind of knowledge," although, to be sure, not as exact as "proof" would be. Aristotle found himself in a blind alley, and sought escape in induction; Husserl believed he had avoided this plight in his doctrine of the intuition of essences.

St. Thomas Aquinas was interested in "essentiality." According to him, essential Being is "won" in the act of reflection or "abstraction." This meant that knowledge of principles "arises" through "reflection" on Ideas. As contrasted with this, Husserl had Ideas, or *Eidos,* as the content of experience. In other words, the *Idee* is not only the "means" whereby transcendent objects become known, but is itself an object of a priori knowledge. His essentiality, then, as contrasted with St. Thomas's, is not won but experienced or, more properly, *discovered* in experience.

St. Thomas likewise contended that the "intellect" distinguishes material things from those of fantasy, and this happens, once again, through "abstraction": first, things are sensibly perceived, then the intellect busies itself with them and abstracts the *forma rei;* in this way they become, through reflection, objects of knowledge. This is possible by means of the "species." The *prima intentio* directs itself to things themselves, then the *secunda intentio* intends the universal. This faculty for directing itself to the universal he called the *intellectus agens.* The "sensible faculty" knows only the particular, the individual, i. e., the psychological datum as matter; this datum, the object of sense, is "metaphysically" the principle of individuation. St. Thomas clearly reverted to Aristotle's metaphysics of the relation of universal and particular, and contained in his outlook is the idea of a power of abstraction in possession of subsisting Ideas. In this way Idea as Being was made an object of knowledge.

With the scholastics, the Idea is known in the *secunda intentio,* and accordingly knowledge of principles is dependent upon sense as a means. It would follow from this that the experience of sense objects is not only temporally prior to the knowledge of principles, but actually conditions it.[29] The knowledge process begins with sensible things, seizes essentialities, makes judgments, then culminates in the drawing of conclusions. The first judging following upon knowing essentialities is termed *prima principia.* In these there is a relation between subject and

[29] Husserl agreed with this, insofar as sensory perception was concerned. But he held that the realm of factual (space-time) objects of knowledge was only one of many kinds (axiological, religious, mathematical, logical, and so forth).

predicate, indeed, an analytical relation, on the basis of which "propositions" are "immediately given" and clarify everything. Yet, since only in the *secunda intentio* does the Idea become an object of knowledge, it is clear that principles are reached through reflection alone or, more properly, through *ontological* reflections that direct themselves toward the act, insofar as it is Idea of the object.

Plainly, Husserl could have nothing whatever to do with such an epistemology. In common with the scholastics he has his "absolute"; but it is not "outside," rather is it "immanently given." It is not "attained" by, in, or through reflection [30] or any other kind of mental or intellectual calisthenics, but is "seized" or, in words more phenomenologically descriptive, it is *experienced* in a peculiar kind of spiritual activity, intuition. Arguing in the line of the scholastics, essence is known "in" the Idea, just as though the Idea itself were absolute. Yet the scholastics said that the Idea is only a "means" whereby we know transcendent objects. On the basis of such an argument, the a priori would be subjective; as already remarked, for Husserl it is "objective."

Finally, the contrast between the two can be seen even more clearly in a consideration of the idea of Being as held by the scholastics. According to them, there is immediately given, upon, after, and *due to* reflection on the *Idea,* the proposition, *Impossible est esse et non esse simul;* St. Thomas called this the *principium firmissimum.* Compare this with Husserl's "principle of all principles," already quoted above. It affirms

that every original given intuition is an authentic source of knowledge, that everything that presents itself in primordial intuition (so to speak, in bodily reality) is to be accepted

---

[30] It must be remarked that "reflection" meant for Husserl eidetic intuition, and, moreover, he used the term to describe his method, not perception.

simply as it gives itself, although only within the limits in which it gives itself.[31]

Could that possibly be interpreted as "Scholasticism"? Reflection upon the implications of this statement unquestionably forbids such a classification. The Husserlian and scholastic theories of *Eidos* were not the same; moreover, the great disparity between the two concepts of how Ideas are cognized must not escape notice.

§ 3. *How Is Phenomenology Anti-Kantian?*

It would obviously be impossible (and needless), within the scope of this study, to include a comprehensive comparison of Kant and Husserl; yet it might assist in clarifying the phenomenological position if some matters of contrast were touched upon succinctly.[32]

Although Husserl rarely explicitly attacked Kant or any form of Kantianism (except, of course, that he classified *Psychologismus* as Kantian), even a cursory glance at his works is sufficient to indicate that he was an antagonist of Kantianism in practically every respect. With the publication of the *Philosophie der Arithmetik* Husserl had once betrayed his allegiance to the Kantian tradition. Yet not long after, with the publication of *Logische Untersuchungen*, it became evident that he had taken a position diametrically opposed to that found in his first publication. As the fruition of his thought is studied, it is readily seen that, *generally speaking*, Husserl could not share (to mention only three) the traditional Kantian concepts of a priori and a posteriori, the distinction between noumenon and phenomenon, and the nature and role of the Ego.

In *Treatise of Human Nature*, Hume had considered

---

31 *Ideen*, p. 43.
32 For a thorough and excellent comparison of these two philosophers, see Ehrlich, *Kant und Husserl*. There is no pretext that the following sketch is a comprehensive treatment of Kant's system.

the problem of a universal causal principle by asking, Must events always be causally determined? Since the mind can in no way see "a necessary connection" between effect and cause, the causal relation must necessarily be reduced to a "psychological prejudice." Our human nature habitually uses the principle as instrumental in the organization of sense experience. After reflection on the results of *Inquiry Concerning Human Understanding*, in which Hume further had elaborated his skepticism, Kant bethought himself of the possibility of conceiving the mind as equipped with a priori syntheses which would transmute the series of events into a "knowable" world. Apparently he agreed with Hume on at least two salient points, viz., (1) the data of all knowledge are furnished by sense experience; (2) no causal connection is observable in sense experience. But Kant was interested, among other things, in "scientific knowledge," and reasoned that although all scientific knowledge required sense experience as a source of its data, there were additional principles of synthesis which could not be subject to doubt. Hume had declared these principles to be psychological; Kant avowed that synthesis was rational and a priori, which characteristic of reason's synthetic activity is displayed in its "universality" and "necessity." He argued further that synthetic a priori judgments were necessary to the constitution of experience as it actually is. Once he had accepted the "indispensable need" of the concept of cause, Hume's real problem, as Kant saw it (according to Husserl) was "whether that concept could be thought by reason a priori, and consequently whether it possesses an inner truth, independent of all experience, implying a wider application than merely to the objects of experience." [33] In short, the a priori as Hume understood it is not found in experience, and Kant accepted this while insisting that, since necessity

[33] *Prolegomena*, p. 7.

and universality are not given in sense experience, they must be "imposed" by the mind, and, moreover, that such additions were essential to the existence of a knowable world. Kant's examination of experience thus arrived at the a priori somewhat as follows. The "matter" of experience is given as sensations to the mind; sensations are purely subjective; the matter of experience exhibits only sequences and no necessary connections (Hume). But as scientific and knowable experience nevertheless require necessary connections, they must be furnished by the mind (Kant). Thus was a new science of epistemology grafted on to the atomic psychology of Hume, an epistemology equipped with a host of synthetic principles a priori which alone made scientific knowledge possible. By accepting Hume's psychological analysis of mind and its experience, which in truth was a probing into the growth of knowledge, Kant offered a *logical* analysis of the mind and its knowledge in answer to Hume's psychological questions. The "a priori" is "imposed" on experience; it is not a datum of any kind of experience whatever.

Kant began with accepting the general principles of Humian epistemology and devoted much time and effort to solving some of its inherent problems. Husserl, as a young mathematician, began his philosophic career as a member of the Kantian school of psychologism, but soon deserted the circle altogether. The clue to the marked difference between the two can thus be discovered by recalling how each treats of "experience."

Both Kant and Husserl agree that knowledge begins with experience. As contrasted with Kant, however, Husserl not only defined "experience" more broadly, but held that all knowledge begins, remains within, and ends in experience. He flatly rejected the Kantian principle that all experience is limited to Humian sensations, and held that there is a "variety" of experiences, e. g., perceptual, essential, logical, and mathematical. By "experience" Husserl meant nothing less than a direct "contact" or relationship with objects other than the Ego and its psychophysical constitution, through which relationship objects are known *as they are*. To be known is to be experienced; only that which is experienced can be known. This is not to argue, of course, that everything has already been known, but that if and when something is known it will be so because of its being a datum of *some kind of experience*.

Husserl could thus have nothing to do with Kant's distinction between "a priori" and "a posteriori," although he occasionally used the terms. The a priori, for him, was a well-defined datum of experience and not something which the mind employs to organize a chaos of sensations; it referred not to "forms" or "functions" of reason, but to a certain kind of experience, namely, the experience of essentiality, of *Eidos*. He used the words, then, to distinguish, broadly speaking, two kinds of experiences, that of essence (a priori experience) and that of "existence" (a posteriori). By so doing, he escaped the psychological skepticism of Hume and the logical impossibilities of Kant. In addition, he was never harassed by the threat of a "noumenon" escaping our experience.

When the Kantian distinction between noumenon and phenomenon is examined, it is found that things, or the objects of sensory knowledge, have no existence in space or time except insofar as they come into the cognitive relation. But even such a relation does not endow them with a "place" in which to be, or a "time" in which to be members of an event, since (so far as we can possibly know) they are not "objectively" real in the sense of enjoying existence independently of the mind. To be sure, the sensibility always displays objects as "in" space or time, or as having spatial and temporal form; it receives the materials of knowledge, yet before passing them on to the understanding, these materials are made into "percep-tions." As the understanding receives nothing more with which to work, clearly objects are not seen as they are in themselves, but as they are "made into" perceptions with spatial and temporal forms. Objects are appearances, phe-nomena. Even the "understanding" with its categories tells us nothing more of those objects because it cannot penetrate behind the phenomena into something (the alleged "cause") which is not given to it by the sensi-bility. Yet Kant says there is much more in the constitu-tion of objects than that which appears to us. Two prob-lems thus present themselves, viz., (1) What are noumena or things-in-themselves; and (2) What is the justification for assuming the existence of the noumenal realm when all knowledge and experience are limited to the phenomenal world? [34] In answer to the first question, Kant said the only knowable objects are those which come into the range of sense experience; nothing, absolutely nothing, can be said of the nature of the noumenal world and its objects; noth-ing can be known of "what" it is or "where" it is.

In answer to the second problem, Kant seemed to as-sume the existence of a *Ding-an-sich*. At least two good reasons for this contention can be gleaned from his general theme. First, it would be pure presumption to believe that our mode of knowledge is the only kind possible. From this it is not hard to take the next step and assume that even as there are other conceivable modes of knowledge, there may be other kinds of objects to be known. Per-haps, if we were not limited to sense experience for the data of knowledge, we would find ourselves in relationship with the noumenal world.

Second, and more important, it must be remembered

34 Professor Edgar S. Brightman, while reading the manuscript, an-swered these questions with "We can think what we cannot know." Then Husserl would have asked, "But what guarantee would you have that your thinking had objective reference or verifiable validity?"

that only the "form" of knowledge is conditioned by and grounded in our nature. Whence the content given to us in sensations? It cannot be said that sensations are "just there." They need a cause, for did not Kant say something to the effect that objects as "things-in-themselves" give the matter of empirical perception; that they contained the ground for determining the faculty of imagination according to sensibility? To be sure, this is a contradiction of his general concept of causality as applicable to nothing outside of sense experience, since it means an unwarranted transcendent use of the category of causality; yet this contradiction demonstrates his dissatisfaction with Humian sensationalism.

Another indication of Kant's desire to escape this sensationalism is his doctrine of the Ideas when resolving the problem of phenomenal and noumenal existence. In the "transcendental dialectic" it is argued that reason has the concepts or ideas of the absolute or thing-in-itself, the soul, the universe, and God. These ideas are purely "regulative" but perform the added duty of reducing the sundry judgments to a "system." Yet, *as absolute,* they cannot be objects of reason; from this it would follow (on Kantian grounds, since we "know" them) that they cannot be said to have existence independently of thought. They are the a priori syntheses of reason and consummate the work of sensibility and understanding. They supply the demand of reason for "absolute totalities." As inherent in the nature of reason, they supply final unity as found in the demand for the first cause, absolute beginnings of space and time, and so forth.

The truth is, Kant at this point unwittingly contradicted the conclusions of the first *Critique,* and all his attempts in the *Critique of Practical Reason* to justify a belief in their objective validity proved futile. Regulative of knowledge they remained, since constitutive character was denied them. As such, they might form the basis of (flimsy and uncertain) "belief," but there can never be any surety that they take us beyond the world of phenomena. They are "supreme norms," corresponding to which there are no scientifically knowable or provable "realities" (and Kant was really interested primarily in "scientific" knowledge). The universe, the soul, and God cannot, on the grounds of sense experience and scientific knowledge, be said to exist. They can, to be sure, be *postulated* as objects of the "practical reason" and as derivatives of the "supreme law of duty." Indeed, they *ought* to be, but beyond that it is impossible to go. The "practical reason" of the second critique failed utterly to circumvent the metaphysical skepticism of the first. God, freedom, and immortality remained "postulates," and as such beyond the scope of scientific proof.

The upshot of the Kantian doctrine of a priori and a posteriori, of noumenon and phenomenon, was a thorough-going skepticism. Husserl from the very beginning, with the publication of his *Logische Untersuchungen,* had fought this. He reversed the Kantian use of phenomenon and noumenon, and, in his doctrine of essence and intuition, that which he calls phenomenon or essence is really the thing-in-itself and therefore what Kant would have called "noumenon." For the phenomenologist there is no such thing as an "unknowable" object; hence he will not even speak of an object which is not experienced. Husserl agreed with Kant that all knowledge begins with experience, but, in addition to redefining experience, he further affirmed that it endures and ends in experience. He completely disavowed sensationalism and, in its stead, held that sensations constitute the least significant part of the world of experienced objects; and, indeed, rather than arousing rational activity on the part of the Ego, they merely announce the "existence" or presence of an object and give occasion for the instituting of intuitive activity which, in reality, is a definite and peculiar kind of experience of a realm of essence-objects. Instead of "categories," "forms," analytical and synthetic judgments, understanding, and the like, Husserl contended for intuition.

Finally, what of the Kantian Ego? It is nothing more than a "logical unity," or logical subject of experience. It is a necessary assumption, if knowledge is to be considered possible. As contrasted with this, Husserl's Ego is something in and for itself. Perhaps it is not a "substance," as Leibniz would have had it, but it is much more than a mere logical unity.[35] Indeed, it is not a mere assumption, but it is that of whose existence we are the most certain. In the mind of Husserl, this Ego, "self," "personality," or whatever it is desired to call it, is in no manner to be brought into doubt.[36] Experience (of every description) demands an experient as well as an object experienced, even as knowledge requires a knower and an object known by my Ego or some other.

Although he never attempted in any way to cast doubt upon the "independent" existence of the world, Husserl, as emphasized above, contended that such *Evidenz* of the Ego is, of all things, the most indubitable of all our knowledge. The world, because of its contingent character, does not contain the certainty of existence (for the Ego) that the Ego itself, for which the world is there, does. As contrasted with its knowledge of the "contingent," and even essential world, knowledge of its own existence brings with it a necessity so indisputable as to make all attempts at denial seem nothing less than foolhardy. This contention alone would suffice to mark the deep cleavage between Kant and Husserl.

[35] I have already adduced sufficient evidence for interpreting Husserl as holding that the Ego is a substance.
[36] *Ideen*, p. 85.

Both Kant and Husserl had the objective of examining the foundations of science, as well as investigating the nature and justification of experience. They likewise shared a disposition to invent their own terms, which they use ambiguously as part of an already tedious method. Owing to this, the principal ideas in each one have undoubtedly been distorted and subjected to misinterpretations which could have been avoided if they had been more careful in their terminology and more explicit in their procedure.

The contrast between the two can be summed up somewhat as follows.

First, Each assumed that knowledge begins with experience: according to Kant, that which is given is "sensory," a sort of *Konglomerat von Mannigfältigkeiten;* according to Husserl, that which is given is not mere sensations, but is of the nature of eidetic content as well.

Second, Knowledge, according to Kant, begins *and ends* in sense experience; Husserl avowed that knowledge begins, remains within, and ends in multifarious experiences; his concept of the breadth of experience was thus much more inclusive than that of Kant.

Third, Each drew a distinction between "a priori" and "a posteriori" knowledge; whereas Kant meant by this to emphasize that all experience suffers a restriction to sense data (concept of a posteriori), Husserl used the terms to show that the a priori, rather than a mere "form," is an object of direct, immediate cognition (intuition of essences).

Husserl, in short, reversed in its entirety the Kantian philosophy. There is no place in his phenomenology for Humian sensationalism, Kantian "categories," forms of understanding, and the like. With this complete reversal of outlook, phenomenology is ineluctably antagonistic to any tradition suckled on Kantianism.

§ 4. *Phenomenology and Realism*

It is common knowledge that modern realism,[37] now divided against itself in the forms of "new realism" and "critical realism," came into prominence about the turn of the present century as a revolt against all kinds of idealism. In 1902 appeared R. B. Perry's "Royce's Refutation of Idealism," in *The Monist;* in 1903, in *Mind,* G. E. Moore's "The Refutation of Idealism"; a year later William James's "Does Consciousness Exist?" in the *Journal*

[37] Needless to say, it is both impossible and unnecessary for the purpose of this discussion to deal with each man singly, or even with new realism and critical realism separately. As a matter of expediency, then, the term realism will be used frequently to include the general ideas found in the principal books and articles of the following men:

William James, "Does Consciousness Exist?" *Journal of Philosophy,* Sept. 1, 1904.

New Realism:

Ralph Barton Perry, "Royce's Refutation of Realism," *Monist,* 1901–2; "The Egocentric Predicament," *Journal of Philosophy,* 1910; *Present Philosophical Tendencies,* 1912, Parts III and V; *Philosophy of the Recent Past,* Part V.

E. B. Holt and others, *The New Realism,* 1912; E. B. Holt, *The Concept of Consciousness,* 1914.

Bertrand Russell, *Scientific Method in Philosophy,* 1914; "Philosophy in the Twentieth Century," in *Skeptical Essays,* 1928, pp. 68 f.

J. E. Boodin, *A Realistic Universe,* 1916. (Since the publication of this book, Boodin has become known in certain quarters as a critical realist.)

Critical Realism:

Durant Drake and others, *Essays in Critical Realism,* 1920; Durant Drake, *Mind and Its Place in Nature,* 1925.

John Laird, *A Study in Realism,* 1920.

Charles A. Strong, *Essays on the Natural Origin of the Mind,* 1930; "On the Nature of the Datum," *Essays in Critical Realism,* 1920, pp. 223 f.; "Is Perception Direct, or Representative?" *Mind,* Vol. XL, 1931.

Roy W. Sellars, *Evolutionary Naturalism,* 1922; "A Re-Examination of Critical Realism," *Philosophical Review,* Vol. XXXVIII, 1929; *The Philosophy of Physical Realism,* 1932.

C. D. Broad, *The Mind and Its Place in Nature,* 1925.

George Santayana, *Skepticism and Animal Faith,* 1923; *The Realm of Essence,* 1927.

W. P. Montague, *Ways of Knowing,* 1925.

At this point I want to acknowledge my indebtedness to Charles W. Morris's *Six Theories of Mind* for a clarification of the various realistic positions, as well as the problems to which he calls attention. His inadequate treatment of Husserl's "Intentionalism" will be mentioned later.

of Philosophy; a few years previous to that, in 1874, Franz Brentano's *Psychologie vom empirischem Standpunkt* had attracted wide attention and stimulated, among other works, Alexius Meinong's *Gegenstandstheorie*[38] and, not long after, Edmund Husserl's *Logische Untersuchungen.* Little imagination is required to understand how, in Germany, America, and England this phenomenon appeared simultaneously. The world of philosophy was in revolt against the suzerainty of idealism.

Since 1900, and particularly during the prewar period, such new realists as Ralph Barton Perry, Edwin B. Holt and E. G. Spaulding have been attracting wide attention. More recently, but certainly with no less vigor, Charles A. Strong, Durant Drake, Roy W. Sellars, Samuel Alexander, John Laird, C. Lloyd Morgan, and many others, who style themselves "critical realists," have been contesting the claims of both idealism *and* new realism. However all these men may differ in detail, both in their theory of mind and epistemology, there are certain viewpoints which they hold in common. For the purposes of discussion, it should be understood, then, that in the following remarks (unless otherwise specified) realism will be used as a term to denote that group of philosophers holding the following tenets:

1. The dementalization of the world; the universe is not of the nature of mind; or at least of mind alone.

2. The dementalization of mind itself; this is a denial of any and all substance theories, as well as that mind is different from the world of objects (new realism) on the one hand and the body, or the physical organism (critical realism), on the other.

3. The objects of knowledge do not depend on mind or perceiving or knowing for their existence or nature.

4. Objects must be experienced to be known, but, as in

38 See bibliographical list in Acknowledgments.

the case of item (3) above, this experience adds nothing to the object as regards its existence or nature.

5. Objects are known, or appear directly, as they are; they are not "ideas" or fabrications of mind or any mental activity.

As a matter of expediency, the following procedure will be adopted: first, it will be shown in what respects Husserl's phenomenology agrees with realism; and then, second, it will be indicated how it is in opposition to it. In the latter case, this opposition will be shown under two headings, viz., (1) "Realism's theory of mind or consciousness" (both schools of realism), and (2) "Epistemology" (principally critical realism).

As far back as the writing of his *Logische Untersuchungen,* Husserl was a rabid opponent of every kind of subjectivism and traditional idealism. This is clear from the manner in which he controverted *Psychologismus.*[39] Husserl would have seen nothing strange or novel, then, in Montague's statement that "realism is opposed to subjectivism or epistemological idealism which denies that things can exist apart from an experience of them, or independently of the cognitive relation."[40] Long before the contemporary realists had gained renown, Husserl had been a strong contender against all philosophies which would make the world dependent upon or a creation of mental activity.

From this it naturally follows, although he did not invent such tricky phrases, that Husserl would share with Perry his disgust with "the fallacy of argument from the egocentric predicament,"[41] and "the fallacy of exclusive particularity."[42] What Perry and his colleagues mean in the first instance is nothing more than that it is impos-

[39] Cf. *supra,* chap. ii, § 2, pp. 30–48.
[40] *The New Realism,* p. 474.   [41] *Ibid.,* p. 11.   [42] *Ibid.,* p. 14.

sible to argue from the necessity of a knower in perception, observation, and experience, that the objects and
events or situations in such relation depend upon this
condition for their existence or nature. In the second case,
particularly as regards not only ordinary sense perception
but such entities as logical and mathematical objects,
Husserl had long argued, ever since his *Logische Untersuchungen,* that the terms involved could "belong to several contexts."[43] As will shortly be seen, the difference between him and the realists lies in the fact not only that
he posits a substantial Ego, but that he does not agree
with them as to *how* the Ego knows its world and the
manner in which objects are publicly shared.

As far as epistemology is concerned, Husserl had long
contended, before and in concurrence with Marvin, Montague, Pitkin, Spaulding, Sellars, Perry, *et al.,* that perceiving adds nothing to what is known; that the Ego does
not "create" its objects or its world; that there can be
drawn no satisfactory distinction between primary and
secondary qualities; and, finally, that objects are known
as they are.[44] It will soon be shown, however, that the real
difference between him and them is to be found, not in
these ideas, since most of them were his long before they
appeared in publications by realists, but in their respective concepts of how these things are possible.

Although he agreed with realism on these terms, Husserl nevertheless is not to be classified with either new or

---

[43] *Ibid.*

[44] Principally in *Ideen,* especially §§ 42, 43, and 44. *Es ist also ein prin-
zipieller Irrtum zu meinen, es komme die Wahrnehmung (und in ihrer
Weise jede andersartige Dinganschauung) an das Ding selbst nicht heran.*
It might be remarked here that Husserl used such terms (and their sig-
nifications) as "intention," "mean," and "essence" before the appearance
of *Essays in Critical Realism* and other works by critical realists. But he,
as contrasted to them, went all the way in following out the implications
of these terms. He did not end, for instance, in "conceptualistic nominalism," as did Sellars and Drake.

critical realists,[45] for the very reason that what they consider their choicest contributions he viewed as *unsinnig*.
For instance, it was anathema to Husserl for anyone to
assert that

Any class that is formed from the members of a given manifold by some selective principle which is independent of the
principles which have organized the manifold may be called
a cross-section. Any such a thing is consciousness or mind,—a
cross-section of the universe, selected by the nervous system.
The elements or parts of the universe selected, and thus included in the class mind, are all elements or parts to which
the nervous system makes a *specific response*. It responds thus
specifically to a *spatial* object if it brings the body to touch
that object, to point toward it, to copy it, and so forth.[46]

Even stranger would Durant Drake's statement have
sounded to Husserl:

I suggest that the mind *is* the brain; i. e. that it is that cerebral mechanism which receives impressions from the outer
world and evokes adjustments of the organism. In using the
term "mind," we are conceiving these cerebral events as they
are on the inside, so to speak; i. e. we are thinking of their
substance. When we use the term "brain," we are looking at
them from the outside, through our sense-organs; that is, we
are exteriorizing our own mental states and thinking of the
brain in terms of *them*.[47]

Husserl could not share, moreover, the new realists'
claim that there is no difference between subject and ob-

[45] Nor with idealists, either. In 1930 ("Nachwort," p. 560) Husserl said:
"*ich nach wie vor jede Gestalt des üblichen philosophischen Realismus
für prinzipiell widersinnig halte, nich minder jeden Idealismus, zu welchem
er sich in seinen Argumentationen in Gegensatz stillt, den er 'widerlegt.'*"

[46] E. B. Holt, *Concept of Consciousness*, p. 353.

[47] "What Is a Mind?" *Mind*, XXV, 1926, p. 234. Perry has the same
viewpoint. Cf. *Present Philosophical Tendencies*, pp. 271 f. Montague's
"Hylopsychism" would be considered by Husserl as very little improvement; it is noteworthy only for its greater ambiguity: "The potentiality
of the psychical is the actuality of the physical" (*The New Realism*,
p. 281).

ject. Perry might have believed that his "theory of immanence" overcame "the duality of mind and body" and established a monism of knower and object known;[48] but Husserl could view this more as a forensic triumph than a philosophically substantiated insight.

It should likewise be clear that Husserl's doctrine of essence has no affinity whatever with that of Russell, Santayana, Drake, and Strong; or the "subsistences" of Holt's earlier viewpoints. It is needless to remark, moreover, that Husserl never shared the realist's enthusiasm over seeking succor from the special sciences, particularly psychology, physiology, and biology.

All these points, as well as others, will now be taken under consideration.

(a) *Realism's theory of mind or consciousness.*—One of the cardinal points of the new realism is that mind, since it has nothing intrinsically its own, must be looked upon and defined in terms of something else.[49] The first thing to be noticed about this "something else" is that it constitutes the contents of mind; in fact, mind is nothing more, nothing less than an aggregate of such contents, however defined. Mind, as opposed to all idealisms, is of secondary importance, and that which is commonly called mental is really comprised of certain parts of "physical nature" to which the nervous system has somehow selectively responded. Mind, then, is "a complex so organized as to act desideratively or interestedly." [50] Perry's whole argument is summarized by himself in the statement that

48 *Present Philosophical Tendencies,* pp. 306 f. Cf. Holt's *Concept of Consciousness,* pp. 282, 287 f.

49 In the following, I rely for my materials principally on the new realists, Perry and Holt, and the critical realists, Drake, Strong, and Sellars. This is no reflection on the other eminent thinkers of these two schools, since those included were taken not for their superiority of doctrine or cogency but because they have succeeded, through various means, in calling greater attention to their theories than have their colleagues.

50 Perry, *Present Philosophical Tendencies,* p. 304.

the natural mind as here and now existing is thus an organization possessing as distinguishable but complementary aspects, interest, nervous system, and contents. Or if interest and nervous system be taken together as constituting the action of mind, we may summarize mind as action and contents.[51]

This is in concurrence with Holt's definition in *The New Realism*[52] of consciousness as

a cross-section of the universe selected by the nervous system. The elements or parts of the universe selected, and thus included in the class mind, are all elements or parts to which the nervous system makes its specific response.

Where is consciousness? Obviously "out there wherever the things specifically responded to are." [53] The word "mind," then, does not denote a substance in contradistinction to the world. It means nothing for the new realists but the *response* of the organism, particularly the brain and nervous system, to certain parts of the environment. This response comprises, or rather *is,* a peculiar "relation" of certain objects of the environment.

The organism, too, is a part of the environment. What role does it play? It is merely a *condition* for the selection of certain parts of the universe, or environment. Once this viewpoint is accepted, it would likewise have to be granted that the mind is purely incidental; that the organism does not "have a mind" with which to govern its selective responses or to control its neural reactions. There can hardly be any doubt about this position when one reads Holt's statement in *Concept of Consciousness*[54] that "in the organ of response (the brain and other nerve tissues) nothing, *absolutely nothing,* is to be looked for except just an organ of response . . . the house of the brain is not haunted." So much for the "relational" theory of mind.

---

[51] *Ibid.,* p. 304.
[53] Holt, *The New Realism,* p. 354.

[52] Page 354.
[54] Page 310.

Curiously enough, critical realism came into existence principally as a protest against new realism's concept of consciousness, prompted by the feeling that it failed to recognize the dignity and role of mind (sometimes called by the critical realist "awareness"). Owing to this, there had been a failure to make a close enough distinction between the means or "vehicle" of knowledge and the object known, which had made it practically impossible to explain, among other things, error.

C. A. Strong, for instance, in his *Essays on the Natural Origin of the Mind,* when considering the matter of "givenness," believes that we are forced to the conviction that experience shows that there is awareness or consciousness. To ask the simple question, "What is givenness?" is in fact to ask, "How is something given?" To which Strong replies, through a "vehicle" not itself given, which vehicle is a "psychic state." That Strong admits the impossibility of defining a psychic state, or what makes it so, is unimportant for the present.[55] To be sure, there are sensations, but sensational data are given, not as they are in themselves, but "through" the psychic states. Sensations become data simply by acquiring a certain status or meaning while passing through the vehicle of givenness. How is this possible? This query leads to Strong's concept of the self, or, as he puts it, the "psyche." The self, be it first noted, is not a substance in the sense that it has a nature different from the objects (or contents) which it cognizes, although, to be sure, it is "a substantive." Yet, in the last analysis, a careful consideration of Strong's self-styled "double-knowledge approach"

[55] "I have never said what it is beyond referring the reader to introspection; for any attempt to express it in words is apt to lead to misunderstanding" (*Essays on the Natural Origin of the Mind,* p. 234). It might be noted, in passing, that the critical realist is not as averse to using the method of introspection as are Perry and Holt. Strong's theory of "givenness" will be treated later under "Epistemology."

permits of no other interpretation of his standpoint except that psyche and the body are metaphysically identical. As he himself says, in effect: the self as the sum-total of the psychic states at any given moment means nothing but the manner in which psychic states appear "from the inside"; the body is the appearance of the psyche to the "outer senses." [56] In common with Sellars' "consciousness" as the "brain-mind" (this concept will be treated at length below), Strong's self or mind-stuff or "sentience" is, by definition, of the nature of space and time, and no cognitive or volitional characteristics can be attributed to it.[57] But whence its unity? In the "extended brain." And, it may be inquired of Strong, is thinking reducible to that which somehow comes into existence when the brain happens to be functioning in a certain way while concerned with certain parts of the environment? How else could he answer but in the affirmative?

This purported improvement over the new realism's concept of mind does not become less ambiguous when one turns to Durant Drake, let alone Sellars' viewpoints as found in *Evolutionary Naturalism,* and *The Philosophy of Physical Realism.*[58] It has already been noticed that Drake holds that mind *is* the brain; now it appears that Sellars would improve upon the new realism by a mysterious enlargement of our conception of the brain to include both "activity" and "content." Mind, he avers, "is sensory-motor, ideo-motor; it is a stream of tendencies lit up by consciousness." [59] In another place he defines consciousness in the sense of a denotative term, as "the total field of a person's experiencing as it shifts and

[56] *Essays on the Natural Origin of the Mind*, pp. 182 f.

[57] "I define 'sentient' as whatever nature is necessary in things in order that, when they get together in the form of an organism, there may be consciousness" (*ibid.*, p. 268).

[58] And "Knowledge and Its Categories," *Essays in Critical Realism*, Drake and others, pp. 187 f.

[59] *Evolutionary Naturalism*, p. 302.

changes." [60] This changing field of experience is "existentially dependent upon the organism. It is here that *knowledge* arises and is understood." [61] Consciousness, then, is an "event" and not a thing or stuff and, as such, "it is an event adjectival to the brain. It is in this latter that we find enduring patterns and principles of integration." [62]

How does Sellars answer the problem of the relationship between consciousness and the brain? The brain is obviously of the nature of space; is consciousness likewise spatial? The answer, of course, is in the affirmative. Consciousness is both temporal and spatial since, as an event, it is "a feature of a physical event. . . . Consciousness is a qualitative dimension of cerebral activity." [63] The spatiality of consciousness is conclusively demonstrable (to his satisfaction), when it is remembered that "perceiving and thinking are organic acts . . . the experiences integral to them are extended in the brain." [64] Nevertheless, he warns that "we must never confuse the characterization of physical bodies with the characterization of any bit of consciousness." [65] This, he believes, could never happen, since perceiving involves "interpretative operation, using categories such as thinghood and causality which arise from complex acts and complex experiences." [66]

Now it is seen from the above that, although they may differ in terminology and in certain details in their concept of mind, both schools of realism actually are in agreement on at least three points. First, mind is not a substance; second, body or physical organism is mind "from the outside"; third, consciousness, or mind, has its setting in the brain, or rather in the total nervous system, including the cerebrum.

60 *The Philosophy of Physical Realism*, p. 407.
61 *Ibid.*   62 *Ibid.*, p. 408.   63 *Ibid.*, p. 424.
64 *Ibid.*, p. 426.   65 *Ibid.*   66 *Ibid.*, p. 427.

PHENOMENOLOGY

Husserl, by implication and explication, was opposed
from the very beginning to all such viewpoints, although,
to be sure, in the *Logische Untersuchungen* he did not explicitly formulate his concept of consciousness or mind.
In the *Ideen,* however, as already noted, he devoted a
great deal of attention to the problem. He would say of
realists that they are still in the "natural standpoint"; that
they have been unable to disentangle themselves from the
world of concrete facts.[67] After all, the brain and nervous
system are just as much "particular" empirical facts as the
objects of the environment which allegedly comprise consciousness. As constitutive of environmental components,
clearly mind has no "other than" qualities. Yet the realists
use such words and phrases as "unity," "coherence," "activity," "volition," and "my mind *possesses* sense contents";[68] and they hold that the mind is the "constant
feature" of the relationship between knower and objects
known. In short, the realists, on the one hand, would de-
spoil the mind of its dynamic character; yet, on the other,
they would attribute to it the capacity of "selectively" responding and reacting to the environment. Husserl would
have no quarrel with the viewpoint that mind cannot be
viewed as something apart from its environment,[69] as possessing a mysterious quality which makes it an alien in
nature. But he would nevertheless inquire of the realists,
as so many have done, How can mind, which is purely incidental, be so active and dynamic, particularly when it is
allegedly nothing more than the accidental or at least incidental matrix, or complex, of a small part of that very environment itself? In short, how can the mind do so much
when it is nothing at all? Mind has everything done to it,

[67] The realists, of course, would probably say they have no desire to
do so.

[68] Perry, *Present Philosophical Tendencies,* p. 293. Italics mine.

[69] Although, of course, he would necessarily refuse to define environment as do the realists.

yet at the same time can do nothing. Mind as the organism viewed "from the inside" is, after all, nothing but a space-time object, the same as any other object-content within our experience. Moreover, since within the organism we have other kinds of spaciotemporal objects, such as nervous system, spinal cord, and brain, it is futile to attempt, for purposes of clarification, to choose either the brain or the nervous system, or the two together as that part of the bodily organism which makes possible the environmental objects creating or bringing into existence that which, at least on Husserlian grounds, is capable of nonspatial and nontemporal activity, e. g., perceiving, remembering, willing, and intuiting. Idealism may have difficulty explaining the union between the psychical and physical; of a certainty, realism has no less difficulty explaining the union of objective neutral (or physical) entities which, in certain relations, miraculously constitute ("mental") consciousness. For instance, in Montague's concept, who or what joins present and absent realities and potentialities to make consciousness the union of the "potential" and "physical"?[70]

Husserl, too, employed the concept of selectivity, but called it by another name, "intentional activity." It has been noted how intentional activity makes intuition possible and how it is the vehicle through which objects disclose themselves. It would be impossible for the realist, and particularly the new realist, with his doctrine of mind as a complex of neutral entities, to account for *any* activity, let alone intentionality of consciousness. If he made a place for it, he would have to change his whole concept of the nonsubstantiality of consciousness. If he adopted it —and there seems to be good reason to believe that the principle of selectivity is analogous to, if not identical with, the intentional activity of phenomenology—he must abandon his position that mind is nothing more than the

70 Montague. *The New Realism*, p. 281.

response of a nervous system to physical objects. Certainly Perry's importation of the element of "interest" in no way solves the problem, since he is helpless to clarify the origin, let alone the active quality, of the organism's *taking* an interest. Husserl, as contrasted with this standpoint, would hold that mind, rather than being a mere relation of neutral entities, determines and specifies what relations it shall have with the objective environment. Mind is more than an incident.

This means, in short, that realism cannot explain the dynamic character of mind as disclosed in remembering, willing, imagining, and in inventive and creative capacities. Realism's "principle of selectivity" (Sellars, Montague, and others) or "interested action" (Perry) is, on their own arguments, an impossibility. First, we are told that mind is the matrix or complex of objects; then, second, that this *results from* the selective response of the organism. But this is obviously incredible since, by definition, there is nothing to respond or institute selectivity, for it has not yet come into existence. If selectivity is made the *condition* of a matrix being found, there is a certain prior "plus" unaccounted for on realistic grounds; if "response to" and "selection" are discarded as the condition, then clearly the matrix could never (on realism's grounds) come into being at all.

Arguments have already been given to show how Husserl held that mind acts in many respects entirely without reference to space-time objects. In the last analysis, all spaciotemporal objects are "present," or contemporary, but surely no one would argue that a *remembered* datum is present except insofar as it is conjured up by the remembering Ego. Even Bertrand Russell, to whom so many look as an improvement over the new realism, cannot solve this problem and is apparently willing to admit defeat when, in *The Analysis of Mind,* he argues that

When I say that the stuff of the mind consists only of sensations and images, I doubt whether what I am saying is more than verbal. Mental phenomena, like all other phenomena, consist of particulars variously related. Sensations and images are merely names for these particulars, sensations being those that have proximate causes outside the brain, and images being all the rest.[71]

It can be inferred from this statement, since the term "image" includes "all the rest," that remembering, volitional activity, and abstract ratiocination are not to be *dynamically* characterized. The viewpoint here exemplified serves no purpose but to render the realistic position more bewildering.

It is while dealing with the problem of meaning that Husserl's "idealism," insofar as it concerns the place given to the pure Ego, becomes so evident. Meaning, it will be recalled, is conferred by the Ego through intentional activity, and in this sense, *and this sense alone,* can it be said to constitute reality. Aside from the question of the relevancy of this viewpoint, the fact remains that, as contrasted with the new realism, Husserl's phenomenology contains, in common with critical realism, a dualism, since the acts of the pure Ego are psychical. Experience in general, in fact, has the dual character of (subjective) noesis and (objective) noema. This was Husserl's way of differentiating between experiencing and experienced, or consciousness and the object of consciousness.[72] The impor-

---

71 Taken from Morris's *Six Theories of Mind,* p. 137.

72 Morris, in *Six Theories of Mind,* chap. iv, pp. 149 f., says that Husserl was here not so much drawing a distinction between psychical and physical, but simply "that of the psychical as opposed to the meaning or intending an object . . . since the object proper, conceived naturalistically, is not itself part of the experience" (*ibid.,* p. 174). I am rather inclined to view this as a misinterpretation of Husserl's position, traceable, very likely, to Morris's failure to make a thorough study of *Ideen,* although his familiarity with *Logische Untersuchungen* is indisputable. As I interpret him, Husserl would define as physical that in which is manifested the essence "physical." Cf. chap. v, § 5, "Fact and Essence."

tant thing to remember, however, so far as concerns the problem at hand, is that although all knowledge of the objective world is, on Husserlian arguments, passive in the sense that it is a revelation of objects to the Ego, this itself is made possible by the intentional act of the pure Ego, which lives in and glances through all experiences to the eidetically composed object.

Since Husserl refused to make of the Ego a matrix of objectivities of the physical environment, he could more readily explain the self-identity of consciousness. Perry, as already noted, refers to mind as the "constant feature of experience." It seems hardly necessary to call attention to the absurdity of holding for the constancy of that which is the product of changing entities and events (objective objects). This is the problem from the standpoint of the environment. When we turn to the realistic concept of mind as identifiable with the nervous system or brain or, taken together, the organism, the problem becomes even more acute, since the organism itself is at least in continual temporal flux. The organism, on the realist's own grounds, is a part of the physical environment. Yet somehow, miraculously, the mind, which is avowedly a component of the environment, remains identical or constant. Husserl did not fall into this trap, since he gave reasons, at least to his own satisfaction, for believing that the Ego is not of the nature of space and time, although it is a part of the universe in general. Ultimately, of course, his theory of essences made it impossible to call the world "physical" in the commonly accepted sense of the word.

Perhaps one of the reasons there is such a wide divergence between the realists and Husserl is that the former are disposed to lean so much upon the natural sciences.[73]

---

[73] In *Essays in Critical Realism* constant reference is made to the contributions of science in supporting critical realism. Drake, Sellars, and Pratt are especially eager to plead their case this way. Sellars (p. 191)

It should now be clear not only that Husserl did not do this, but why he could not. He would say it was this tendency on the part of realism that led it mistakenly to view consciousness as definable in terms of the brain or nervous system. Husserl was convinced he had escaped this when he bracketed the natural standpoint and all the sciences that have to do with it. It would follow from this that he would not be required to rest his theory of mind upon what psychology (however defined) said about physiological reactions of the organism to a space-time world. There may be a place for and value of psychology as an empirical science, but there is no evidence to show that one must use psychology as a starting-point for philosophy, let alone, as Sellars seems so disposed, to rest one's case entirely on it. Moreover, Husserl would hold it as pure prejudice to maintain, as Perry does, that there is nothing private about psychical activity; or as Holt holds, that there is nothing, *"absolutely nothing,"* to look for except cerebral and neural processes. As a matter of fact, on grounds of his investigation of psychologism in *Logische Untersuchungen*, it can be said without fear of exaggeration that Husserl would brand all forms of the new realism as psychologistic; by the same token he could reject it as completely and with the same arguments as he did its nineteenth-century precursor. If realists considered this classification an affront, Husserl could say that it was left to them to demonstrate the invalidity of his claim that

---

says, "If you would really know the world, it is felt you should find out what science has to say about it." They all (with the possible exception of Strong) incline to tag along behind science, waiting for its latest definitions of "physical realities and processes external to the percipient organism" (p. 192). In one place (p. 208) Sellars says, "In a very real sense, epistemology only supplements psychology, since cognition is a function within the *organized* psychical." It is my impression that the case is just the opposite. Pratt stakes his case on Ward, Stout, and Titchener (pp. 92 f.). Husserl, of course, would interpret all this as one more bit of conclusive evidence that philosophy is ready to admit that it cannot stand on its own feet.

perceptual objects, and mathematical and logical laws and propositions, are known by intuition of essences.

From the standpoint of empirical science, which realists choose to adopt to support their claims, the organism for Husserl remains nothing but another "fact," and certainly, in view of this, he could challenge the realists to show how a "mind" of this sort could be in relation with and cognize a realm of nonspatial and nontemporal entities (mathematics and logic again). Or, if such entities were denied existence or subsistence, the realist must show how the laws and propositions of mathematics and logic, not to mention ordinary sense qualities, are of the nature of space and time. In truth, one of the greatest problems confronting the realist is to verify and account for the universality and indubitability of those very laws and propositions which the sciences of psychology, physiology, and biology themselves employ, and upon which the realist relies so wholeheartedly. Husserl believed he had accomplished it with his doctrine of essences and intuition. If the realists controvert this, they must explain away the eidetic realm, deny its existence, or else abandon their own position.

What, then, was Husserl's attitude toward the bodily organism? He never dealt with this specific problem, but it can be inferred from his general outlook that he viewed it as a means whereby the realm of essences announces its presence through concrete manifestations, commonly referred to as "sense qualities." Owing to our particular frame of reference, it is apparently necessary to be in possession of an organism through which space-time objects can make their *Dasein* known. It has already been indicated how Husserl believed that, with the exception of the realms of mathematics and logic, essences must make themselves known through the concreta of space-time experience. But, as also shown, it does not follow from this, at least on Husserlian premises, that these space-time objects consist *only* of the existential properties commonly called empirical.

Husserl would likewise take the realist to task for attempting to dementalize the world. He would view the substitution of such words as "nervous system" and "organism" for mind and Ego not only as pure verbalism but a verbalism hardly based on ordinary facts or scientific evidence. It may be good "common sense" (Sellars and Drake), but common sense meant for Husserl the naïve "natural standpoint," wholly unworthy of the philosopher. He always viewed as pure prejudice the concept that we must limit the world of experience to that which can be mediated only through the senses. Yet, on the other hand, it cannot be inferred from this that Husserl meant to mentalize the world, i. e., to hold that the world is of the nature of mind alone. He preferred rather, beginning with the *Ideen,* to use the word eidetic, and meant thereby, of course, of the nature of essences, which are neither mental nor physical. Eidetic, however, cannot be identified with "neutral," since by the wildest stretch of the imagination the new realist does not mean by his term "of the nature of essences."

The affinities and differences between Husserl's and the realist's theory of consciousness may be summarized in this way. Husserl agreed, and said long before Perry and the other new realists did, that the world is not dependent upon the Ego for its existence or nature and that things can pass in and out of a relation to mind, yet remain unchanged. He would have no quarrel with realists that it is absurd for idealists to argue, from the fact that to be known an object must be in relation with a knower, that it must perforce be further held that the object gained thereby something besides the advantage of being known. But Perry and his fellow realists, as Morris so aptly points out in *Six Theories of Mind*,[74] end up with a deadly body-centric predicament. This, in the mind of Husserl, would be a greater logical absurdity than the idealistic position. It is clear, moreover, from Husserl's position, that Perry's doctrine of the externality of relations is not the only way to defeat idealism, and that it is not necessary to employ it to escape the egocentric predicament.

(*b*) *Epistemology.*—It would probably be generally agreed that a theory of mind is basic to an epistemology. This is certainly the case in the instance of Husserl, and without doubt it accounts for the prominence of his theory of the pure Ego in his phenomenology.

If, as in the case of Perry, in *Present Philosophical Tendencies,* a theory of mind must be developed before proceeding to epistemology, it is clear from the foregoing that, since Husserl would have to view the new realism's theory of mind as a travesty, he would likewise hold that the epistemology based upon it was equally absurd. It is impossible on phenomenological grounds for the new realism to have any kind of epistemology whatever, since what is known already constitutes, as a matter of fact, the knower; by definition, then, there is no knower to be conscious of anything, let alone that which has allegedly comprised it. Even if the new realist rejected the prepositional character of cognition for Perry's theory of immanence, it would still be impossible to explain the presence of a knower which somehow is brought into existence by its own contents.

It has already been remarked and emphasized that Husserl's phenomenology is in agreement with both kinds of realism on the independence of objects, both for their existence and nature. It concurs, moreover, with critical real-

74 Pages 107 f.

ism's demand for a dualism.[75] This means, in the eyes of Husserl, a necessary differentiation between the subjective and objective poles of knowledge. This is found in his doctrine of the "transcendence" of objects known.[76] In addition to this he would likewise say with realism that perception, knowing, and *all* forms of cognition must be viewed, if not as processes, certainly as *conditions* in which objects, however defined, make themselves known. This discussion, then, can be restricted to two of Husserl's tenets, and to a comparison drawn between them and the realist's position, i. e., the concept of consciousness and cognition and, second, the concept of experience and realms known.[77]

It has already been noted that Drake identifies mind and brain. Strong likewise rejects any theory which holds that the self is a substance. But his mind-stuff, or psyche, since it is "extended brain," is no improvement over Drake's definition. It is futile to turn to Sellars's "double-aspect" theory for succor, since, although he would im-

[75] As Drake points out in the first essay in *Essays in Critical Realism*, all critical realists, while holding for a certain kind of duality between subject and object, do not agree on the precise nature of the division. But they do agree, as opposed to the new realism, that there must be drawn a sharp differentiation between the knower and what is known. Drake is particularly eager to insist that by dualism he and his colleagues do not mean that we first know a mental state and then infer the existence and nature of the physical object. Critical realism's dualism consists in distinguishing between "the cognitive state which is the vehicle of knowledge" and "the object known" (*ibid.*, p. 4 n). All may not agree with Sellars, Lovejoy, and Pratt "that although what is *given* is a mere character-complex, it is in reality *in toto* the character of the mental state of the moment, and so *is* an existent, in spite of the fact that its existence is not given"; but all accept that we cognize or *know* "the independent object itself" (*ibid.*). New realism, critical realism, and phenomenology are in agreement here (cf. *The New Realism*, pp. 472, 474, 476, 477, 478). The real problem, of course, is *how* this is possible.

[76] Cf. *Ideen*, § 41, pp. 73 f., *"Der reele Bestand der Warhnehmung und ihr transzendentes Objekt."*

[77] Aside from those mentioned incidentally, the theories of Strong, Drake, and Sellars will be taken as representative epistemologies of the critical realists,

pute activity to consciousness, it is still identifiable as
a "continuant" of the brain. Consciousness would be
an abstraction "if conceived apart from a mind-brain
event." [78] When elaborating his epistemology he inquires,
to be sure, "How could we know if there were nothing to
know?" Husserl would inquire, How could we know if
there were no knower? Later on,[79] when discussing Hock-
ing's antagonism toward realism, and while arguing
against substantializing the mind, he defines mind as

complex experiences in which judgments about external things
and about the self dominate . . . the mind as a continuant is
the brain and the brain is spatial and in spatial relations with
other physical systems.[80]

Then he declares that "the psychical is a condition of the
brain alone as a focus of stimuli and response . . . thinking
as a process involves the whole organism. But thinking
comes to a head in the brain." [81]

It is interesting to see that, although Sellars and his
fellow realists abhor the thought of the substantiality of
mind, it seems impossible for them to escape the use of
such terms as judging, directing, thinking, willing, and so
forth, all of which are imputed to a psyche or, in the words
of Sellars, a self.[82] Now although it would be nonsense to
try to argue from linguistic necessity to metaphysical or
ontological proofs of the self, it is nevertheless important
to observe that in this point is found one of the most
serious problems facing critical realism. It wants to have a
duality of experience; it insists upon the activity of the
subjective side of that experience, yet it is reluctant to
grant that that side, as contrasted with the objective aspect,

[78] *Philosophy of Physical Realism*, p. ix.
[79] *Ibid.*, p. 440.   [80] *Ibid.*, p. 434.
[81] *Ibid.*, p. 440. Does he not mean, rather, that thinking comes to a
brain in the head?
[82] Cf. *Essays in Critical Realism*, p. 198: "the object must be known in
terms of the content which is given to the *knowing self*." Italics mine.

has any ontological status of its own. This may be traceable to its disdain of metaphysics, but Husserl would hold it as unfounded, since he is not only willing to grant the independence theory insofar as it affects the objective side of experience, but insists upon applying it to the Ego likewise. As contrasted with Sellars, consciousness is not "secondary to being." Husserl would interpret this as no different from Holt's statement that

it is not that we have two contrasted worlds, the "objective" and the "subjective"; there is but one world, the objective, and that which we have hitherto not understood, have dubbed therefore the "subjective" are the subtler workings of integrated objective mechanisms.[83]

Husserl would hold, for instance, that the realist has aggravated the problem rather than solved it by holding for such a position when arguing against the idealistic concept that the self or Ego makes possible being. He saw no reason why the two should not be given an equally independent ontological status.

His theory, although to be sure not without its problems, makes it possible, as contrasted with that of Sellars and his colleagues, to account for the dynamic character of mental life. Without going into detail, it might be remarked that it has been shown in previous chapters that (1) the world is knowable because it is experienceable, its experienceability is traceable to the intentional character of consciousness, and this intentionality can be defined briefly as the prepositional character of knowledge;[84] (2) the Ego's activity includes a "glancing of the Ego toward something," a directedness of attention which makes it possible for objects to announce their presence to it; and (3) intuitive activity makes it possible for objects to announce their eidetic qualities. In addition to these, Husserl emphasized that experience, since it has

[83] *The Freudian Wish*, p. 93.   [84] Chap. v, § 4, pp. 170–76.

unity and coherence, reflects the Ego's property as a uni-fying factor.[85] The Ego, in short, is the condition of all experiences, since it is the presupposition of all knowing, and, as the realists say, it is folly to speak of anything either existing or subsisting which cannot be experienced or known. If a decision were necessary regarding the pri-macy of objective being or consciousness, it is evident that in the light of these remarks Husserl would say that reality really lacks "independence." Reality, taken as single ob-jects and "the whole world," means what is real for the self, and from his doctrine of intentionality it clearly fol-lows that

it is not in itself something absolute, binding itself in a second-ary way to another; absolutely speaking, it is nothing at all. It has no "absolute essence" whatsoever. It has the essentiality of something which in principle is *only* intentional, *only* known, as an appearance consciously presented.[86]

The spaciotemporal world, in short, is *intentional* Be-ing, and as such

has only the secondary relative sense of existence *for* a con-sciousness. It is a Being which is posited by consciousness in its own experiences. In principle it is intuitable and determi-nable only as the element common to the motivated appear-ance-manifolds; *over and beyond* this it is just nothing at all.[87]

Husserl, then, long before the time of critical realism, maintained that the world is not dependent for its ex-istence or quality properties on the self or its activities. But it should be equally clear wherein Husserl differed from realism in his theory of the self, or Ego. It is now pertinent, however, to inquire of Husserl, How is it pos-sible for the Ego to cognize or know that which by defini-

[85] *Encyclopaedia Britannica*, 14th ed., XVII, 700.   [86] *Ideen*, p. 94.
[87] *Ibid.*, p. 93. It must be emphasized that in the light of the foregoing this is not "idealism" in the sense that the world is dependent upon in-tentional activity. Husserl here is merely emphasizing that the world as "my" *world of objects* is a world of intentional objects.

tion neither creates it nor is dependent upon it? This can best be answered by first treating briefly the realist's answer to the problem of what constitutes knowledge. Once again Strong and Sellars will be taken as typical examples.[88]

It has just been depicted how Strong conceives of the self as a complex of psychic states. Actually now, what role does the psychic state play in knowledge? Strong feels it is necessary to "assume" psychic states since sensational data cannot give us the object. It is in the problem of "givenness," then, that the psychic state is brought to the fore as the vehicle of sensational content. He draws a distinction between "physical objects," on the one hand, and "the appearances of psychic states," on the other. These appearances, or *sensa,* are not then to be attributed to the physical object itself. As such they are nonexistential.[89] Yet experience does have meaning, and in order to account for it he brings in what he calls "essence." Closer examination shows, however, that what he means by essence is simply psychic state, or, as he sometimes calls it, "phantasm." This is the inevitable outcome of his biological concept of mind. Perception, then, involves this state and the physical object, as a result of which there appears "the thing." Yet somehow there is a mysterious connection between the real or physical thing and this product of

[88] Even though they disagree on the concept of "datum," the "given," there is no need to turn especially to Durant Drake's epistemology (except his "essences"), since, on the whole, it is the same as that of Strong and Sellars. I would like to acknowledge here my indebtedness to Bernard Bosanquet's *Contemporary Philosophy,* particularly chap. vii, for an elucidation of the critical realist's position.

[89] See Strong's remarks in *Essays in Critical Realism.* pp. 223 f. In many respects (although I doubt if he would view it as complimentary) Strong agrees with Husserl. This is particularly true of his doctrine of the "given" as essence and not existential datum. In this sense they both opppose Sellar's and Drake's representationism. The real point of difference between Strong and Husserl is to be found in the answer to the problem, how essence is known—due, of course, to their respective concepts of the self or Ego.

psychic states, for "we not only 'have to do' with the real thing, but 'apprehend' it, and that directly." [90] In this way he believes that he avoids a representational theory of knowledge, even though there is obviously a complete cleavage between the object as it is and the object as known (as it appears). But to say that there is an essence involved in the explanation of meaning is fruitless when it is remembered that a careful scrutiny of his theory shows essence to be nothing but a mental projection. It is an *imputation*. He identifies datum and essence, but in the last analysis "datum" is "idea." [91] And that makes essence an idea.

Nor can satisfaction be found in Durant Drake's theory of the realm of essence, since he never shows *how* an essence is given. As a matter of fact, with both Strong and Drake, the word essence means nothing whatever but something which is imputed to sense data, i. e., it is nothing but the psychic state's activity when engaged with the emanations of the physical object which itself remains unknown.[92]

If an appeal is made to Sellars, very little improvement over Strong and Drake is found. His desire to attribute creativity, activity, and other comparable characteristics to the mind-brain, attractive as it might sound to those who feel the need of something to solve their epistemological difficulties, is an expression rather of a great hope to overcome the difficulties inherent in the new realistic position than an accomplished fact.[93]

[90] *Essays on the Natural Origin of the Mind*, p. 109.

[91] *Ibid.*, pp. 112 f.

[92] George Santayana's theory of "symbolic essence" cannot rescue the critical realist from this predicament since, after all, it is nothing but an assumption grounded in "animal faith." Cf. *The Realm of Essence*, and *Skepticism and Animal Faith*.

[93] "The human mind-brain is creative, and this creativity is causally controlled and socially conditioned" (*The Philosophy of Physical Realism*, p. 205).

We must [he enjoins us] forget Cartesian dualism and start afresh on the basis of naturalism. Away with Transcendental Egos and things-in-themselves! The whole terminology must be forgotten. We are conscious organisms, thinking the things around us in accordance with our nature and theirs.[94]

A great hope, indeed. Perhaps he does forget about his "Cartesian" dualism; but is it not true that he himself is dualistic—if in another way? Perhaps, once again, we should forget about things-in-themselves; but is it not true that he himself, although finding Kantianism unacceptable, ends with an unknowable thing-in-itself? True, the whole terminology may be forgotten. It is questionable, however, whether the *import* of the traditional terminology is escaped in his critical realism. This is the only interpretation which can possibly be given to such affirmations as "the idea which gives the content of knowledge (the *esse intentionale* of the scholastics) is other than the object of knowledge," [95] and "It is pretty clear, then, that there are two elements in perception: *the affirmation of a co-real and the assigned set of characters or aspects.*"[96] The former he would call the "object," the latter, the "content" of perception. "The content is intuited; the object is reacted to and affirmed."[97] Yet critical realism (according to Sellars) claims to *know* physical objects although "we *intuit* only contents."[98]

Sellars finds the new realism's neglect of the knower irritating. He rejects Drake's making of sense-data and meanings spaceless and timeless essences. What does he offer in their place? What does he attribute to the knower's capacities which new realists would not? An analysis of his theory of knowledge, particularly as found in his *Philosophy of Physical Realism,* Chapters IX and X, dis-

94 *Ibid.,* p. 217. How do we know "their" nature?
95 *Essays in Critical Realism,* p. 190.
96 *Ibid.,* p. 196. Note his emphasis upon *assigned.*
97 *Ibid.,* p. 196.   98 *Ibid.,* p. 193.

covers the following basic tenets. Perception is referential. As a form of knowledge, it is knowledge of, or knowledge about. It is not, however, knowledge of universals or essences. (Then what, one is constrained to inquire, is "intuited"?) With Drake and Strong, it must be granted, indeed insisted upon, that perceptual experience has meaning or meanings, but, as contrasted with them, meanings cannot exist apart from events.

I hold that the reference of meanings as experienced events does rest upon the persistence of cerebral pattern as intrinsic to a physical system. Here we get to something upon which the character of successive events rests, in other words, to substance.[99]

How meanings, which, as will be seen, are categorial, or a matter of the knower's imputative powers, can be the object of "experienced events" remains known to Sellars alone. What "substance" is, remains even more obscure, particularly if it is that which the physical sciences deal with, since by definition, in accordance with Sellars's dualism, the geometrico-mathematical realm of physical objects is beyond the possibility of human experience and ken. Nevertheless, this much is to be emphasized: knowledge is not to be reduced to crass sense data. *Intellection* is involved. "We are aware of relations, comparison, meanings, attitudes, references." [100] Why, Husserl would ask, does he use "awareness" when, as a matter of fact, relations, meanings, and the like are categorial imputations of the biological organism? But granting this kind of awareness had objective reference, what would be the difference between it and the awareness of existential data? Is that what he means by "intuition"? What role do sense data play? Simply that of a stimulus, and this stimulus with its proper cerebral effect "is just the starting-point of all sorts of directed and massive operations." [101] In this way intellection is given "operational activity." Perceiving is much more than awareness of sense data (perceiving is "always thicker"!). Sense data do not stand alone, but are enveloped "in a directed complex of meaning in the perceptual evidence." [102] This, we are led to believe, is not hard to understand when we remember that perceiving involves organic response.

The upshot of Sellar's epistemology up to this point is that sense-data are not enough to acquaint us with the world; there is much more involved, namely, the *operational, meaning-giving, referential activity* of the organism which he calls, in sum, "intellection." Yet this is not the whole story. After calling attention to the great difference between the employment of the intellect in its concern with logical entities or propositions, on the one hand, and empirical affairs, on the other, he continues in this vein by insisting that in the latter the human organism is concerned with existential matters: "the knower is concerned with things, events, and actual affairs. Such knowing involves judgments and the use of ontological categories such as space, time, thinghood, causality, event." [103] Sense-data, then, are "worked on" as it were, by the intellect when it is concerned with empirical affairs, and the instruments of such intellection are these ontological categories. They represent the equipment of the organism to deal with what would otherwise be an unintelligible world. (Husserl would call this sheer Kantianism.) As a result of this categorial intellection, our world resolves itself into a system of concepts. Fortunately for us, the organism is so equipped as to be provided with an organic act "with characteristics of a unitary synthetic art." [104] Clearly, from this, objects do not announce themselves either as qualities or exist-

---

101 *Ibid.*, pp. 202–3.   102 *Ibid.*, p. 202.   103 *Ibid.*, p. 207.
104 *Ibid.*, p. 209. The word "art" may be a misprint, but obviously its import is that of property or kind.

ences, but are what they are because of the judgmental, synthetic activity of the organism. Sellars himself says that in perceptual experience

> I denote and characterize an external thing made an object of my perceiving. It is equally clear that, for this position, concepts are not mere copies of sense-data but they are more of the nature of operative patterns.[105]

In this statement, of course, concepts are used synonymously with categories and are not to be viewed as ideational products. At any rate, Sellars believes that in this way he escapes the causal theory of sensationalism. That may be, but it is made at a great sacrifice, since, although he might refute sensationalism, he obviously falls into a form of subjective idealism, something which for him is presumably anathema.

What role, then, do sensory presentations serve? To control rational intellection, not to tell us anything of objects. This is evident from the judgmental character of perceptual experience, which somehow mysteriously "takes in the relations of things to one another." [106] In order to avoid this misunderstanding, however, Sellars hastens to add that this must not be construed as the doctrine of intuition, which holds for an immediate knowledge of the necessary connection between events. Quite the contrary, since the "judgmental character" of such experience means "only to perceive the spatial, temporal and executive order of molar bodies. This means that I employ categories of this type in my interpretation of things." [107] Data are given in and by the sensory field; they must be interpreted and related and organized by the use of categorial meanings, which are the property of the physical organism. Yet note how Sellars insists that his is a theory of "direct"

---

105 *Ibid.*, p. 209. Did he not mean, "made an object *by* my perceiving"?
106 *Ibid.*, p. 210.   107 *Ibid.*, p. 210.

knowledge. "We mean independent objects and we interpret these objects in terms of ideas." [108] But we intuit only data from the physical realm.[109] There must be drawn, to be sure, a distinction between the givenness of content and knowledge of the physical thing. Is the realm of existence "inferred"? Not at all. It is *affirmed* "through the very pressure and suggestion of our experience." [110]

But does he ever solve the problem of what objects are and how we know them? Hardly. Notice the ambiguity of his statements: only content is intuited, but "internally or in the percipient himself, we have the content of perception." [111] It follows, naturally, that "the content with which we automatically clothe these acknowledged realities is subjective." [112] First content is intuited (whatever that can possibly mean in his system), then it is described as subjective, something with which we embellish reality. The knowledge relation is allegedly "direct." Content, now subjective, hence our own operational product, now objective, hence other than the percipient, is somehow assigned to the object itself. There is no other way to interpret such observations as, "Knowledge is just the insight into the nature of the object that is *made possible by the contents which reflect* it in consciousness." [113] In this way he allegedly repudiated the new realism. He is willing to admit "the fact of causal mediation while yet proclaiming that the object affirmed and intended is known in terms of the content presented to the knowing self." [114] Presented by what? Perhaps God—since he draws such a cleavage between content and physical reality. But no, that would be Berkeleyanism. Yet note that "the content given is the essence of the object." [115] Sellars goes on to

108 Sellars, *Essays in Critical Realism*, p. 194.   109 *Ibid.*, p. 195.
110 *Ibid.*, p. 195.   111 *Ibid.*, p. 196.   112 *Ibid.*, p. 197.
113 *Ibid.*, p. 200. Italics mine.   114 *Ibid.*, p. 200.   115 *Ibid.*

explain that "the content is relevant to the object, that it has a sort of revelatory identity with the object, that it contains its structure, position, and changes." [116]

It can readily be seen that these doctrines of Sellars would be acceptable to most idealists, particularly absolute idealists.[117] In fact, his viewpoint is strictly that of absolute idealism until, apparently faced with the problem of clarifying the relational and organized character of experience, he betrays his previous standpoint and, instead of saying that it is the physical organism or mind-brain that is responsible for the world announcing itself as an organized whole, he affirms in no uncertain terms that things are in dynamic relation "because they are so disclosed by our data." [118] This is obviously vacillation pure and simple. First we are led to believe that relations are categorial, and that means judgmental, coming from the subjective whole of experience; then it is affirmed that these dynamic relations are *disclosed* by the sense-data. This might be a source of much-needed comfort to the new realists, did Sellars not go on to say that even though our interpretive judgments possess objective reference, in no case whatever should this be described as meaning that "we literally intuit the object of perceiving." [119] As he himself says, in agreement with Hume, causal propositions are empirical and synthetic, but, as contrasted with Hume, they are also "perceptual and transcendent. In them we are judging perceptually the relation between thing and events." [120] In short, causal propositions are not a priori in any sense of the word, although referentially objective; in any particular case they may be rejected.

In this way Sellars believes that he escapes both sensa-

[116] *Ibid.*
[117] As pointed out by Bosanquet in *Contemporary Philosophy,* pp. 127 f.
[118] Sellars, *Philosophy of Physical Realism,* p. 211.
[119] *Ibid.*
[120] *Ibid.,* p. 212.

tionalistic empiricism and Platonic rationalism. Taking the perceptual experience as he finds it, he purports to have found in it simultaneously "sense-data, concepts and categories, all of which are founded on the organism and its situation." [121]

Lest it be thought, however, that the categories have no objective reference, it should be remembered that "the categories arise in us as expressions of ourselves as operationally immersed in the sea of being." [122] Our categories are well *founded* and therefore valid, since "Nature conforms to them because nature is their foundation." [123] How we can possibly know this conformity, when, by definition, all knowledge is judgmental and therefore, as with the idealists, a complex of ideas constructed of subjective patterns and categories, is left to the imagination of the reader. Does Sellars solve the problem merely by arguing that the mind is the brain and that its patterns are developed under control "and in relation to the organism as a whole"? [124] What Sellars actually means to say, of course, is that the organism is a part of this physical world and that he perforce must reject that sort of dualism which would make mind alien to the world of nature. Admirable as this may be, it nevertheless fails to explain the integral relationship between the categorial equipment of the organism and the world as a whole. This he could never do, since we cannot on his own arguments know the world *per se*. Moreover, Sellars never answers satisfactorily the problem of why we as human beings have such peculiar instruments of knowl-

---

[121] *Ibid.*, p. 213. Cf. *Essays in Critical Realism*, pp. 197–98, in which the "factors" of knowledge are "(1) the affirmation of an object or ideatum; (2) the idea or content given to the knowing self; and (3) the interpretation of the first in terms of the second."

[122] Sellars, *Philosophy of Physical Realism*, p. 216. See also his remarks on categories in *Essays in Critical Realism*, p. 204.

[123] Sellars, *Philosophy of Physical Realism*, p. 216.

[124] *Ibid.*, p. 216.

edge, while it is very obvious, judging from their behavior, that they are absent in other creatures whose organic constitution is so similar to ours.

Although, as is now widely known, Sellars rejects Drake and Strong's theory of essence, as well as that of Santayana,[125] it can be said, nevertheless, that, insofar as mind and cognition are concerned in general, they are all in agreement. In the first place, the theory of mind as substance is rejected in favor of that of mind as "mind-stuff" or brain or physical organism considered *in toto*. Second, each ends in a dualism between the perceived object-as-known and the (unknowable) physical object as it is in itself. Whereas Drake and Strong would bring psychic states or essences into the picture to explain how the inadequacy of sense data is overcome in perception, Sellars, according to the foregoing, utilizes categories. As a matter of fact, of course, there is not much difference, not only because of their common subjectivity, but because in both instances there is an additional (and foreign-to-reality) element brought in to explain knowledge *of*. Third, it follows that the things or objects of ordinary perception can in no manner be conceived as self-contained entities, as something in themselves and possessing certain qualities of their own. Consequently, fourth, the world of physical objects of science remains forever and absolutely separated from the things of normal intercourse with the world. Yet, fifth, the scientific, physical objects are somehow the cause of the things of normal perception. Finally, sixth, since the object of thought is in reality something that we cannot think about, *ex hypothesi* the realm of physical objects remains transcendent to every kind of experience. It is a *Ding-an-sich*, inaccessible to any kind of perception.

[125] *Ibid.*, pp. 163, 202, 416 f. The problem of essences as it concerns other critical realists will be considered later.

It need hardly be said that this in an impossible theory for phenomenology to accept. It is not made more attractive to Husserl whether sensible qualities are called secondary, or, as in the case of others, they remain in the domain of the physicist and hence of a geometrical and mathematical character. Aside from his refusal to attribute subsistential, existential, or any other kind of existence to the realm of essences, Husserl would find it impossible *on grounds of critical realism itself* to believe that there is any evidence that the objects of perception are in any way of the nature of the "physical" reality. He would consider ludicrous realism's use of the term "essence," since it is given no ontological status, yet performs the miracle of making all existence intelligible. The critical realist, to be sure, would urge that knowledge is prepositional, and with this Husserl would certainly agree. But the greatest difference between him and them is the *nature* of this prepositional property of knowledge, since, in the last analysis, the real question is not only the process of cognition but what is cognized. Husserl's treatment of such problems will become clear from the following considerations.

In his *Ideen,* Husserl called attention to the inadequacies of realism when he pointed out its definition of the physical thing, for which the thing that appears in sense perception must function, as nothing but mere appearance and therefore purely subjective. This he called the "image theory," and put realism in the same group as using the sign theory of perception.[126] Realism (as he interpreted it)

126 See particularly *Ideen,* § 43, pp. 78 f., and § 52, pp. 97 f. Husserl mentioned neither the new realism nor critical realism by name. This is difficult to understand since he vigorously attacked "realism" in *Ideen,* first published in 1913. He must have known of the new realism's "The Program and First Platform of Six Realists" (1910) and *The New Realism* (1912). He could not, of course, have referred to *Essays in Critical Realism* (1920). Yet strangely enough, in *Ideen* he gave (and attacked) the arguments of "Realism" as found in later critical realism (§ 52, pp. 97 f.). It

affirms that "what is really perceived (and, in the primary sense of the term, something appearing) is to be regarded from its side as appearance, i. e., the instinctive substructure of something else inherently alien to it and separated from it." [127] That of which perception's contents is the appearance is a concealed *cause* (*verborgene Ursache*) to be characterized only "indirectly" and "analogously" through mathematical concepts. Husserl believed that such theories were possible

only so long as we fail to keep persistently in mind, and to establish scientifically, the meaning of thing-givenness which lies in the *essentiality* of experience, and therefore likewise of "thing-in-general" the meaning which comprises the absolute standard of all reasonable statements concerning things.[128]

Yet, Husserl argued, it can easily be shown that if this "unknown cause" which has been assumed to exist, exists at all, "it must be *in principle* perceptible and experienceable—if not by us at least for other Egos who see better and farther than we do."[129] Then, second, it must be demonstrated "that the possible perception itself again, and with essential necessity, must be a perception through appearances, and that we have therefore fallen into an inevitable *regressus in infinitum.*"[130] Finally, third, it would be necessary to point out that in principle there is a great difference between "an explanation of the perceptually given events through causal realities hypothetically assumed, i. e., through unknown entities of the nature of a thing," and that which is allegedly "an explanation in the

---

might be that he was referring to G. E. Moore's "The Refutation of Idealism" (1903), William James' "Does Consciousness Exist?" (1904), or even Brentano's *Psychologie;* in a different connection he mentioned K. Twardowski's *Zur Lehre vom Inhalt und Gegenstand der Vorstellungen* (1894), a "realistic" development of the implications of Brentano's psychology. Cf. Morris, *Six Theories of Mind*, pp. 110 f., in which it is said there is no evidence of specific influence from the Germans, although Pitkin (a new realist) was a student of Husserl.

[127] *Ideen*, p. 97.   [128] *Ibid.*, p. 98.   [129] *Ibid.*, p. 98.   [130] *Ibid.*

sense of a physical means of explanation after the style of atoms, ions, and so forth." [131]

Now (he continued) let us take the position "that in physical method *the perceived thing itself* is always and in principle precisely the thing which the physicist studies and scientifically determines." [132] But this, of course, would be inadmissible to Husserl. In the first place, there is involved a separation between primary and secondary qualities, which he rejected because of his persuasion that knowledge is *knowledge of the object,* i. e., of its essential characteristics. There is no reason to believe that the sensational content of the physicist's experience is any more primary or of the nature of the object than that of normal apprehension. The so-called qualities of the physicist on these grounds would be just as much "copy" and "sign" theories as the appearances of normal sense perception.

The difficulty with an image or a sign is that, by hypothesis,

it signifies something that lies beyond it, which, could it but pass over into another form of presentation, into that of a dator intuition, might "itself" be seized. A sign or copy does not "reveal in itself" that which is signified (or copied).[133]

Actually, when this realistic theory is subjected to close scrutiny, it is seen that a thing which appears to sense, which has the sensory properties of shape, color, and so forth, is in fact not a sign for something else at all but *only a sign for itself*. This, then, would oppose Husserl's conviction that "it is a fundamental error" to suppose that perception "does not contact the thing itself." [134] As far as the physicist is concerned, the thing which allegedly appears with or in such sensory qualities is governed by him and makes its appearance under certain physical conditions created and fixed by him on general lines; these in turn serve as "the sign and symbol for a wealth

[131] *Ibid.*   [132] *Ibid.*, p. 99.   [133] *Ibid.*, p. 99.   [134] *Ibid.*, p. 78.

of causal properties for this identical thing, which as such affirm their presence in specific and familiar relations of dependence upon appearances." [135] But what is there declared—even when revealed in intentional unities of conscious experiences—is obviously, *in principle, transcendent.* This makes it clear that even in the so-called "higher transcendence" of the knowledge of the physicist, there is no reaching out beyond the world on the part of the Ego or its consciousness.

The consequence of this whole argument is that, for Husserl, physical thought builds itself on natural experience following the "rational motives" which the connections of experience possess or suggest; there is a compulsion to adopt certain forms of apprehending its data; a construction of such intentional systems as are demanded by the instance; a utilization of them for the "theoretical determination" of things as experienced through the senses. Hence the opposition between the thing of plain sensory *imaginatio* and the thing of the physical *intellectio.* "The world" becomes *eine unbekannte Welt von Dingrealitäten an sich,* "a hypothetical substructure devised to give the *causal* explanation of appearances." [136]

Sensory things, in short, are *widersinnigerweise* connected with physical things *through causality.* This is the standpoint of realism. What is the explanation of its difficulties? It confuses, by reason of their "mere subjectivity," sensory appearances, i. e., "the appearing objects *as such* (which are in fact already transcendent) with the absolute experiences which constitute them." [137] And then absolute experiences are further confounded with experiences of the appearing, of empirical consciousness generally. Causality becomes a mythical bond of union between physical being and subjective being, the latter of which "appears" in immediate experience; the so-called subjective things

[135] *Ibid.,* p. 100.   [136] *Ibid.,* p. 101.   [137] *Ibid.,* p. 101.

of sense are then declared to be "secondary qualities."
Ultimately, then, causality plays the role of a mysterious
bond between physical being, on the one hand, and absolute consciousness or, more specifically, the pure experiences of the experiencing consciousness, on the other. The
absoluteness of physical being is thereby allegedly established. This was an absurdity to Husserl, since it amounts
to transforming physical nature which, on realism's own
arguments, is the "intentional correlate of logically determining thought," [138] *into an absolute* which itself is
"unknown" and thereby can never be itself apprehended.
By the nature of the case, we are so far separated from it
that we can know nothing of it; yet causality is attributed
to it. But this is logically inconsistent since, on realism's
own arguments, causality *in principle* belongs only to the
constituted world—for Husserl this meant, of course, "the
constituted intentional world." [139] Pratt's concept of "givenness" [140] is a typical example of the sort of realism Husserl was here controverting. In the first place, he looks to
natural science (particularly physiology and psychology)
for his materials. Then, second, when discussing "datum,"
he tells us "meaning" is "that which we find directly given
to our thought," [141] although meaning had already been
described as something "attributed" to sensory data.[142]
But note this contradiction: as the "active side" of perception meaning is endowed by the perceiver; yet it has
"outer references or *attribution* to some existent outer object. . . . (Datum) is unreflectively affirmed of some physical object existing in an external spatial world." [143] Now
how can anything be both *given* and *attributed?* Pratt's
theory is nothing but the time-worn "sign" theory. A
quality group *"means more than it is."* [144] While repre-

---

[138] *Ibid.*

[140] Pratt, *Essays in Critical Realism*, pp. 85 f.

[142] *Ibid.*, p. 89.   [143] *Ibid.*, p. 92.

[139] *Ibid.*, p. 101.

[141] *Ibid.*, p. 90.

[144] *Ibid.*, p. 96.

senting or referring to a physical object, the quality group itself is not physical. It is a sign or "token," since it means or implies the presence and "to a considerable extent" the nature of some active entity outside it. First, quality group or datum is given; now it is declared the *means* of "perceiving the object." [145] "To mean" signifies the outer reference of cognition, the "innate tendency to attribute the datum to some external object." [146] The object is "transcendent," the datum tells us of it, yet the datum (or "quality group") is of our own making, and is "attributed" to the unknown object!

Husserl's answer to realism is, of course, to be found in his doctrine of intuition of essences in perception. It will be remembered how he broadened the concept of experience to include much more than the critical realists allow, i. e., he viewed empirical experience involving the bodily organism not only as just one kind of experience but as playing a minor role, even in sense perception. To be sure, without a bodily organism there could be no perception of empirical objects. But does that mean that the bodily organism is in any way responsible for, let alone constitutive of the objects of sense experience? Might as well say that because a carpenter needs tools to construct a house, the house comes into being *because* of those tools alone. In sense perception the body plays the part only of permitting the Ego in this particular frame of reference to be spatially located in its activities. In other words, the body receives certain sense impressions from objects which are of like nature; but these sense impressions, these "vibrations" *considered in themselves,* are actually "neutral" and tell us nothing about anything. Sense data serve the sole purpose of announcing the *Dasein* of objects. The real problem of an epistemology of perception is what there is in the perceiving process which makes possible *meaning*

[145] *Ibid.*, p. 96. [146] *Ibid.*, p. 97.

or whatness. This is evident when one follows Husserl's analysis of perception of things and sees that, since a thing is given necessarily in mere "modes of appearing," the sense object considered as sense data is perspectival. Yet perception itself is not perspectival insofar as meaning is concerned. Hence, if it be granted that perception says something about the object, or rather (on grounds of phenomenology) that it allows the object to say something of itself, and that meaning is not perspectival, it follows that Husserl must define sense perception in a way radically different from every kind of realism. The presentationalism of new realism falls when an analysis of sensations is made; the representationalism of critical realism collapses when one considers the absolute severance between the appearance and the reality of things. The real concern for the epistemologist is to show how it is possible (if idealism is to be avoided) to know the thing itself in perception. Husserl believed that he did this with his doctrine of essences and intuition.

It should be clear from the foregoing why Husserl would consider the concept of essences as held by Sellars, Santayana, Drake, Strong, *et al.* as impossible.[147] In the last

147 With the possible exception of Strong's concept as found in *Essays in Critical Realism*, pp. 223 f. (in which is found, if I interpret him correctly, a theory of essences radically different from that in *A Theory of Knowledge* and *Essays on the Natural Origin of the Mind*). At any rate, Husserl would agree with Strong (in *Essays in Critical Realism*), on the following points: (1) we must distinguish between the "that" and the "what"; (2) essences are not to be identified with the *existential* thing perceived; (3) essence is the concrete nature of things; (4) the *datum* of sense perception is "the logical essence of the real thing" (p. 223); (5) essence represents the logical or *essential* identity of the real thing; (6) essence is a universal, and hence "the essence given and the essences embodied in the object are not two but one" (p. 241); (7) sense perception, so conceived, *can* "rest directly on the object" (p. 241). These concepts are radically different from those of essence as "psychic state" or an "imputation" (*Essays on the Natural Origin of the Mind*), with which Husserl would disagree. Morris, in *Six Theories of Mind* (p. 230), says that Strong has repudiated his "precious conception" of essence which he had borrowed from Santayana (*Essays in Critical Realism*, p. 224 n.).

analysis, if the above is an accurate interpretation, essence means for them nothing but a psychological or subjective imputation of something that has somehow been
brought into actuality through the activity of the self, in
order to organize what would otherwise be a group of
chaotic sensations. In Husserl's case, essence was a datum
of direct intuition, not something gratuitously given by
the self. For realism, essence is adventitious to objects; for
Husserl essence *is* the object, its intrinsic nature. In short,
he would reject the realists' doctrine of essence for the
same reason that he rejected most idealistic viewpoints and,
as just seen, Sellars's idea of a categorial organism.[148] They
all amount to the same thing, viz., the separation of the
subject from the object, the unbridgeable abyss between
what appears in sensibility and the cause of the appearance.

In the final analysis all of these theories, on Husserlian
grounds, are based on nothing but pure prejudice, namely,
that organic, empirical experience is the only kind admis-
sible. This was just too naïve for Husserl; it was relying entirely too much upon common sense.[149]

What, in normal perception, does the Ego have as content? What is commonly referred to as *sensa;* but this term
means for Husserl *eidetic* qualities, which are not to be
defined in terms of space and time, even though they comprise, in a particular space and time-spot, the object *per
se.* What role does the Ego play? Does it create its ob-

[148] What Sellers calls "categories" is for Husserl essences. Cf. chap. v,
§ 5, pp. 177–204, in which I show Husserl's distinction between formal
(unity, multiplicity, identity, and so forth) and material (nature, race,
perceptual qualities, and the like) essences. The real difference between
the two, of course, is that Sellars's categories are concepts, whereas Husserl's essences are directly intuited data or objects of a realm existing in
its own right, hence not "mental constructions."

[149] On the other hand, it is obvious that Husserl would have nothing
to do with idealism in the traditional sense, except insofar as he affirmed
the indubitability of the Ego or self (*Ideen,* pp. 85 f.).

jects? No, this would be idealism. Does it initiate any activity? Yes—intentional activity, which makes possible intuitive cognition of the essences. In this sense and *in this sense alone* can the Ego be said to constitute its objects. But on Husserlian grounds knowledge is still knowledge *of*. In this sense he agreed with the realists. Hence it is in his concept of intuitive cognition and his broadening of experience, his definition of the Ego, and his doctrine of essences that we find what sharply differentiates him from both the realist and the idealist.

§ 5. *Phenomenology as a Science*

Of all the charges brought against phenomenology, probably the most preposterous is that which claims it is psychology, or more particularly, "descriptive psychology." Every careful student of phenomenology would agree that such a statement is the result not only of an inadequate understanding of Husserl's position but of the nature of psychology as well. This was a matter of deep concern to Husserl, and he went to great lengths to dispel the misinterpretation. On one occasion he wrote, in fact, as follows: [150]

Among those who thrust aside the phenomenological reduction as a philosophically irrelevant eccentricity (whereby, to be sure, they destroy the whole meaning both of the work and my phenomenology, and leave only an a priori psychology) it happens frequently that this residual psychology is identified essentially with Franz Brentano's psychology of intentionality. While I remember my genial teacher with profound respect and gratitude, and view his transformation of the scholastic concept of intentionality into a descriptive fundamental concept of psychology as a great discovery, through which alone phenomenology is possible, it is nevertheless necessary to distinguish sharply between the pure psychology implicitly contained in my transcendental phenomenology and

---

[150] "Nachwort," pp. 564–65.

Brentano's psychology. The same is true of his "psychognosis," limited as it is to pure description in the region of inner experience. It is indeed "phenomenological" psychology if, as has so frequently occurred at the present time, there is given the title "phenomenological" to every psychological investigation conducted within the sphere of "inner experience" and, grouping together all such studies, one speaks of a phenomenological psychology. Then the latter (quite part from its name) leads us naturally to John Locke and his school, including John Stuart Mill. One can then say that there is found in D. Hume's *Treatise* the first systematic sketch of a pure (although not eidetic) phenomenology, and particularly that of the first volume wherein is found the first sketch of a phenomenology of experience. Certainly the Humian designation of psychology conceals the hitherto unremarked fact that Hume (according to commonly accepted opinion) was in no way a psychologist but that his *Treatise* is much more an actual "transcendental" phenomenology although perverted with sensualism. Like his great predecessor, Berkeley, he is regarded as a psychologist and as such has wielded his influence. Hence, excluding all transcendental questions it is this whole "phenomenological" school alone which demands our consideration. Characteristic of it and of its psychology is the concept contained in Locke's "white paper" simile of the pure soul as a complex or conglomerate of temporally contemporaneous and successive data, which run their course according to rules partly their own and partly psychophysical. Descriptive psychology would have, then, the role of distinguishing and classifying the fundamental types of these "sense-data," data of "inner experience" as well as the elementary basic forms of their complexes. Explanatory psychology would discover the rules of genetic formations and transformations—as in the case of natural science, with similar methods. Quite naturally . . . since pure psychical being or the psychical life is regarded as a nature-resembling flow of events in a quasi-space of consciousness. On grounds of principle, it obviously makes no difference whether psychical "data" are blown together "atomistically" like heaps of sand (although according to empirical laws) or whether they are viewed as parts of wholes which, by empirical or a priori necessity, can alone come forward as such parts, and supremely, perhaps, within the whole of the entire consciousness, fettered rigidly as it is to a form of the whole. In short, both atomistic and *Gestalt* psychology remain, in principle, psychological "naturalism" (as defined above) which, remembering what has been said of the "inner sense," may be termed "sensationalism." Clearly Brentano's psychology of intentionality is a part of this inherited naturalism, although a reforming factor in this sense, that it has introduced into psychology the universal and descriptive root-concept of intentionality.

Psychology is a "positive" science with objects of the "natural" world as materials of investigation; its interest is in experience (*Erfahrung*); it is a science of "facts" (*Tatsachen*) in Hume's sense of the word. In brief, it is a science of "realities" dealing with psychologically "real" events.

Unquestionably the stigma of descriptive psychology is traceable not only to Husserl's appropriation, to a certain extent, of Brentano's psychology of intentionality, but also to Husserl's careless use of the term in his earlier writings (particularly the first edition of *Logische Untersuchungen*) to define his own position. Yet the mere fact that phenomenology has to do with "consciousness," with all types of psychical experiences, including acts and their correlates, is no ground for such a charge. Phenomenology claims a "new" way of establishing the concept of pure consciousness and its contents and, as has been already seen, by consciousness it does not mean the empirical consciousness of the psychophysical organism in relation to a physical world, the field which psychology investigates, but "pure" consciousness of the *geistig* Ego. "Transcendental" phenomenology is not a science of facts, but a science of eidetic Being (the "content" of pure consciousness), and aims exclusively at substantiating and clarifying *Wesenserkenntnisse,* knowledge of essences. Moreover, the phenomena of transcendental phenomenology are "irreal," non-real (a concept abhorrent to Brentano); they are in-tuitively experienced and transcendentally "reduced," not factually experienced and empirically "observed." As early as 1903, in order to avoid any misunderstanding in this regard, Husserl had written that

Phenomenology is no longer to be described as "descriptive psychology." In the strictest sense of the word it is not. Its descriptions are not of experiences or classes of experiences of empirical persons; for it knows nothing about, or concerns itself with nothing of, persons or the I or other I's or personal experiences, as well as the experiences of others. . . . Phenomenological description investigates in the strictest sense that which is given, and experience as it is in and of itself. It analyzes, for instance, the real appearance, not that which appears in it, and it thrusts aside those apperceptions by virtue of whose appearance and appearing it is related to the I to which it appears. The critical clarification built upon such an epistemological analysis is nothing more than intuitive, adequate abstraction which embraces in phenomenological fixation the universal essence, and brings "the true and proper content of logical concepts and laws to consciousness, and with it, clear and insightful understanding."[151]

Since Husserl's indebtedness to Brentano is not only acknowledged by him but well known in philosophic circles, regard should be given to at least four essential differences between the two, and a careful consideration of these should convince with finality anyone that psychology and phenomenology are in no way to be identified.

First, there is the manner in which each defines "phenomena." Said Brentano, "The entire world of our appearances falls into two great classes: those of physical, and those of psychical phenomena."[152] To elaborate his position, he described the "psychical" in this manner.

---

[151] From *"Bericht über deutsche Schriften zur Logik," Archiv für systematische Philosophie,* IX (1903). After the first edition of *LU,* Husserl dropped the term "descriptive psychology" altogether.

[152] *PES* I, 109. Cf. pp. 109 f. for his lengthy discussion of the concept of "phenomenon."

An instance of psychical phenomena is found in every idea arising through sensation or phantasy; and I understand here under idea not that which is ideated but the *act of ideating*. Some examples of what I mean are the hearing of a tone, the seeing of a colored object, having a sensation of cold or warmth, including similar products of phantasy; also there is the thinking of a universal concept. . . . Further, every judgment, memory, expectation, inference, conviction, or opinion, every doubt—each is a psychical phenomenon. Moreover, so is every emotion, joy, sadness, fear, hope, courage, despair, anger, love, hate, desire, will, intention, astonishment, wonder, contempt, etc.[153]

Psychical phenomena are "ideas," and as such they have ideas as their "foundation." All the rest are "physical." All psychical phenomena are "without extension." Yet this does not completely define them, since they also have "intentional inexistence," i. e., *die Beziehung auf etwas als Objekt*.[154] Furthermore, the psychical is exclusively the object of "inner" perception for it alone is perceived with immediate evidence; as a matter of fact, *it alone is perceived in the strict sense of the word*. Hence only those phenomena corresponding to the psychical, in addition to possessing "intentional inexistence" are also of "real existence." Moreover, psychical phenomena appear as a "unity": "The entire multiplicity of psychical phenomena which appear in inner perception disclose themselves always as a unity, while physical phenomena, which simultaneously are seized through so-called external perception, do not appear as a unity."[155]

Of "physical" phenomena, Brentano said, "there are a color, a figure, a landscape, which I see; a chord which I hear; warmth, cold, smell which I sense; included are similar forms which appear to me in phantasy."[156] Brentano thus means by physical phenomena those that are

153 *Ibid.*, p. 112. This quotation, I know, has already been given but it is repeated because of its importance.
154 *Ibid.*, p. 137.   155 *Ibid.*, p. 135.   156 *Ibid.*, p. 112.

given *anschaulich,* perceptually: *Es handelt sich bei all dem um Objekte unserer Empfindungen, um Empfundenes.*[157] We do not "see" a landscape, but something "extended," "colored," and so forth:

"Landscape" is no sensory quality and above all not an object of sense perception. That which one sees when one "sees" a landscape is forms of colors, expanded and extended. Everything else is a matter of judgment and conceptual interpretation of judgment.[158]

By "idea," then, Brentano meant not that which is ideated, but *the act of ideating,* e. g., hearing and seeing, and "thinking" of universal concepts.

Illustrative of physical phenomena are color, figure, cold, and warmth, i. e., every image that appears in fantasy or imagination; after Aristotle: *per accidens sensibel.* It follows from this that, in the last analysis, physical phenomena, those of so-called external perception are, strictly speaking, not "perceived" objects at all, since they are really grounded in psychical phenomena. As objects of "inner perception," psychical phenomena alone are perceived *"mit unmittelbarer Evidenz;* they alone are perceived in the strict sense of the word." [159] Ideating constitutes the ground of all psychical acts, of all experiences. Physical phenomena are actually only "content" or "object" of psychical phenomena. "Belief" in the psychical is self-evident and easy; belief in the physical, which itself is ideated, must be "forced." There can be no certain assurance of the existence of physical phenomena. To the psychical alone, in addition to intentional existence can be attributed *"wirkliche Existenz."*

Brentano denied "ideal, timeless, universal objects," while Husserl affirmed that essences are just as "real" as any other kind of "object." *Eidos,* however, is neither "psychical" nor "physical." It is simply the object of a

157 *Ibid.,* p. 266.   158 *Ibid.,* p. 267.   159 *Ibid.,* p. 137.

peculiar kind of experience, intuition. Clearly, Brentano could never countenance this. *Wesenschau* would be regarded by him as a *Fiktion* unless it meant no more than "abstracting, simplifying, generalizing, ideating, i. e., ideating which only individualizes the thing (realities) *in specie specialissima.*" [160] But Husserl certainly meant much more than that by his concept.

Husserl drew no distinction of any kind between "psychical" and "physical" phenomena. Everything is a "phenomenon" which "presents itself." Moreover, as seen in the discussion of "Fact and Essence," ultimately phenomenon means *essence,* which, of course, could not be defined now as "psychical," now as "physical." Essences are neither.

Husserl, then, as contrasted with Brentano, was interested in "transcendentally pure" phenomena, or, more properly, essences, which are the content of "pure" consciousness, and are "intuited" as a result of intentional activity directed by the pure Ego. The phenomenological reductions, he believed, render it possible that these phenomena are "purified" and the whole world "bracketed," essences so becoming the objects of a special kind of examination.

Second, both Brentano and Husserl had consciousness as an object of investigation, yet, as against his teacher's interest in "empirical" consciousness, Husserl's ultimate objective was the consciousness that experiences "pure" objects, which has as its object and content nonspatial and nontemporal (irreal) essences. Husserl, of course, always acknowledged his indebtedness to Brentano for calling his attention to the "intentional character" which psychical phenomena have as their peculiarity, particularly in respect to their character of being experienced, *Erlebtwerdens.* Contained in this concept is the differentiation

[160] *Ibid.,* p. xix.

between the subjective act of experiencing and the objective object or content to which the act is intentionally directed. To be sure, Brentano himself later changed this to state that only the "real" can be the object of our representation, and then the terminus, object, or content, must be systematically taken as "expression." Consciousness, on this basis, would be not a relation but a *relativeness*. In either instance, however, the "natural" attitude is still there, since actually the spaciotemporal world is the only (object) world. This is precisely the point of departure for Husserl. Abstract from these experiences all contingency, all relation to the empirical "I" and its body, and one arrives at the pure essence of experiences, the residue that is known and seized by pure consciousness. These he makes his principal object of investigation. Furthermore, real consciousness is "conditioned" by pure consciousness; empirical consciousness, as interred in the spaciotemporal world, is conditioned by it and by a body. Brentano, as against this, had denied any consciousness and any objects other than the empirical, but according to Husserl pure consciousness is *"Urkategorie des Seins überhaupt,"* in which all Being is rooted.[161] Since Brentano had denied essence and eidetic experience, he likewise disdained the value of his student's phenomenology as a science of *Wesenserkenntnis.*

Third, relative to method, Brentano studied empirical experience and was interested only in the contingent "here and now," in that which is given in the experience of "matters-of-fact"; his psychology is *"die Wissenschaft von den psychischen Phänomenon."* [162] As opposed to this, Husserl's interest lay not in the contingent here and now, and inevitably he could not employ any method which had contingency as the object of study. His explicit purpose, among others, was greater, deeper *Einsicht* into es-

sences, and to accomplish this he employed intuitive ideation alone which, indeed, is an integral part of the
method of the reductions. He would investigate "absolute
experience" and the contents of pure consciousness. He
not only scorned Brentano's emphasis upon empirical experience; he bracketed it entirely.

Finally (fourth), Brentano's psychology is clearly *Tatsachenwissenschaft,* a science of facts. But Husserl's phenomenology is *Wesenswissenschaft,* and it would divorce
itself completely from all contingency and deliberately
direct itself to the *Nichttatsächliches.* This is necessary in
order to seize upon the essentiality of a thing "in its
purity." Even in *Logische Untersuchungen,* when Husserl committed the blunder of calling his phenomenology
"descriptive psychology," he meant thereby a "pure" psychology, which would be a priori because of its interest
in pure inner experience, in pure intentionality, and the
pure components yielded in such a study.

These observations should make it clear that Husserl's
phenomenology cannot be described as "descriptive" (or
any other kind of) "psychology."

As a science, phenomenology thus aims at *Wesenserkenntnis,* and as such "its sole task and service is to
clarify the meaning of this world, the precise sense in
which everyone accepts it, and with unquestionable right,
as really existing." [163] In this statement of aim there are
at least three important implications. First, there is a
"universe," a "natural world" (*Natur*), which exists (*ist*);
second, this world has meaning and significance; finally,
and most important of all, both the world and its meaning
are accessible in experience to our (eidetic) apprehension and comprehension. Among other things, Husserl's
punctum saliens was to emphasize the *experienceability*
of the world and its essence-structure, as well as to insti-

163 "Nachwort," p. 462.

tute an investigation of its essentiality and the possible fruits of such knowledge.

Husserl, while elaborating his method of phenomenological reductions, not only drew a distinction between fact and essence, but went further and differentiated between "exact" or mathematical essence and "vague" or morphological essence.[164] The exact essence is related to a definite manifold; vague essence is related to an indefinite manifold. Possibly an elaboration of this distinction will assist in elucidating Husserl's concept of phenomenology as a science.

Obviously, Husserl must not only distinguish between empirical and eidetic sciences, but, owing to the aforementioned differentiation between exact and vague essence, he is required to describe more sharply the sciences investigating them. Husserl developed his position in this regard by first defining, as regards exact essence, what he meant by "definite manifold," or "mathematical manifold in the pregnant sense of the term." [165] How he did so can be best described in his own words.

It is sharply characterized as follows, that a finite number of concepts and propositions, which are drawn as required from the essential nature of the domain under consideration, determines completely and unambiguously, on lines of pure analytic necessity, the totality of all possible formations in tne domain, so that in principle, therefore, nothing further remains open.

It can also be put this way: a manifold of this type has the distinctive property of being "mathematically exhaustively definable." The "definition" lies in the system of axiomatic concepts and axioms; the "mathematically exhaustive" element lies herein: the definitive assertions in the relation to the manifold imply the greatest conceivable prejudice—nothing further remains undetermined.

[164] Cf. *Ideen,* §§ 72–74, and pp. 133 f.
[165] *Ideen,* p. 135.

An equivalent of the concept of a definite manifold lies also in the following propositions:

Every proposition constructed out of the specified axiomatic concepts, and in accordance with any logical form whatsoever, is either a pure formal-logical implication of the axioms, or is the opposite of what they imply, and formally derivable from these, that is, formally contradicting the axioms; the contradictory opposite would then be a formal-logical implication of the axioms. In a mathematically definite manifold the concepts "true" and "formal-logical implications of axioms" are equivalent, and likewise are the concepts "false" and "formal-logical opposite of the axioms."

I also call a system of axioms which, on purely analytic lines, "exhaustively defines" a manifold in the way described, a *definite system of axioms;* every deductive discipline which rests on such a system is a *definite* discipline, or one that is *mathematical* in the pregnant sense of the term.[166]

Geometry is an example of a science of exact essence, and it is representative of a "material" mathematics. Once again, let Husserl speak for himself.

If we now glance at the familiar eidetic sciences we are struck by the fact that they do not proceed *descriptively,* that, for instance, geometry does not in single intuitions seize, describe, and classify according to order the lowest eidetic differences, i. e., the innumerable spatial figures that can be drawn in space—as do sciences in respect of empirical, natural formations.

Geometry, on the other hand, gives a few types of basic constructions, e. g., the ideas of body, surface, point, angle, etc., the same which play the determining role in "axioms." With the help of axioms, i. e., of primitive laws of Essentiality, it is now in the position to infer inductively, in the form of exact determining concepts which represent essences that in general remain alien to our intuitions, *all* forms that "exist" in space, i. e., all spatial forms that are ideally possible and all the essential relations belonging to them. The essential

166 *Ibid.,* pp. 135–36.

generic nature of the sphere of geometry, and accordingly the pure nature of space, is so constituted that geometry can be fully certain of controlling, with precision, through its method, all possible cases.[167]

In short, the great variety of spatial formations has "a remarkably logical basic property" which Husserl called "definite" manifold. Such a manifold is the object of geometry, a concrete, eidetic discipline. Its data are "experiential" essences, they are *Konkreta;* they are "mathematically, exhaustively definable."

Since he had drawn the distinction between exact and vague essence and the sciences thereof, Husserl inquired, Is the stream of consciousness a genuine, mathematical manifold? Does it actually resemble physical nature? Is it a concrete definite manifold? He answered that the stream of consciousness, as datum, *cannot be examined or known as are the data of mathematics.* The stream of consciousness is an "indefinite manifold," and can be characterized by the fact that it excludes any "exhaustive" determination out of a finite number of concepts and propositions. Any formulations about it would therefore be, in principle, "inexact," and, accordingly, anything known about it and said about it would be "inexact." The essence of the stream of consciousness can be known only through ideation; on the other hand

Geometrical concepts are "ideal" concepts, they express something which one cannot "see"; their "origin," and therefore also their content, is essentially other than that of the descriptive concepts which express the essential nature of things as taken directly from simple perception, and not anything "ideal." Exact concepts have their correlates in essences, which have the character of "ideas" in the Kantian sense. As against these ideas or ideal essences stand the morphological essences, as correlates of descriptive concepts.[168]

---

[167] *Ibid.*, p. 135.
[168] *Ibid.*, p. 138.

Exact sciences have a "constancy" and "pure distinguish-ability" of generic concepts or generic essences, having their scope within the "flux of things" (*im Fliessenden*), which are totally lacking in "purely descriptive sciences." Exact and descriptive sciences cannot supplant each other, although they can "unite" their energies for certain ends. It is clear, however, that no matter how far exact science develops, since it operates "with ideal substructions," it can never dispose of the original and authentic tasks of pure description.[169]

Phenomenology, then, can be only "descriptive." Its "field," the essence of "pure transcendental experiences," is such that it cannot be a *Geometrie der Erlebnisse*. Its province is to seize "eidetically in pure intuition" "re-duced" experiences. In order to demonstrate that phenom-enology, although not "exact," "has its own justifica-tion," [170] Husserl argued that one of the peculiar aspects of consciousness is that it is perpetually "fluctuating in different dimensions"; from this it follows that it would obviously be impossible to fix any of its "eidetic con-creta" or any of their constitutive momenta with "concep-tual exactness." Take, for example, an experience of the genus "imagery of a thing" (*dingliche Phantasie*), whether it be given in phenomenologically immanent perception or in a "reduced" intuition. What would be the object of phenomenological examination? The "phenomenological particular," i. e., the *eidetic particularity,* the *Dingphan-tasie*

in the complete fullness of its concretion, precisely as it enters into the flow of experience, with the exact determinacy or in-determinacy with which it allows its thing to appear now from this, now from that side, and with that clearness or obscurity, that fluctuating distinctness and intermittent obscurity, etc., which are peculiar to it.[171]

---

169 *Ibid.,* p. 139.   170 *Ibid.,* pp. 139 f.   171 *Ibid.,* pp. 139–40.

Phenomenology ignores only the individuation, the particular element, while bringing into "eidetic consciousness" the whole "essence-content" in the fullness of its concreteness. This essential content it sees insightfully as an "ideally identical essence," which, as with every essence, could particularize itself not only *hic et nunc,* but in innumerable instances. Unquestionably from this standpoint it would be impossible to establish a conceptual or "terminological" fixation of this or any other similarly flowing concretum, and the same applies "to each of its immediate, but none the less flowing, parts and abstract aspects." [172]

The foregoing has to do with Husserl's description of his phenomenological determination of "eidetic singularities." What, he asked, of the essences "of higher levels"? [173]

First of all, they are capable of "stable distinction, identifying perpetuity, strict conceptual apprehension, and of analysis into component essences." [174] Accordingly, they could be made the subject of comprehensive scientific description.

Thus, second, the "generic essence of perception in general" can be described and determined with *strict* concepts; the same can be done with "subordinate species," e. g., perception of physical "thinghood" and animal natures, of memory, empathy, and will. But the "highest generalities," according to Husserl, are "experience in general, *cogitatio* in general, which make possible the comprehensive descriptions of essences." [175] Curiously enough, inherent in the nature of apprehension, analysis, and description of essences is "no corresponding dependence of accomplishments at higher grades on what is done at the lower." [176] No systematic inductive procedure, no

[172] *Ibid.,* p. 140.   [173] *Ibid.,* pp. 139 f.   [174] *Ibid.,* p. 140.
[175] *Ibid.*   [176] *Ibid.*

"gradual ascent up the ladder of generality," can be demanded as method.

It would follow from this (third) that "deductive theorizing" plays no role in phenomenology. Husserl did not mean, to be sure, that "mediate inferences" are categorically forbidden; his point here was simply that since all knowledge of scientific phenomenology is "descriptive," i. e., adjusted purely to the immanent sphere, inferences are valueless because they are "unintuitable" ways and means of description. If they have any function at all, it is only that of a "methodological meaning," namely, the role of an introduction to "facts" which ensuing direct essence-insight must "bring to givenness." Analogies and conjectures about "essential relations" there may be, from which inferences might be drawn, but in the end the conjectures "must be redeemed" by the "real vision of essence-connections." [177]

Husserl, then, viewed as a "misleading prejudice" the supposition that the methods of historical a priori sciences, which are entirely *exact* ideal sciences, are the only authentic patterns of procedure. "Exactness" is not enough, since, considered in its historical sense, it is not even necessary (let it not be concluded from this, however, that Husserl was not an "exact" thinker!) . Transcendental phenomenology, as the descriptive science of eidetic Being, of *Wesen*, "belongs to a main class of eidetic science totally different from that of which mathematical sciences are a member." [178]

Since the stream of consciousness is not a "definite manifold," phenomenology, from the standpoint of method, is a descriptive doctrine of essences of pure experience.

The above should serve to explain on what grounds Husserl's eidetic phenomenology claimed to be the Sci-

[177] *Ibid.*, p. 141.   [178] *Ibid.*

ence of all sciences. As such, of course, it would be unique, it would be "a science covering a new field of experience, exclusively its own, that of 'transcendental subjectivity.' " [179] This "transcendental" yet direct experience would be subjected to a method of examination, which, as we now know, he called phenomenological reduction. His phenomenology is "a priori" because it is an "eidetic" science "directed upon the original, intuitable universal." [180] Furthermore, phenomenology would be purely "eidetic description," and would restrict itself "to the realm of immediately insightful essential structures of transcendental subjectivity." [181]

Husserl meant that phenomenology was a "Science of science" because it examined, among other things, the *bases* of all positive sciences, whether psychical or physical. All scientific investigation and knowledge, he averred, really "assume" eidetic knowledge as the basic instrument of work. As Boyce Gibson so aptly expresses it, since Husserl was in quest of a "pure logic" of Ideas or meanings, phenomenology would accordingly deal with "pure meanings in their logical interrelations, i. e., with pure ideal content only. . . . Every science presupposes the validity of science itself, and therefore all the implied notions of truth, proposition, subject, predicate, object, property, relation, etc." [182] As a philosophy, its task would be to study the necessities and laws and identities resident in the pure experiences of the Ego, and to do this is to employ intuitive ideation as an instrument for investigating the realm of essences. Husserl held that his phenomenology discovered that the essentialities of everyday experience, as well as those of scientific investigation, are "intuited" contents, i. e., data of pure consciousness. As the discipline

179 "Nachwort," p. 552.   180 *Ibid.*   181 *Ibid.*, p. 553.
182 Gibson, "The Problem of the Real and Ideal in the Phenomenology of Husserl," p. 314.

designed to discover the foundation of all principles and
bases of other sciences, it would thus be "a science of the
conditions upon which the very intelligibility of science
itself depends." [183]

Recalling what was said of the natural standpoint and
the empirical sciences and how they are to be held in
contrast to phenomenology and its standpoint, it is clear
that phenomenology would never have to presuppose or
have recourse to "scientific" knowledge. All positive sciences deal with the *Tatsachenwelt* or, better still, each
science deals with a "part" of it. But once there is effected
a change to the phenomenological attitude, even the
world and the results of positive science are "bracketed"
and no judgment made about them. There is an eidetic
connection which obtains between particular objects and
essences and which is such that "to each individual object
there belongs, as *its* essence, a state of essential Being just
as, conversely, to each essence there corresponds possible
particulars as its factual instances." [184] Here, according to
Husserl, is the ground for a corresponding reciprocal relationship between sciences of fact and sciences of essence.

To be sure, Husserl has granted that there are already
pure sciences of essential Being, such as pure logic, pure
mathematics, time theory, space theory, and theory of
movement. These are all free from any positings of actual
fact, for in them there is no experience *qua* experience.
The geometer, for instance, does not study "actualities"
but *"ideal possibilities,"* not *"actual"* but "essential" relationships; in his case "essential insight, not experience, is
the act which supplies the ultimate grounds." [185] The same
holds true with all eidetic sciences. All mediated essential
contents are grounded in essential contents or in eidetic
axioms which are seized by immediate insight. Consequently, the procedure of every eidetic science is exclu-

183 *Ibid.*, p. 315.   184 *Ideen*, p. 16.   185 *Ibid.*, p. 17.

sively eidetic. As contrasted with this, the student of nature "observes" and "experiments"; he establishes what is "concretely" there, just as it is experienced by him; for him, "experience" supplies the grounds. If this viewpoint of Husserl's is at all acceptable, it is clear that "the meaning of eidetic science excludes in principle every assimilation of the theoretical results of empirical sciences." [186] Yet the very opposite obtains with the "sciences-of-fact" themselves.

On this point Husserl reasoned in the following manner. Empirical science proceeds in its judgments according to "formal principles" of formal logic, and since it is directed *toward objects,* "it is bound by the laws pertaining to the essence of *objectivity in general.*" [187] Empirical science thereby enters into relation with the group of formal-ontological disciplines, which includes not only formal logic in the narrow sense of the word, but those disciplines which figured formerly under the formal *"mathesis universalis,"* e. g., arithmetic, pure analysis, and theory of manifolds. Furthermore, "every fact includes a *material* essential element, and each eidetic truth that pertains to the pure essence so included must furnish a law to which is bound the given concrete instance and, generally, every possible one as well." [188]

Phenomenology thus investigates the "instruments" used by natural science in its theoretical work. Even pure mathematical disciplines, whether material, such as geometry or kinematics, or formal (i. e., purely logical), e. g., arithmetic and analysis, do not proceed "empirically." They are not grounded in "observations" and "experiments" on figures, movements, and the like, as presented in concrete experiences. In short, they are not empirically "real," and according to phenomenology, which assumes the task of investigating the bases of these principles, they

[186] *Ibid.,* p. 18. [187] *Ibid.* [188] *Ibid.*

are known as "valid" *because of intuitive insight.* Every empirical science possesses essential theoretical bases in eidetic ontology, and phenomenology has as one of its tasks to ascertain more precisely what that is.

Husserl justifiably contended, then, that phenomenology, as a science of *Eidos,* as a science of essential Being, must avoid any use whatever of the findings of positive science, since the two are, in fact, examining two entirely different realms. Although it is true (on phenomenological grounds) that whenever an object is given to consciousness in "sensory perception," it is understood and has meaning because of intuitive content seized by the Ego's intuition, it does not follow from this that the perceived object *as such* could possibly add to any knowledge of essences and qualities constituting it; it follows (once more, on phenomenological grounds) that no positive science dealing with objects as mere "facts" could add to such knowledge. Since essences and further knowledge of them are gained only in intuition, no amount of studying the hyletic content of sensory perception could yield anything in addition. Were anyone to hold that it could, it would be nothing short of making of intuition a matter of rationalizing about concrete empirical facts. Now if, as Husserl has long contended, intuition alone is the means of insight into principles, propositions, universalities, and the like, and all rationalizing *presupposes* such insights, it is clear that intuition itself could never be a matter of "rational activity." Insight into mathematical principles, for instance, could never be facilitated or enriched by examining any conceivable number of objects of sense perception. Briefly, neither conceptual nor perceptual activity could modify or correct that which has been learned in intuitive ideation; by the same token, any science built upon their content could be of no value to eidetic phenomenology.

Phenomenology, then, is the Science of essences. As "transcendental," it deals with pure consciousness, transcendental subjectivity, and its peculiar content, eidetic Being. As the Science of science, it investigates the acts and experiences that make empirical sciences possible. As a science of essentials, it is a science of *Eidos*. If this claim of Husserl has the slightest vestige of validity, he was justified in calling phenomenology the essential science.

Which is to be considered of greater importance, phenomenology as *science,* or phenomenology as *epistemology?* Husserl, it is certain, would avow that his establishment of a Science of science was the important thing and that his epistemology was purely incidental. Curiously enough, however, not everyone would agree with him. Perhaps, indeed, no decision can be made in this matter, since without his development of philosophy as a science there would have been no "phenomenological" epistemology, and, on the other hand, without a theory of knowledge his *phänomenologische Wissenschaft* would be of very little, if any, practical value. Of what service would a science of knowledge be which disclosed nothing of what is known and the manner of its being known?

Be that as it may, there are many who consider Husserl's real contribution to lie in his theory of knowledge. They view him as the one who has opened a realm of *geistig* experience too long closed to us by Kant and his disciples. The world of *Eidos,* the realm of essences, opens possibilities of experience and investigation hardly dreamed of since the time of Plato. Phenomenology, in short, affords a "reasonable" justification for "belief" in a "substantial" Ego, a moral order, and a divine relationship forever proscribed to him who would restrict the human mind to experience of crass "sensations," emanating from no one knows what or where. Very likely this was the reason that Husserl has attracted such a large group of eminent scholars to his phenomenology. He has not offered philosophy merely a new method, a new discipline. Husserl's doctrines of the intuition of essences and values, of pure spiritual experiences, and, by implication, of immediate, direct experienceability of the Divine, have given man new grounds for his perennial faith in his capacity to construct for himself a reasonable and comprehensive *Weltanschauung.*

BIBLIOGRAPHY

This bibliography is made possible not only by personal collection of data, but also by the bibliographies found in Werner Illemann's *Husserls vorphänomenologische Philosophie*, Friedrich Weidauer's *Kritik der transzendental Phänomenologie*, and Jan Patocka's "Bibliographie," *Revue internationale de philosophie*, January, 1939.

1. Edmund Husserl's Writings and Publications

"Beiträge zur Variationsrechnung." Dissertation, Wien, 1882 (unpublished).
   Ueber den Begriff der Zahl (Habilitationsschrift), Halle, F. Beyer, 1887.
Philosophie der Arithmetik, Vol. I. Psychologische und logische Untersuchungen, Halle. Pfeffer, 1891.
"Folgerungskalkül und Inhaltslogik," *Vierteljahrsschrift für wissenschaftliche Philosophie*, XV (1891), 168–69, 351–56.
Besprechung: "E. Schröder, Vorlesungen über die Algebra der Logik," I, Göttingische Gelehrte Anzeigen, 1891, pp. 243–78.
   "A. Voigts Elementare Logik und meine Darlegungen zur Logik der logischen Calculs," *Vierteljahrsschrift für wissenschaftliche Philosophie*, XVII, 11–120, 508–11.
"Psychologische Studien zur elementaren Logik," *Philosophische Monatshefte*, XXX (1894), 159–91.
"Bericht über deutsche Schriften zur Logik aus dem Jahre 1894," *Archiv für systematische Philosophie*, III (1897), 216–94.
Logische Untersuchungen, Vol. I, Prolegomena zur reinen Logik, 1900; Vol. II, 1901, Halle a. S. Niemeyer. Selbstanzeige: *Vierteljahrsschrift für wissenschaftliche Philosophie*, XXIV (1900), 511; XXV (1901), 260–63. Second edition, Vols. I and II, Parts 1 and 2, Halle a. S., Niemeyer, 1913; third edition, 1922; fourth edition, 1928. Russian transla-

tion, Vol. I, E. A. Bernstein, St. Petersburg, 1909. Spanish translation, Goas, Madrid, 1928.

Besprechung: "M. Palagyi, Der Streit der Psychologisten und der Formalisten in der modernen Logik," *Zeitschrift für Psychologie und Physiologie der Sinnesorgane,* XXXI (1903), 287–93.

"Bericht über deutsche Schriften zur Logik 1895–1898," *Archiv für systematische Philosophie,* IX (1903), 113–32, 237–59, 393–408, 523–43.

"Bericht über deutsche Schriften zur Logik 1895–1899," *Archiv für systematische Philosophie,* X (1904), 101–25.

"Philosophie als strenge Wissenschaft," *Logos,* I (1910), 289–341.

Ideen zu einer reinen Phänomenologie und phänomenologischen Philosophie, Part I, *Jahrbuch für Philosophie und phänomenologische Forschung,* Halle, Niemeyer, 1913, 1928; Ausfürliches Index, Gerda Walther, 1923. English translation, W. R. Boyce Gibson, entitled *Ideas,* New York, 1931. Original Preface by Husserl.

"A. Reinach. Ein Nachruf," *Kantstudien,* XXIII (1919), 147–49.

"Erneuerung. Ihr Problem und ihre Methode," *Japanische Zeitschrift Kaizo,* 1922, pp. 84–92; Japanese translation, 1923.

"Idee einer philosophischen Kultur," *Japanisch-deutsche Zeitschrift für Wissenschaft und Teknik,* 1923, pp. 1, 45–51.

"Phenomenology," article in Encyclopaedia Britannica, 1927, 14th edition, Vol. XVII, 699–702.

"Vorlesungen zur Phänomenologie des inneren Zeitbewusstseins," edited by Martin Heidegger, *Jahrbuch für Philosophie und phänomenologische Forschung,* IX (1928), 367–496.

"Formale und transzendentale Logik," *Jahrbuch für Philosophie und phänomenologische Forschung,* X (1929), xi–298.

"Nachwort zu meinen Ideen zu einer reinen Phänomenologie," *Jahrbuch für Philosophie und phänomenologische Forschung,* XI (1930), 549–70.

Méditations cartésiennes. Introduction à la Phénoménologie, Paris, A. Colin, 1931. Translated by Gabrielle Pfeiffer and Em. Levinas.

"Brief an den VIII. internationalen Kongress für Philosophie in Prag," *Proceedings of the Eighth International Congress of Philosophy*, Prague, 1936, xli–xlv.

"Die Krisis der europäischen Wissenschaften und die transzendentale Phänomenologie," Part 1, *Philosophia*, Belgrad, Vol. I, 1936, 77–176.

Erfahrung und Urteil. Untersuchungen zur Genealogie der Logik. Edited by Ludwig Landgrebe. Prague, Academia-Verlag, 1939.

"Die Frage nach dem Ursprung der Geometrie als intentional-historisches Problem," *Revue internationale de Philosophie*, January, 1939.

"Grundlegende Untersuchungen zum phänomenologischen Ursprung der Räumlichkeit der Natur." Philosophical Essays in Memory of Edmund Husserl, Harvard University Press, 1940.

"Notizen zur Raumkonstitution." Philosophy and Phenomenological Research, Vols. I and II, September and December, 1940. With a preface by Alfred Schuetz.

2. JAHRBUCH FÜR PHILOSOPHIE UND PHAENO-MENOLOGISCHE FORSCHUNG

Edited by Edmund Husserl in collaboration with M. Geiger (München), A. Pfänder (München), A. Reinach (Göttingen), M. Scheler (Berlin). Halle a. S., Max Niemeyer.

Vol. I (1913):
E. Husserl, "Ideen," I; A. Pfänder, "Zur Psychologie der Gesinnungen," I; M. Geiger, "Beiträge zur Phänomenologie des ästhetischen Genusses"; M. Scheler, "Der Formalismus in der Ethik und die materiale Wertethik," I; A. Reinach, "Die apriorischen Grundlagen des bürgerlichen Rechtes."

Vol. II (1916):
P. F. Linke, "Phänomenologie und Experiment in der Frage der Bewegungsauffassung"; M. Scheler, "Der Formalismus in der Ethik und die materiale Wertethik," II.

Vol. III (1916):
A. Pfänder, "Zur Psychologie der Gesinnungen"; D. v. Hildebrand, "Die Idee der sittlichen Handlung"; H.

Ritzel, "Ueber analytische Urteile"; H. Conrad-Martius, "Zur Ontologie u. Erscheinnungslehre der realen Aussenwelt."

Vol. IV (1921):

M. Geiger, "Fragment über den Begriff des Unbewussten und die psychische Realität"; A. Pfänder, "Logik"; J. Hering, "Bemerkungen über die Wesen, die Wesenheit und die Idee"; R. Ingarden, "Ueber die Gefahr einer Petitio principii in der Erkenntnistheorie."

Vol. V (1922):

E. Stein, "Beiträge zur philosophischen Begründung der Psychologie und der Geisteswissenschaften"; R. Ingarden, "Intuition und Intellekt bei H. Bergson"; D. v. Hildebrand, "Sittlichkeit und ethische Wertureile"; A. Koyre, "Bemerkungen zu den Zenonischen Paradozen."

Vol. VI (1923):

G. Walther, "Zur Ontologie der sozialen Gemeinschaften"; H. Conrad-Martius, "Realontologie"; Fritz London, "Ueber die Bedingungen der Möglichkeit einer deduktiven Theorie"; O. Becker, "Beiträge zur phänomenologischen Begründung der Geometrie und ihrer physikalischen Anwendungen"; H. Lipps, "Die Paradoxien der Mengenlehre."

Vol. VII (1925):

E. Stein, "Eine Untersuchung über den Staat"; R. Ingarden, "Essentiale Fragen. Ein Beitrag zu dem Wesensproblem"; D. Mahnke, "Leibnizens Synthese von Universalmathematik und Individualmetaphysik"; A. Metzger, "Der Gegenstand der Erkenntnis. Studien zur Phänomenologie des Gegenstandes," Part I.

Vol. VIII (1927):

M. Heidegger, "Sein und Zeit," Part I; O. Becker, "Mathematische Existenz."

Vol. IX (1928):

Fritz Kaufmann, "Die Philosophie des Grafen P. Yorck von Würtenburg"; L. Landgrebe, "W. Diltheys Theorie der Geisteswissenschaften"; E. Husserl, "Vorlesungen zur Phänomenologie des inneren Zeitbewusstseins" (Ed. by M. Heidegger).

Vol. X (1929):

E. Husserl, "Formale und Transzendentale Logik"; C. V.

Salmon, "The Central Problem of David Hume's Philosophy"; Festschrift E. Husserl zum 70. Geburtstag gewidmet. Erganzungsband zum Jahrbuch für Philosophie und phänomenologische Forschung, 1929; H. Amann, "Zum deutschen Impersonale"; O. Becker, "Von der Hinfälligkeit des Schönen und der Abenteuerlichkeit des Künstlers"; L. Claus, "Das Verstehen des sprachlichen Kunstwerks"; M. Heidegger, "Vom Wesen des Grundes"; G. Husserl, "Recht und Welt"; R. Ingarden, "Bemerkungen zum Problem 'Idealismus-Realismus'"; Fritz Kaufmann, "Die Bedeutung der künstlerischen Stimmung"; A. Koyre, "Die Gotteslehre J. Bomes"; H. Lipps, "Das Urteil"; Fr. Neumann, "Die Sinneinheit des Satzes und das indogermanische Verbum"; E. Stein, "Husserls Phänomenologie und die Philosophie des heil. Thomas v. Aquino"; H. Conrad-Martius, "Farben. Ein Kapitel aus der Realontologie."

Vol. XI (1930):
H. Spiegelberg, "Ueber das Wesen der Idee"; E. Fink, "Vergenwärtigung und Bild"; H. Morchen, "Die Einbildungskraft bei Kant"; O. Becker, "Zur Logik der Modalitäten"; E. Husserl, "Nachwort zu meinen Ideen zu einer reinen Phänomenologie und phänomenologischen Philosophie."

3. WORKS ON EDMUND HUSSERL

Adorno, T. W., "Husserl and the Problem of Idealism," *Journal of Philosophy*, Vol. XXXVII, No. 1, 1940.
Ammann, Herman, Die menschliche Rede, Vol. I. Lahre i. B., 1925; Vol. II, *ibid.*, 1927.
— Besprechung: "Die Idee der Sprache und das Wesen der Wortbedeutung," von Friedrich Kreis, *Kantstudien*, Vol. XXXII.
— Vom Ursprung der Sprache, Lahr i. B., 1929.
Anschütz, G., Spekulative, exakte und angewandte Psychologie. Leipzig, 1912.
Aster, E. von, Prinzipien der Erkenntnislehre. Leipzig, 1913.
— Geschichte der Philosophie. Leipzig, 1932, 373 ff.
— Philosophie der Gegenwart. Leiden, 1935.
Astrada, Carlos, Idealismo fenomenologico y Metafisica existencial. Buenos Aires, 1936.

Baade, W., "Aufgaben und Begriff der 'darstellenden' Psychologie," *Zeitschrift für Psychologie,* Vol. LXXI.

Bagdasar, N., "Edmund Husserl," *Revista de Filosofie,* Bukarest, 1928.

Banfi, A., "La Tendenza logistica della filosofia tedesca contemporanea e le Richerche logiche di E. Husserl," *Revista di Filosofia,* Milano, 1923.

—"La fenomenologia pura di E. H. et l'autonomia ideale della sfera teorica," *ibid.,* 1923.

—"La fenomenologia pura dell Husserl," Principii di una teoria della Ragione, 1926.

—"Filosofia fenomenologica," *La Cultura,* 1931, n. s., X.

—"La fenomenologia e il compito del pensiero contemporaneo," *Revue internationale de philosophie,* No. 2, January 15, 1939.

— E. Husserl. Civilta Moderna, 1939.

Bannes, J., Versuch einer Darstellung und Beurteilung der Grundlagen der Philosophie Edmund Husserls. Borgmeyer, Breslau, 1930.

Baumgardt, "Das Möglichkeitsproblem in der Kritik der reinen Vernunft, der modernen Phänomenologie und der Gegestandstheorie," *Kantstudien,* 1920, Erg.-Heft 51.

Beck, Maximilian, "Ideelle Existenz," *Philosophische Hefte,* Vol. I, 1929–30, Nos. 2 and 4.

—"Der phänomenologische Idealismus, die phänomenologische Methode und die Hermeneutik (NB. Heideggers) im Anschluss an Theodor Celms, 'Der phänomenologische Idealismus Husserls,'" *Philosophische Hefte,* Vol. II, 1930–31, No. 2.

Becker, Oskar, "Die Philosophie E. Husserls," *Kantstudien,* 1929, Vol. XXXV.

—"Ueber den sogenannten Anthropologismus in der Philosophie der Mathematik," *Philosophische Anzeiger,* 1929, III.

—Besprechung: "G. Günther, Grundzüge zu einer neuen Theorie des Denkens in Hegels Logik," 1933, *Deutsche Literatur-Zeitung,* 1934.

—"Husserl und Descartes. Im Anschluss an Husserls Méditations cartésiennes," *Archiv für Rechts- und Socialphilosophie,* 1937, Vol. XXX.

Behn, Siegfried, "Ueber Phänomenologie und Abstraktion," *Philosophischer Jahrbuch der Görresgesellschaft,* Vol. XXXVIII, 1925.

Berger, Gaston, "Husserl et Hume," *Revue internationale de Philosophie,* No. 2, January 15, 1939.

Berl, H., E., "Husserl oder die Judaisierung des Platonismus," *Menorah,* Vol. X, Wien, 1932.

Binswanger, Ludwig, Einführung in die Probleme der allgemeinen Psychologie. Berlin, 1922, 391 ff.

—"Ueber Phänomenologie," *Zeitschrift für die gesammte Neurologie und Psychiatrie,* Vol. LXXXII.

— Ueber Ideenflucht. Zurich, 1933.

Bixler, J. S., "Germany's 'Quest for an Absolute,'" *The International Journal of Ethics,* Vol. XLI, No. 1, October, 1930.

—"German Phenomenology and Its Implications for Religion," *Journal of Philosophy,* Vol. IX, 1929.

—"A Phenomenological Approach to Religious Realism," Religious Realism, D. C. Macintosh and others, New York, 1931.

Bobbio, "La filosofia di Husserl e la tendenza fenomenologica," *Revista di Filosofia,* 1935.

Bosanquet, B., "The Meeting of Extremes in Contemporary Philosophy." London, 1924.

Brecht, F. J., "Festschrift, E. Husserl z. 70. Geburtstag gewidmet," *Kantstudien,* Vol. XXXVI, 1/2.

Bréhier, E., "Histoire de la Philosophie." II. Philosophie moderne. Paris, 1932.

Brightman, E. S., "The Finite Self," in Contemporary Idealism in America, edited by Clifford Barrett, 1932. Deals with Franz Brentano.

Brentano, Franz, Psychologie vom empirischen Standpunkt. Edited by Oskar Kraus. Felix Meiner, Leipzig, 1924. 2 vols.

Brock, Erich, An Introduction to Contemporary German Philosophy, Cambridge University Press, 1935, 164 ff.

Brück, Maria, Ueber das Verhältnis Edmund Husserls zu Franz Brentano vornehmlich mit Rücksicht auf Brentanos Psychologie. Konrad Triltsch, Würzburg, 1933.

Bühler, F., Sprachtheorie. Die Darstellungsfunktion der Sprache. Jena, 1934.

Burgert, H., "Zur Kritik der Phänomenologie," *Philosophischer Jahrbuch der Görresgesellschaft,* Vol. XXXVIII, 1925.

Burloud, A., La Pensée d'après les recherches expérimentales de H. J. Watt, de Messer et de Bühler. Paris, Alcan, 1927.

Caspary, Adolph, "Ueber Phänomenologie," *Geisteskultur,* Vol. XXXVI, 1927.

Celms, Theodor, Der phänomenologische Idealismus Husserls. Riga, 1928.

Cerf, Walter H., "An Approach to Heidegger's Ontology," *Philosophy and Phenomenological Research,* Vol. II, December, 1940.

Chandler, A., "Professor Husserl's Program of Philosophical Reform," *Philosophical Review,* 1917, Bd. 26, 634 ff.

Chestov, Leon, "Momento mori," *Revue philosophique,* January, 1926. (See also "Schestow.")

Clauss, F., Die nordische Seele. Halle, 1923.

Cohen, H., Logik der reinen Erkenntnis. Berlin, 3d Ed., 55 ff.

Cornelius, H., "Psychologische Prinzipienfragen," *Zeitschrift für Psychologie,* Vol. XLII–XLIII.

Delbos, Victor, "Husserl. La Critique du psychologisme et sa conception d'une logique pure," *Revue de metaphysique et de morale,* 1911.

Demuth, M., "E. Husserl." Lektorenkonferenz der deutschen Franziskaner für Philosophie und Theologie, III, Werl, 1926.

Dessoir, Max, "La Phénoménologie de Husserl," *Revue internationale de Philosophie,* January 15, 1939.

Driesch, Hans, Die Logik als Aufgabe. J. C. B. Mohr, Tübingen, 1913.

— Philosophische Forschungswege. Leipzig, 1930.

— "Die Phänomenologie und ihre Vieldeutigkeit," Proceedings 7th International Congress of Philosophy, Oxford University Press, 1931.

Ehrlich, W., Kant und Husserl. Kritik der transzendentalen und phänomenologischen Methode. Halle, 1923.

— Besprechung: "Egon von Petersdorff," *Kantstudien,* 1924, Vol. XXVIII.

— Das unpersonale Erlebnis. Einführung in eine neue Erkenntnislehre. Halle, 1927.

— Intentionalität und Sinn. Prolegomena zur Normenlehre. Halle, 1934, 48.

Eisler, Rudolph, "Phänomenologie," Handwörterbuch der Philosophie, 2d ed. E. S. Mittler & Son, Berlin, 1922.

Elsas, A., "Husserls Philosophie der Arithmetik," *Philosophische Monatshefte,* Vol. XXX, 1894.

Elsenhans, Th., "Phänomenologie und Empirie," *Kantstudien,* Vol. XXII, 1918.

— "Phänomenologie, Psychologie, Erkenntnistheorie," *Kantstudien,* Vol. XXII, 1924.

Engel, W., "Zur Kritik der Phänomenologie Husserls." Dissertation, Prag, 1929.

Enyvvari, E., "Zur Phänomenologie der Ideation," *Zeitschrift für Philosophie und philosophische Kritik,* 1914.

Erckmann, R., "Husserl und Hans Hörbiger." Schlussel zum Weltgeschehen, Vol. V, 1919.

Ertel, Chr., "Von der Phänomenologie und jüngeren Lebensphilosophie zur Existentialphilosophie M. Heideggers," *Philosophischer Jahrbuch der Görresgesellschaft,* LI.

Ettlincer, Max, Geschichte der Philosophie von der Romantik bis zur Gegenwart. München, 1928, 308 ff.

Ewald, O., "Die deutsche Philosophie im Jahre 1907," *Kantstudien,* 1908, Vol. XIII.

Eyser, Ulrich, "Phänomenologie. Das Werk E. Husserls," *Mass und Wert,* 1928, Vol. II.

Farber, M., "Phenomenology as a Method and as a Philosophical Discipline," Dissertation, University of Buffalo, 1928.

— and others, Philosophical Essays in Memory of Edmund Husserl. Harvard University Press, 1940.

— "Edmund Husserl and the Background of his Philosophy." Philosophy and Phenomenological Research, Vol. I, September, 1940.

Feldkeller, P., Sinn, Echtheit, Liebe nach Paul Hofmanns Sinnanalyse. Berlin, 1931.

Fels, H., "Bolzano und Husserl," *Philosophischer Jahrbuch der Görresgesellschaft,* 1926.

Fink, Eugen, Was will die Phänomenologie Edmund Husserls? Junker und Dunnhaupt, Berlin, 1934.

— Die phänomenologische Philosophie Edmund Husserls in der gegenwärtigen Kritik. Pan-Verlagsgesellschaft, Berlin, 1934. Foreword by Husserl.

— "Das Problem der Phänomenologie Edmund Husserls," *Revue internationale de philosophie,* January 15, 1939.

Folwart, Helmut, Kant, Husserl, Heidegger. Breslau, 1936.

Freund, Ludwig, Philosophie ein unlösbares Problem. München, 1932.

Frischeisen-Köhler, Max, "Philosophie und Psychologie," Die Geisteswissenschaften, Vol. I, 1914.

Fritsch, W., Die Welt "einklammern," eine philosophische Frage an Edmund Husserl. Reclams Universum, 1931.

Fulton, Street, "Husserl's Significance for the Theory of Truth," *The Monist*, July, 1935.

— "The Cartesianism of Phenomenology," *The Philosophical Review*, May, 1940.

Gehlen, Arnold, Wirklicher und unwirklicher Geist. Leipzig, 1932.

Geiger, Moritz, "Zum Problem der Stimmungseinfiehlung," *Zeitschrift für Aesthetik und allgemeiner Kurstwissenschaft*, Vol. VI.

— "The Philosophical Attitudes and the Problem of Subsistence and Essence," *Proceedings 6th International Congress of Philosophy*, London, 1927.

Geyser, J., Neue und alte Wege der Philosophie. Münster i. W., 1916, 302 ff.

— Ueber Wahrheit und Evidenz, Freiburg, 1918.

— Eidologie, Freiburg, 1921.

— Erkenntnistheorie, Freiburg, 1922.

— "Ueber Begriff und Wesensschau," *Philosophischer Jahrbuch der Görresgesellschaft*, 1924, Vol. XXXIX.

— Auf dem Kampffelde der Logik. Freiburg i. Br., 1926.

— "Besprechung: W. Meckauer," *Kantstudien*, 1929, Vol. XXXIV.

— "Besprechung: W. del Negro," *Kantstudien*, Vol. XXXIV.

Gibson, Boyce, "The Problem of Real and Ideal in the Phenomenology of Husserl," *Mind*, Vol. XXXIV. See also "1. Edmund Husserl's Writings."

Ginsburg, E., "Zur Husserlschen Lehre von Ganzen und Teilen," *Archiv für systematische Philosophie*, 1929.

Gotesky, Rubin, "Husserl's Conception of Logic as Kunstlehre in the Logische Untersuchungen," *The Philosophical Review*, July, 1938.

Grasselli, G., "La fenomenologia di Husserl e l'ontologia di M. Heidegger," *Rivista di Filosofia*, Milano, 1928.

Grassi, E., La fenomenologia di E. Husserl. Dell 'apparire e dell' essere. Firenze.

Graumann, Heinz, "Versuch einer historisch-kritischen Einleitung in die Phänomenologie des Verstehens." Dissertation, München, 1924.

Grimme, A., "Die frohe Botschaft der Husserlschen Philosophie," *Der Falke,* 1917, Vol. I.

Groethuysen, B., La Philosophie allemande depuis Nietzsche. Paris, 1927.

Gronau, G., Die Philosophie der Gegenwart, Langensalza. 1922.

Gründler, Otto, "Die Bedeutung der Phänomenologie für das Geistesleben," *Hochland,* Vol. XIX, 1921–22.

— Elemente zu einer Religionsphilosophie auf phänomenologischer Grundlage. München, 1922.

— Besprechung "Chr. Herrmann," *Kantstudien,* Vol. XXXIII.

Grundwaldt, H. H., "Ueber die Phänomenologie Husserls." Dissertation, Berlin, 1927.

Gurvitch, Georges, "La Philosophie phenomenologique en Allemagne: Edmund Husserl," *Revue de metaphysique et de morale,* 1928.

— Les Tendances actuelles de la philosophie allemande. Paris, 1930.

Guthrie, Hunter, "Max Scheler's Epistemology of the Emotions," *The Modern Schoolman,* Vol. XVI, 1939.

Hamilton, K. G., "Edmund Husserl's Contribution to Philosophy," *Journal of Philosophy,* Vol. XXXVI, 1939.

Hartmann, Nicolai, Grundzüge einer Metaphysik der Erkenntnis. W. de Gruyter, Berlin, 1925.

— Zur Grundlegung der Ontologie. 1935.

— Ueber die Erkennbarkeit des Apriorischen, *Logos,* Vol. V.

Heber, Johannes, "Die phänomenologische Methode in der Religionsphilosophie. Ein Beitrag zur Methodologie der Wesensbestimmung der Religion." Dissertation, Leipzig, 1929.

— Besprechung: (a) "Robert Winkler," Blätter für deutsche Philosophie, Vol. V, 1931–32. (b) "Christentum und Wissenschaft," 1929.

Heidegger, Martin, Die Kategorien- und Bedeutungslehre des Duns Scotus, Tübingen, 1926.

Heim, K., Psychologismus oder Antipsychologismus? Berlin, 1902.

Heimsöth, H., "Die Philosophie im XX. Jahrhundert," In Windelband, W., Lehrbuch der Geschichte der Philosophie, Tübingen, 1935.

Heinemann, Fritz, Neue Wege der Philosophie. Leipzig, 1929.

— "Les Problèmes et la valeur d'une phénoménologie comme théorie de la réalité. Etre et apparaitre," *Travaux du IXe Congres international de Philosophie*, Paris, 1937.

Heinrich, E., Untersuchungen zur Lehre vom Begriff. Göttingen, 1910.

Héring, J., Phénoménologie et Philosophie religieuse. Paris, 1926.

— "Sub specie aeterni. Réponse à une critique de la philosophie de Husserl," *Revue d'histoire et de philosophie religieuse*, 1927.

— "La phénoménologie d'Edmund Husserl il y a trente ans," *Revue internationale de philosophie*, January 15, 1939.

Heyde, G., "Vom philosophischen Ausgang: Die Grundlegung der Philosophie, untersucht am Beispiel der Lehren von J. Rehmke, H. Driesch, E. Husserl, J. Volkelt und H. Rickert." Dissertation, Leipzig.

Hicks, George Dawes, "The Philosophy of Husserl," *The Hibbert Journal*, Vol. XII.

— "Survey of Recent Philosophical Literature," *The Hibbert Journal*, XXXVII, October, 1938.

Hofmann, H., "Ueber den Empfindungsbegriff." Dissertation, Göttingen. *Archives für die gesammte Psychologie*, 1913.

Hudeczek, P. M., "Ontologické základy pravdivosti poznàni," *Filosoficka Revue* (CSR), Vol. X.

Hufnagel, A., Intuition und Erkenntnis nach Thomas von Aquin. Münster, 1932.

[Husserl, E.], Notes Concerning Husserl by W. P. Montague, Charles Hartshorne, Andrew D. Osborne, Horace L. Freiss, Dorion Cairns, *Journal of Philosophy*, Vol. XXXIV, No. 9, 1939.

Husserl, G., Rechtskraft und Rechtsgeltung. Berlin, 1925.

— Besprechung: "Prof. C. Brinchkmann," *Kantstudien*, Vol. XXXIII.

Illemann, Werner, Husserls vorphänomenologische Philosophie. Hirzel, Leipzig, 1932.

— Besprechungen: (a) "von A. Kofevnikoff," Recherches philosophiques, III; (b) "Ludwig Landgrebe," Kant-

studien, 1933; (c) "O. Becker," *Deutsche Literaturzeitung,*
1934.
Ingarden, Roman, Ueber die Stellung der Erkenntnistheorie
im System der Philosophie. Halle, 1926.
— "O poznawaniu dziela literackiego." Lwów, 1927.
— "Das literarische Kunstwerk. Eine Untersuchung aus dem
Grenzgebiet der Onotologie," Logik und Literaturwissen-
schaft, Halle, 1931.
— Besprechung: "von A. Kojevnikoff," Recherches phi-
losophiques, II.
Jakowenko, Boris, "Was ist die transzendentale Methode?"
Bericht über den III. international Philosophenkongress in
Heidelberg, Heidelberg, 1909, 787 ff.
— "Filozofija E. Husserlja," *Novyja idei v filozofii,* Vol. II.,
St. Petersbourg, 1912.
— "Il commino della conoscenza filosofica," *Logos,* Vol. V,
1922.
— Vom Wesen des Pluralismus. Prague, 1928.
— "Edmund Husserl und die russische Philosophie," Der
russische Gedanke, 1929, Vol. I.
— "Kritische Bemerkungen über die Phänomenologie," *Pro-
ceedings of the Seventh International Congress of Phi-
losophy,* 1930.
— "Zur Kritik der Logistik, der Dialektik und der Phänome-
nologie." Bibliotheque internationale de Philosophie, Prag,
1936.
Janssen, D., Vorstudien zur Metaphysik. Halle, 1921.
Jaspers, Karl, Psychologie der Weltanschauungen. Berlin, 1919.
Jerusalem, W., Der kritische Idealismus und die reine Logik.
Wien, 1905.
— Einleitung in die Philosophie.
Joël, K., "Die Ueberwindung des XIX. Jahrhunderts im
Denken der Gegenwart," *Kantstudien,* Vol. XXXV, 35.
Husserls Phänomenologie, 510 ff.
— "Die philosophische Krisis der Gegenwart." Rektoratsrede,
1914.
Jones, W. Tudor, Contemporary Thought of Germany, Vol. I.
Williams Norgate, London, 1930.
Jordan, M., "The Revival of Catholic Philosophy in Ger-
many," *The Catholic World,* 1928.

Kaufmann, Felix, Logik und Rechtswissenschaft. Tübingen, 1922.
— Die Kriterien des Rechts. Tübingen, 1924.
— Das Unendliche in der Mathematik und seine Ausschaltung. Leipzig-Wien, 1930.
— "Die Bedeutung der logischen Analyse für die Socialwissenschaften." *Actes du VIIIᵉ Congres international de Philosophie.* Prague, 1936.
— Methodenlehre der Sozialwissenschaften. Wien, 1936, 331 ff.
— "Truth and Logic," *Philosophy and Phenomenological Research,* Vol. I, September, 1940.
Kaufmann, Fritz, "In Memorian Edmund Husserl," *Social Research,* February, 1940.
— "Spinoza's System as Theory of Expression," *Philosophy and Phenomenological Research,* Vol. I, September, 1940.
Kerler, Dietrich Heinrich, Die auferstandene Metaphysik. Ulm, 1921.
Köhler, W., "Wesen und Tatsachen," *Forschung und Fortschritte, Nachrichtenblatt der deutschen Wissenschaft und Technik.* 8. Jahrg. No. 12.
— The Place of Value in a World of Facts. Liveright, New York, 1938.
— Dynamics in Psychology. Liveright, New York, 1940.
König, Josef, Der Begriff der Intuition. Halle, Niemeyer, 1926.
Köpp, W., Grundlegung zur induktiven Theologie. Kritik, Phänomenologie und Methode des allgemeinen und des theologischen Erkennens. Güterslch, 1927.
Kottje, F., Illusionen der Wissenschaft. J. G. Gotta'sche Buchhandlung, Stuttgart, 1931.
Kraft, Julius, "Die Wissenschaftliche Bedeutung der phänomenologischen Rechtsphilosophie," *Kantstudien,* Vol. XXXI.
— Die Grundformen der wissenschaftlichen Methoden, Wien, *Sitzungsberichte der Akademie der Wissenschaften, hist-phil. Klasse,* Vol. XXIII.
— Von Husserl zu Heidegger. Kritik der phänomenologischen Philosophie. Leipzig, 1932.
— Besprechung: "Springmeyer," *Kantstudien,* Vol. XXXVII.
Krämer, Ernst, Benno Erdmanns Wahrheitsauffassung und ihre Kritik durch Husserl. Blaubeuren, 1930.
Kränzlin, Gerhard, Max Schelers phänomenologische Systematik. Leipzig, 1934.

— Besprechung: "A. Kojevnikoff," *Recherches philosophiques,* Vol. IV.

Kraus, Oscar, "Die Phänomenologie des Zeitbewusstseins." Aus dem Briefwechsel Brentanos und Vorlesungsbruchstück, *Archiv für die gesammte Psychologie,* Vol. LXXV.

— "Franz Brentano," Abt. II: Erinnerungen an F. B. von E. Husserl, 1919.

— Franz Brentanos Stellung zur Phänomenologie und Gegenstandstheorie. Zugleich eine Einleitung in die Neuausgabe der Psychologie. Leipzig, 1924.

— Einleitung zu Brentanos Psychologie III. Leipzig, 1928.

— "Gegen entia rationis, sogenannte irreale oder ideale Gegenstände." Briefe Franz Brentanos, Philosophische Hefte, Vol. I, 1929–1930.

— Einleitung zu: Franz Brentano, Wahrheit und Evidenz. Leipzig, 1930

Kreis, F., Phänomenologie und Kritizismus. Tübingen, J. C. B. Mohr, 1930.

— Besprechung: "Von F. Blaschke, *Blätter für deutsche Philosophie,"* Vol. V, 1931–1932.

Kremer, R., Le Neo-Realisme americain. Louvain, 1920.

Krejci, Fr., Filosofie poslednich let pred valkou. "Philosophie der letzten Vorkriegsjahre," Prag, 1930.

Kröner, Franz, Die Anarchie der philosophischen Systeme. Leipzig, 1929.

Kroner, R., "Ueber logische und ästhetische Allgemeingültigkeit." Dissertation, Freiburg, 1906.

Kuhn, Helmut, Besprechung: "E. Husserl, Méditations cartésiennes," *Kantstudien,* 1933, Vol. XXXIX.

Külpe, O., "Husserls Phänomenologie." Deutschland unter Kaiser Wilhelm II, Part III, 1914.

Kuntze, Fr., Die kritische Lehre von der Objektivität.

Kuznitzky, G. Naturerlebnis und Wirklichkeitsbewusstsein. Breslau, 1919.

Kynast, R., Das Problem der Phänomenologie, Breslau, 1917.

— Intuitive Erkenntnis. Dissertation, Breslau, 1919.

Landgrebe, L., "Die Methode der Phänomenologie E. Husserls," *Neue Jahrbücher für Wissenschaft und Jugendbildung,* 1933.

— "Formale und materiale Normen der Erkenntnis," *Travaux*

du IXe Congres international de Philosophie, Paris, 1937, XI, 34 ff.

Landgrebe, L., "Patocka, J., Edmund Husserl zum Gedächtnis," Zwei Reden. Prag, 1938.

— "Husserls Phänomenologie und die Motive zu ihrer Umbildung," *Revue internationale de philosophie*, January 15, 1939.

— "The World as a Phenomenological System," *Philosophy and Phenomenological Research*, Vol. I, September, 1940.

Landmann, Edith, Die Transzendenz des Erkennens. Berlin, 1923.

Landsberg, Paul L., "Husserl et l'idée de la philosophie," *Revue internationale de Philosophie*, January 15, 1939.

Lanz, Henry, "The New Phenomenology," *The Monist*, XXXIV, 1924.

La Phénoménologie. Journées d'etudes de la Société thomiste, I; Les Editions du Cerfs, Juvisy.

Lapp, A., "Versuch über den Wahrheitsbegriff." Dissertation, Erlangen, 1912.

Leeuw, G. Van Der, Einführung in die Phänomenologie der Religion. 1925.

— Phänomenologie der Religion. Tübingen, 1933.

Legendecker, H., Zur Phänomenologie der Täuschungen. Halle, 1913.

Leisegang, H., Deutsche Philosophie im 20. Jahrhundert. Breslau, 1928.

Lenzen, Wilhelm, "Der Intentionsgedanke in der Phänomenologie und die erkenntnistheoretische Repräsentation." Dissertation, Bonn, 1929.

Levinas, E., "Sur les 'Ideen' de E. Husserl," *Revue Philosophique*, 1929.

— La Théorie de l'intuition dans la phénoménologie de Husserl. Paris, 1930.

— Spanische Uebersetzung V. Carlos Cueto: "Las 'Ideen' de E. Husserl." Letras, 1937.

Liebert, Arthur, "Das Problem der Geltung," *Kantstudien*, Vol. XXXII, 1914.

Linke, Paul F., Die phänomenale Sphäre und das reele Bewusstsein. Halle, 1912.

— "Das Recht der Phänomenologie. Eine Auseinandersetzung mit Theodor Elsenhans," *Kantstudien*, 1916. Vol. XXI.

— "Die Minderwertigkeit der Erfahrdung in der Theorie der Erkenntnis," *Kantstudien,* 1918, Vol. XXIII.
— Grundfragen der Wahrnehmungslehre. München, 1918, I, 1929, 2.
— "Die Existentialtheorie der Wahrheit und der Psychologismus der Geltungslogik," *Kantstudien,* 1924, Vol. XXIX.
— "Beobachten und Schauen," *Vierteljahrsschrift für philosophische Pädagogik,* Vol. II.
— "The Present Status of Logik and Epistemology in Germany," *The Monist,* XXXVI, 1926.
— "Der Satz des Bewusstseins und die Lahre von der Intentionalität," *Atti del V° Congresso internazionale di filosofia in Napoli, 1924,* Neapel, 1927.
— Logic and Epistemology. In E. L. Schaub, Philosophy Today, Chicago, 1928.
— "Gegenstandsphänomenologie," *Philosophische Hefte,* II, 1930–1931.
— Auseinandersetzung: Fr. Krejci, "Parallelistische Phänomenologie" (Paralelisticka fenomenologie), *Ceska Mysl,* 1931.
Löwenstein, K., "Sätze über Phänomenologie," *Zeitschrift für Philosophie und philosophische Kritik,* Vol. CXLVIII, 1912.
Löwith, K., Das Individuum in der Rolle des Mitmenschen. München, 1928.
— "Grundzüge der Entwicklung der Phänomenologie zur Philosophie und ihr Verhältnis zur protestantischen Theologie," *Theologische Rundschau,* 1930.
— Besprechung: "von Fritz Kaufmann," *Kantstudien,* Vol. XXXVII. (Zusammenhang mit Husserl hervorgehoben.)
Lukacs, F. von, "Nachruf für E. Lask," *Kantstudien,* Vol. XXII, 1918.
Mager, Alois, "Phänomenologie und Religionsphilosophie," *Hochland,* Vol. XX.
Mahnke, D., "Eine neue Monadologie," *Kantstudien,* Erganzungsheft XXXIX, 1917.
— Der Wille zur Ewigkeit. Halle, 1917.
— Besprechung: "K. Kesseler," *Kantstudien,* vol. XXXIV.
— Das unsichtbare Königreich des deutschem Idealismus. Halle, 1920.
— Besprechung: "W. Diltheys Gesammelte Schriften," Vol. VII des deutschen Idealismus. Erfurt, 1922.

Mahnke, D., "Von Hilbert zu Husserl." *Unterrichtsblätter für Mathematik und Naturwissenschaften,* Vol. XXIX.

— Besprechung: "W. Diltheys Gesammelte Schriften, Bd. VII." Deutsche Literaturzeitung, 1927.

Maier, H., "Logik und Psychologie." Festschrift für Alois Riehl, Halle, 1914.

Marcuse, H., Besprechung: "E. Husserl, Die Krisis der europaischen Wissenschaften und die transzenidentale Phänomenologie," *Zeitschrift für Sozialforschung,* Vol. VI, 1937.

Maréchal, Joseph, "Phénoménologie pure ou philosophie de l'action?" Festschrift Joseph Geyser. Regensburg, 1931, Vol. I.

Margolin, Julius, "Grundphänomene des intentionalen Bewusstseins." Dissertation, Berlin, 1929.

Maritain, J., "Notes sur la connaissance," *Rivista di Filosofia neo-scolastica,* Vol. XXIV, 1932.

Maticevic, J., Zur Grundlegung der Logik. Ein Beitrag zur Bestimmung des Verhältnisses zwischen Logik und Psychologie. Wien, 1909.

Mazzantini, C., "L'undicesimo volume dell' 'Annuario della scuola fenomenologica' di Husserl," *Rivista di filosofia neo-scolastica,* Vol. XXIII, 1931.

Meckaner, Walter, "Aesthetische Idee und Kunsttheorie," *Kantstudien,* Vol. XXII.

Menzer, Paul, Deutsche Metaphysik der Gegenwart. Mittler und Sohn, Berlin, 1931.

Mertens, Paul, "Zur Phänomenologie des Glaubens." Dissertation, Bonn, 1927.

Messer, A., Empfindung und Denken. Leipzig, 1908.

— "Husserls Phänomenologie in ihrem Verhältnis zur Psychologie," *Archiv für die Gesammte Psychologie,* Vol. XXII, 1912; Vol. XXXII, 1914.

— "Ueber den Begriff des Aktes," *Archiv für des Gesammte Psychologie,* Vol. XXIV.

— Philosophie der gegenwart in Deutschland. Leipzig, 1931.

Metzger, A., "La situacion presente de la fenomenologia," *Revista de Occidente,* Vol. XXII, 1928.

— Phänomenologie und Metaphysik. Halle, 1934.

— Besprechung: (a) "E. Levinas, *Revue philosophique,*" Vol. LXII, 1935; (b) "H. Corbins, Recherches philosophiques," Vol. IV, 1936.

BIBLIOGRAPHY 319

Michaltschew, D., Philosophische Studien. Leipzig, 1912.

Micic, Zagorka, "Fenomenologija Edmund Husserla," *Studija iz savremene filozofije*, Beograd, 1937, 176 ff.

Misch, G., Lebensphilosophie und Phänomenologie; Ein Auseinandersetzung der Diltheyschen Richtung mit Heidegger und Husserl. Teubner, Leipzig, 1931.

— Besprechung: (a) "A. Kojevnikoff," *Recherches philosophiques*, Vol. II, 1934. (b)

Moog, Willy, "Die Kritik des Psychologismus," *Archiv für die Gesammte Psychologie*, Vol. XXXVII.

— "Logik, Psychologie und Psychologismus." Wissenschaftssystemathische Untersuchungen, Halle, 1919.

— Die deutsche Philosophie des XX. Jahrhunderts. Stuttgart, 1922.

Morgenstern, Georg, "Der Begriff der Existenz in der modernen Philosophie." Leipziger Dissertation, Weida, 1917.

Morris, Bertram, "Intention and Fulfilment in Art," *Philosophy and Phenomenological Research*, Vol. II, December, 1940.

Morris, Charles W., Six Theories of Mind. The University of Chicago Press, 1932.

Müller, A., Einleitung in die Philosophie. Berlin, 1931.

Müller-Freienfels, Richard, The Evolution of Modern Psychology. Trans. by W. Beran Wolfe. Yale University Press. New Haven, 1935.

Mundle, W., "Recht und Möglichkeit einer phänomenologischen Betrachtung der Religion," *Theologische Blätter*, Vol. II.

Murphy, Gardner, An Historical Introduction to Modern Psychology. New York, 1932.

Muth, Franz, "Edmund Husserl und Martin Heidegger in ihrer Phänomenologie und Weltanschauung," Münchener Dissertation, Temeswar-Timisoara (Rumanien), 1931.

Natorp, Paul, "Zur Frage nach der logischen Methode." Mit Beziehung auf E. Husserl "Prolegomena zur reinen Logik," *Kantstudien*, Vol. VI, 1901.

— Allegemeine Psychologie, Vol. I. Tübingen, 1912.

— "Husserls Ideen zu einer reinen Phänomenologie," *Die Geisteswissenschaften*, I, 1914, 426 ff. Abgedruckt: Logos, Vol. VII, 1917–1918.

Noel, L., "Les Frontieres de la logique," *Revue neo-scolastique ᵤ ⎺⸍.:losophie*, Vol. XVII, 1910.

Odebrecht, Rudolph, Grundlegung einer ästhetischen Werttheorie. I. Das ästhetische Welterlebnis, Berlin, 1927.

— Besprechung: "Grossart," *Kantstudien*, Vol. XXXV.

Oesterreich, T. K., "Die reine Logik und die Phänomenologie," in Friedrich Ueberweg, Grundriss der Geschichte der Philosophie (12th ed., 1923), IV, 504 ff.

Ogden and Richards, The Meaning of Meaning. London, 1923.

Osborn, Andrew D., "The Philosophy of Edmund Husserl. Dissertation, Columbia University Press, New York, 1934.

Otaka, T., Die Lehre vom sozialen Verband. Wien, 1932.

Palagyi, M., Der Streit der Psychologisten und Formalisten in der modernen Logik. Engelmann, Leipzig, 1902.

Pastore, Annibale, "Verso un nuovo relativismo," *Archivio di Filosofia*, II, 1932.

— "Contributo all' interpretazione dell' ontologicita eidetica di Husserl," *Rivisto di Filosofia*, 1932.

— "Husserl, Heidegger, Chestov," *Archivio di Storia della Filosofia*, 1933. Abgedruckt in La Logica del potenziamento.

Patocka, J., Prirozeny svèt jako filosoficky problém (Die natürliche Welt als philosophisches Problem). Prag, 1936.

Perry, R. B., Philosophy of the Recent Past. Scribner's, New York, 1926.

Pfänder, A., Einführung in die Psychologie. Leipzig, 1920.

Pöll, M., Wesen und Wesenserkenntnis. Untersuchungen mit besonderer Berücksichtigung der Phänomenologie Husserls und Schelers. München, 1936.

Port, K., "Betrachtungen zu Husserls Einteilung der Denkakte und ihrer erkenntnistheoretischen Bedeutung," *Archiv für die gesammte Psychologie*, Vol. LXVI.

Pos, H. J., "Descartes en Husserl," *Alg. Nederl. Tijdschrift*, Vol. XXXI, 1938.

— "Phénoménologie et linguistique," *Revue internationale de philosophie*, January 15, 1939.

Pradines, Le Problème de la sensation. Paris, 1928.

Preti, G., "Filosofia e saggezza nel pensiero husserliano," *Archivio di Filosofia*, 1934.

— "I fondamenti della logica formale pura nella 'Wissenschaftslehre' di B. Bolzano e nelle 'Logische Untersuchungen' di E. Husserl," *Sophia*, III, 1936.

Przywara, Erich, Gott. Fünf Vorträge über die religionsphilosophischen Probleme. München, 1926.
— "Drei Richtungen der Phänomenologie." Stimmen der Zeit, 1928.
— "Die Wende zum Menschen." Stimmen der Zeit, 1929–30.
Read, W. T., Jr., "Aesthetic Emotion," *Philosophy and Phenomenological Research*, Vol. II, December, 1940.
Recktenwald, Friederike, Die phänomenologische Reduktion bei Edmund Husserl. München, 1929.
Reimer, Wilhelm, "Der phänomenologische Evidenzbegriff," *Kantstudien*, Vol. XXIII, 1919.
Reinach, A., Gesammelte Schriften, Halle, 1922.
Reiner, Hans, "Freiheit, Wollen und Aktivität. Phänomenologische Untersuchungen in der Richtung auf das Problem der Willensfreiheit." Dissertation, Freiburg, Halle, 1927.
Reinhardt, Kurt F., "Husserls' Phenomenology and Thomistic Philosophy," *New Scholasticism*, Vol. XI, 1937.
Reyer, W., "Untersuchungen zur Phänomenologie des begrifflichen Gestaltens. Beiträge zur Grundlegung einer eidetischen Intentionalpsychologie." Dissertation, Hamburg, 1924.
— "Ueber das Wesen und die Bedeutung der phänomenologischen Forschung," *Hamburger Universitatszeitung*, Vol. VIII, 1926.
— Einführung in die Phänomenologie. Leipzig, 1926.
Rickert, H., "Zwei Wege der Erkenntnistheorie," *Kantstudien*, Vol. XIV, 1909.
Rovighi, Vanni, "Il 'Cogito' di Cartesio ed il 'Cogito' di Husserl," *Cartesio*, Vol. I, 1937.
Ruggiero, Guido de, "Husserl e la 'Fenomenologia,'" *La Critica*, Vol. XXIX, 1931.
Ryle, G., "Phenomenology," *Proceedings of Aristotelian Society*, suppl. Vol., 1932.
Salmon, C. V., "The Starting Point of Husserl's Philosophy," *Proceedings of the Aristotelian Society*, XXX, 1930.
Sartre, J. P., L'Imagination. Paris, 1936.
— "La transcendance de l' 'Ego,'" *Recherches philosophiques*, Vol. VI, 1938.
Sauer, Friedrich, "Ueber das Verhältnis der Husserlschen Phänomenologie zu David Hume," *Kantstudien*, Vol. XXXV, 1931.

Schaff, W., Beiträge zur Phänomenologie der Wahrnehmung. Halle, 1910.

Schestow, L., "Memento Mori." Potestas clavium. München, Nietzsche Gesellschaft, 1926.

— "Q'est-ce que la vérité?" *Revue philosophique,* 1927.

— Auf Hiobs Wage. Ueber die Quellen der ewigen Wahrheiten, Berlin, 1929.

— "Pamjatnik velikogo filosofa," *Russkija zapiski,* 1938.

Schilpp, Paul, Commemorative Essays. Stockton, California, 1930.

Schmalenbach, H., "Neues zum Problem der Phänomenologie," *Deutsche Literaturzezitung,* Vol. XLIII, 1922.

Schmid-Kowarzik, W., Umriss einer neuen analytischen Psychologie und ihr Verhältnis zur empirischen Psychologie. 1912.

— Phänomenologie und nichtempirische Psychologie. Einfuhrung in die neurere Psychologie. 5th ed., A. W. Zickfeldt, Osterwieck-Harz, 1931.

Schönrock, W., "Das Bewusstsein. Ein psychologisch-phänomenologischer Versuch." Dissertation, Erlangen, 1924.

Schräder, H., "Die Theorie des Denkens bei Külpe und bei Husserl." Dissertation, Münster, 1924.

Schreier, F., Grundbegriffe und Grundnormen des Rechts. Leipzig-Wien, 1924.

Schulz, Julius, "Ueber die Fundamente der formalen Logik," *Vierteljahrsschrift für wissentschaftliche Philosophie,* Vol. XXVII, 1903.

Schunk, K., Verstehen und Einsehen. Halle, 1926.

Schupp, W., Die neue Wissenschaft vom Recht. Eine phänomenologische Untersuchung. Berlin-Grunewald, 1930.

Schütz, Alfred, Der sinnhafte Aufbau der sozialen Welt. Wien, 1932.

— Besprechung: "Méditationes cartésiennes," *Deutsche Literaturzeitung,* 1932.

—Besprechung: "Formale und transcendentale Logik," *Deutsche Literaturzeitung,* 1933.

Schwinge, E., and L. Zimmerl, Wesensschau und konkretes Ordnungsdenken im Strafrecht. Bonn, 1937.

Serrus, Ch., "Le Conflit du logicisme et du psychologisme," *Organe officiell de la Societe,* Vol. I, May, 1928.

— Le Parallélisme logico-grammatical. Paris, 1934.

Siegfried, Th., Phänomenologie und Geschichte. Kairos, 1926.

Sjaardema, Hendrikus, "A critical Examination of the Concept of Understanding in the Psychologies of Wilhelm Dilthey, Eduard Spranger, and Karl Jaspers." Dissertation, University of Southern California, 1939.

Söhngen, Georg, Sein und Gegenstand. Münster, 1930. Veröffentlichungen d. kathol. Institutes für Philosophie in Köln. Vol. II, No. 4.

Souriau, M., "La Matière et le Concret," *Recherches philosophiques,* Vol. II, 1932.

Spaier, La Pensée concrète. Alcan, Paris, 1927.

Spet, G., Javlenie i Smysl. Fenomenologija kak osnovnaja nauka i jeje problemy, Moskva, 1914.

Spiegelberg, H., "Der Begriff der Intentionalität in der Scholastik, bei Brentano und bei Husserl," *Philosophische Hefte,* V Jahrgang, 1/2, 1936.

— "Critical Phenomenological Realism," *Philosophy and Phenomenological Research,* Vol. II, December, 1940.

Ssalagoff, Leo, "Vom Begriff des Geltens in der modernen Logik." Dissertation, Heidelberg, 1910.

Stein, Edith, "Zum Problem der Einfühlung." Dissertation, Freiberg, Halle, 1917.

— "Husserls Phänomenologie und die Philosophie des heilige Thomas von Aquino." Husserl-Festschrife, 1929.

Steinmann, H., "Die systematische Stellung der Phänomenologie," *Archiv für die gesammte Psychologie,* Vol. XXXVI, 1917.

Stenzel, Julius, "Philosophie der Sprache." Handbuch der Philosophie, Vol. II, München-Berlin, 1934.

Straubinger, Heinrich, Einführung in die Religionsphilosophie. Freiberg (Breisgau), 1929.

Temuralq, T., Ueber die Grenzen der Erkennbarkeit bei Husserl und Scheler. Berlin, 1937.

Volkelt, Joh., "Die phänomenologische Gewissheit," *Zeitschrift für Philosophie und philosophische Kritik,* Vol. CLXV.

Vollmer, R., Beiträge zur Kritik der phänomenologische Methode vom Standpunkte der Friesschen Schule aus. Jena, 1929.

Vorländer, Karl, Geschichte der Philosophie. 7th Ed., Leipzig, 1927, Vol. III.

Walther, Gerda, Zur Phänomenologie der Mystik. Halle, 1923.
— Besprechung: "H. Schwarz." *Literarische Berichte aus dem Gebiete der Philosophie,* 1927.
— "Ludwig Klages und sein Kampf gegen den 'Geist,'" *Philosophischer Anzeiger,* Vol. III, 1928.
— Uebersetzt: *Revista de Occidente,* Vol. VI, Madrid, 1928.

Weidauer, Friedr., Kritik der transzendental Phänomenologie Husserls. Leipzig, 1933.
— Besprechung: (a) "L. Landgrebe," *Kantstudien,* Vol. XXXIX, 1934; (b) "A. Kojevnikoff," *Recherches philosophiques,* Vol. III, 1935.

Welch, E. Parl, "Max Scheler's Phenomenology of Religion." Dissertation, University of Southern California, 1934. (First section deals with Edmund Husserl.)
— "Phenomenology and the Doctrine of Man," *Journal of Liberal Religion,* Vol. I, No. 1, 1939.
— Edmund Husserl's Phenomenology. The University of Southern California Press, 1939.
— "Edmund Husserl—An Appreciation," *The Personalist,* Winter, 1940.

Weyl, H., Raum, Zeit, Materie. Vorlesung über allgemeine Relativitätstheorie. Berlin, 1918.
— Philosophie der Mathematik und Naturwissenschaft. München-Berlin, 1927.

Wild, John, "The Concept of the Given in Contemporary Philosophy," *Philosophy and Phenomenological Research,* Vol. I, September, 1940.

Wilming, Josef, "Husserls Lehre von dem intentionellen Erlebnissen." Dissertation, Leipzig, 1925.

Winkler, R., "Das religiöse Urphänomen," *Preussische Jahrbücher,* Vol. LXXXIX.
— Phänomenologie und Religion. Tübingen, 1921.
— "Husserls Programm der Phänomenologie in seiner Bedeutung für die systematische Theologie," *Zeitschrift für Theologie und Kirche,* 1921.

Wissengrund, Theodor, "Die Transcendenz des Dinglichen und Noematischen in Husserls Phänomenologie." Dissertation, Frankfurt, 1924.

Wolff, Gustav, Leben und Erkennen. Vorarbeiten zu einer biologischen Philosophie. München, 1933.

Wundt, W., Kleine Schriften. Vol. I, Leipzig, 1910.

Wust, P., Die Auferstehung der Metaphysik. Leipzig, 1920.

Ziehen, Th., Lehrbuch der Logik. Bonn, 1920.

Zocher, R., Husserls Phänomenologie und Schuppes Logik. Ein Beitrag zur Kritik des intuitionistischen Ontologismus in der Immanenzidee. München, 1932.

— Besprechung: "A. Kojevnikoff," *Recherches philosophiques,* Vol. II, 1934.

INDEX

Abstraction, 60*n*, 103, 181, 226, 227
Act, act-character, 66, 69, 73, 83; meaning of term, 73, 74; nature of, 73, 83–87; relation of ideas to, 74, 86, 94; act-content, 80, 83, 95, 96; matter, 84, 85, 86; quality, 84–86; unity, 86 f., nominal, 87 f.; objectifying, 87 f., 94*n*
Adequation, doctrine of, 95
Alexander, Samuel, 239
Antipsychologizers, Husserl's rejection of, 13, 48 f.
A posteriori, doctrine of, 229 ff., 235, 237
Appearances, 125, 199, 272, 274
Apprehended and intentional, distinction between, 174
Apprehension, two kinds, 99; transformed into comprehension, 176
A priori, doctrine of, 229 ff., 235, 237
Argument, three characteristics of, 23
Aristotle, 284; philosophy of, 224–27 *passim*
Arithmetic, *see* Mathematics
Art, characterization of, 17
Awareness, 169, 174

Bain, Thomas, 32
Being, concept of, 97 ff., 188; essential Being can be known, 140; doubt of, 146; of pure consciousness, 147 ff., 153, 154; meaning of, inverted, 155; contingency is correlative to essential, 184, 204; examples of sciences of, 185; system of experiences called "absolute," 195, 196; two kinds, 196;

Idea as essential, 226; scholastics' idea of, 226, 228
Beiträge zur Theorie der Variationsrechnung, xiv
"Bericht über deutsche Schriften zur Logik aus dem Jahre 1894," 9, 36
Berkeley, George, 280
Bibliography, 301–25; works on realism, 238–79 *passim*
Bodily organism, *see* Organism
Bolzano, Bernhard, xv, 8*n*, 50
Boodin, J. E., 238*n*
Bosanquet, Bernard, xvii, 261*n*
Brain, relation to consciousness, 244 ff. *passim*
Brentano, Franz, 49, 111*n*, 224; tragic personal effects of his opposition to dogma of infallibility, xiv f.; his *Psychologie . . .*, xv, 239, 272*n*; Husserl's studies under, and personal relationship with, xv; early influence upon Husserl, xvi, 5, 6, 8*n*; conception of psychology and its task, 3; doctrine of intentionality, 3, 5, 171, 172, 279, 281; theory of consciousness, 74 ff., 121*n*, 285; on relation of ideas to psychical acts, 74, 86, 94; theory of immanent objectivity, 78; Husserl's indebtedness to, 224, 279, 282, 285; essential differences between his philosophy and Husserl's, 280 ff.
Brightman, Edgar S., 233*n*
Broad, C. D., 238*n*

Cartesian method, Husserl inspired by, 146; *see also* Descartes, René

334   *INDEX*

Organism, mind identifiable with, 244 ff. *passim;* Husserl's attitude toward, 254; categorical equipment, 269
Osborn, Andrew D., quoted, xix
Ostwald, W., 115n
Ought-to-be and is, relation between, 26

Particular, the, and essence, 130
Particular intuition, *see* Perception, sensory
Particulars, relation to species, 183
Patocka, Jan, 301
Paulsen, Friedrich, xiv, xvi
Perception, study of perceiving the task of psychology, 3; term, 67n; role of, 88, 92, 99; expression of, 89; and thing, 186 ff.; perspective variations, 187; distinguished from intuition of experience, 189; content, 194; realists' epistemology of, 264 ff. *passim;* Husserl's contrasted with, 271 ff.; objects of inner, 283, 284; of external, 283
Perception, sensory, 67n, 100, 171, 276; and ideal ideation, 69–72; two elements, 156; the thing-world apprehended in, 188, 193, 194, 196; function of sense data, 197; error in, 215 ff.; what it is, 218; is prior to, and conditions, knowledge of principles, 227; realists' theory, 264 ff.; Husserl's contrasted, 273, 276
Perry, Ralph Barton, 194n, 224n, 238, 239, 240, 241, 242n, 256; theory of mind, 243, 245n, 248n, 250, 252, 253, 255
Personality and self, 157 f.
Perspective variations of perception, 187
"Phänomenologie und ihre Vieldeutigkeit, Die" (Driesch), xvii, xxi
Phenomena, term, 76; psychical, 125 ff., 282; concept of, 137–41; distinction between noumena and, 229, 232–35; concepts of

Brentano and Husserl contrasted, 282–85; physical, 283
Phenomenology, inadequate treatments of, xvii; established as a potent factor in European philosophy, xvii; why so little known in America, xviii; of greater value as science or as epistemology? xix, 298; reached fruition in *Ideen,* xx; Husserl's philosophy before the development of, 3–13; his quasi-phenomenology, 14–53, 55–72; development of a pure logic, 55–72; of epistemology, 72–107; Husserl's transition from earlier philosophy to, 112–34; deals with pure consciousness, 120; psychology's need of a systematic, 131; Husserl devotes rest of his life to, 135; pure, 136–204; the concept of phenomenon, 137–41; twofold culmination of, 137; and Kantianism, 140, 229–37; method: the reductions and the realm of pure consciousness, 141–61, 286; the doctrine of essences and intuition, 143, 161–70; concern of psychology and, differentiated, 158; intuition and intentionality, 170–76; fact and essence, 177–204; basic arguments and principles summarized, 203 f.; problem of error, 207–23; misconceptions of, 207; and scholasticism, 224–29; and realism, 238–79; agreement with realism, 240; their different theories of mind or consciousness, 243–56; of epistemology, 256–79; as a science, 279–99; not to be identified as psychology, 279 ff.; aims, 287 ff.; its field, 291; as the Science of sciences, 293, 298; spiritual faith conferred by, 299; *for detailed entries see subjects listed, e.g.,* Consciousness: Essences: Logic
"Philosophie als strenge Wissenschaft," 111, 112, 132, 201
Philosophie der Arithmetik, xvi, xvii, 6, 9, 12, 49, 229

Realism (*Continued*)
  and their publications, 238 f.;
  tenets, 239; and phenomenology,
  240–79; their agreement, 240;
  their disagreement about mind
  or consciousness, 243–56; about
  epistemology, 256–79
Reality and Being, 155, 156
Reductions as a method, 141–61, 286
Reflection, 60n, 65n, 98, 192; logical, 64–66; distinction between
  content of, and primary contents,
  104; principles reached through,
  226 ff.
Rickert, Heinrich, xvi
Rogers, A. K., quoted, 219
Roman Catholic Church, Brentano
  retired from priesthood and professorship by, xiv f.
"Romantic Philosophy," 113
Russell, Bertrand, 162, 194n, 238n,
  243, 250

Santayana, George, 238n, 243, 262n,
  270, 277
Scheler, Max, xix, 91n
Scholasticism and phenomenology,
  224–29
Schopenhauer, Arthur, quoted, xvii
Science, two aspects of any, 46;
  meaning of exact, 59; nature of,
  61, 62; Husserl's position in respect to, 112–34, 153; philosophy's
  disposition to lean upon exact,
  112 ff.; psychology avowedly a
  natural, 117; how differentiate
  between physical and psychical
  nature, 123; natural, and psychical
  existence, 125; philosophy can be
  free only by emancipation from
  natural, 134; eidetic, those dealing with nature, 153, 160; empirical, 162, 296; natural, as the
  only science, 162; attitude of
  realists toward natural, 252; the
  organism from standpoint of
  empirical, 254; phenomenology as
  a, 279–99; as the Science of
  sciences, 293, 298; relation between exact and descriptive, 291

Selectivity, principle of, 248, 249,
  250
Self, and personality, 157 f.; theories
  of realists and of Husserl contrasted, 246, 258, 260; *see also*
  Ego
Self-evidence, as basis of knowledge,
  22; in judgment, 42; what is
  meant by, 44; in relation to truth
  and error, 209–17 *passim*; kinds
  of, 211; *see also* Insight
Sellars, Roy W., 198n, 238n;
  realism of, 239, 241, 243, 246; its
  epistemology, 257–78 *passim*
Sensations, difference between object and, 79; role of, 217; ideas
  of Hume and Kant contrasted,
  230 f., 234; of Husserl, 235
Sense data, what they are, 139, 194;
  see also Perception, sensory
Sensory and categorical intuitions,
  96–105, 106
Sentient, defined, 246n
Significant content of act, 96
Signification, 93n; opposition be-
  tween intuition and, 105
Sign theory, 271, 273
Sigwart, Christoph, 32, 33, 42n, 43n
Similarity, relation to identity, 68
Six Theories of Mind (Morris), xvii
Skepticism, of Hume, 130, 230, 232;
  of Kant, 235
Sorbonne, lectures at, xxi
Spatiality, 185, 193, 199, 202, 232;
  of consciousness, 247, 249
Spaulding, E. G., 239, 241
Species, 63; ideality of, 66–69; ap-
  prehension of, 67n, 70; relation
  to particulars, 183
Spencer, Herbert, 162
Spiritual experiences and faith, 299
Stout, G. F., 253n
Strong, Charles A., 238n; realism
  of, 239, 243, 245; its epistemology,
  257–77 *passim*
Stumpf, Carl, xvi, 5, 121n
Subjective expressions, 60n
Subjectivity, relation to error, 224n;
  opposition to, 240
Substantiality, 199, 202